A Chanticleer Press Edition

Taylor's Guide to Houseplants

Houghton Mifflin Company Boston 1987

Based on Taylor's Encyclopedia of
Gardening, Fourth Edition, copyright © 1961
by Norman Taylor, revised and edited by
Gordon P. DeWolf, Jr.

Library of Congress
Cataloging-in-Publication Data
Taylor's guide to houseplants.
(Taylor's guides to gardening)
Based on: Taylor's encyclopedia of gardening.
4th edition. 1961
Includes index
1. House plants.   2. Indoor gardening.
3. House plants—Dictionaries.   4. Indoor
gardening—Dictionaries.   I. Taylor's
encyclopedia of gardening.   II. Title: Guide
to houseplants.   III. Series.
SB419.T355   1987   635.9'65   86-20023
ISBN 0-395-43091-7 (pbk.)

Prepared and produced by Chanticleer Press,
Inc., New York
Cover photograph: *Sinningia speciosa*
by Pete Carmichael

Designed by Massimo Vignelli

Color reproductions made in Italy
Printed and bound in Japan

First Editon.

DNP   10   9   8   7   6   5   4   3   2   1

Contents

Introduction
Preface 9
How to Use This Guide 10
Basic Botany 12
Choosing Your Plants 14
Plant Care 19
Potting Plants 26
Propagation 32
Plant Chart 42

The Color Plates
Visual Key 68
Hanging Plants 74
Small Foliage Plants 88
Orchids 118
Bromeliads and Flowers 152
Showy Foliage Plants 200
Lacy Leaves 238
Succulents and Others 254

Encyclopedia of Houseplants
Plant Descriptions A–Z 289

Appendices
Orchids 432
Decorating with Plants 436
Buying Plants 439
Pests and Problems 440
Glossary 450
Index 454

Contributors

Pete Carmichael, the principal photographer for this book, is a professional photographer specializing in nature studies. His work has appeared in *National Geographic, Omni, The Audubon Society Field Guide to North American Shells,* and many other publications.

Gordon P. DeWolf, Jr., Ph.D., is coordinator of the Horticulture Program at Massachusetts Bay Community College in Wellesley Hills, Massachusetts. He revised and edited the fifth edition of *Taylor's Encyclopedia of Gardening,* upon which this guide is based. Dr. DeWolf previously served as Horticulturist at the Arnold Arboretum at Harvard University.

Charles Marden Fitch, author of the orchid descriptions and the essay on growing orchids, is a horticulturist, photographer, and media specialist. His book *All About Orchids* is a guide to growing orchids in the home.

Elvin McDonald, consultant for this guide, is a gardener, writer, and Director of Special Projects at the Brooklyn Botanic Garden. His twice-weekly gardening column is syndicated by King Features.

Dolores R. Santoliquido illustrated the gardening essays and contributed most of the drawings in the encyclopedia section. Her work has appeared in numerous books, including the Audubon Society Field Guides, the Audubon Society Nature Guides, and other volumes in the Taylor's Guide series.

Frances Tenenbaum, author of the gardening essays and editor of the plant descriptions, has edited numerous books on gardening. She is the author of *Gardening with Wild Flowers,* as well as two books on houseplants, *Nothing Grows for You? A Brown-Thumb Guide to Houseplants* and *Plants from Nine to Five: Gardening Where You Work.* She has had years of experience growing her own houseplants.

Katharine Widin is the author of the essay on pests and diseases. She holds an M.S. and a Ph.D. in plant pathology and operates a private consulting firm, Plant Health Associates, in Stillwater, Minnesota.

Some illustrations in the Encyclopedia of Houseplants are by Daniel Allen, Robin Jess, and Mary Jane Spring. The drawings in the essay on pests and diseases are by Mary Jane Spring, and the title page illustration is by Sarah Pletts.

Preface

Ever since Eve, humans have been attracted to gardens and the trees and shrubs and flowers that grow in them. In Eve's part of the world, flowers bloomed all year long; for those of us who live in the temperate zones, our gardening experience is restricted to the warm months. Unless, of course, we bring our plants indoors.

Botanically, there is no such thing as a houseplant. There are no plants native to an environment enclosed by four walls and a roof. Houseplants are simply tropical or semitropical plants that can survive indoors. It was the Victorians who first discovered that plants could enliven the gloom of their chilly homes, and the plants they knew—Boston Fern, Parlor Palm, and the aptly named Cast-iron Plant—are still with us today.

But the Victorians could never have dreamed of the vast number and variety of species, hybrids, and cultivars that today's growers have developed for indoor use. Indeed, if you haven't visited a plant nursery or garden shop within the past five years or so, you may be amazed at the wealth of plants that can be grown in the house. Every year, plant breeders improve old familiar species and produce new cultivars with larger flowers, more compact stems, and improved ability to adapt to relatively inhospitable indoor conditions. The revolution in the world of indoor plants is a particular boon to those of us who have neither ideal growing conditions nor great experience with indoor plants.

On the other hand, the new popularity of solar rooms, garden rooms, and attached greenhouses means that, for the first time, many people have indoor environments conducive to growing even the more difficult and temperamental houseplants.

Whether you are a novice or an experienced grower, you will find a wealth of plants suitable for your needs and desires in this book, along with expert information on how to choose and care for your plants.

How to Use

From a windowsill lined with geraniums to an entire garden room, any decor that includes plants always seems warm and appealing. This book, designed to answer the needs of both beginners and experienced indoor gardeners, makes it easy to choose plants that suit your particular tastes and the conditions in your home.

How This Book Is Organized
This guide contains three types of material: color plates, plant descriptions, and expert articles that guide you through every aspect of growing houseplants.

Color Plates
More than 320 of the most attractive and versatile houseplants in cultivation today are illustrated in the color plates. The plates are divided into seven groups: hanging plants, small foliage plants, orchids (each of which is shown with a detail of its blossoms), bromeliads and flowers, showy foliage plants, lacy leaves, and succulents and others. Within each of these groups the plates are arranged by shape.

The color section opens with a visual key, which shows examples of the plants in each group. Showy foliage plants, for example, include rubber trees, with their large, bold leaves, and stately palms with feather-shaped fronds, along with other striking foliage plants. Another group features bromeliads with colorful bracts and flowering plants from bright, compact African violets to a climbing Black-eyed Susan Vine.

The captions that accompany the color plates provide essential information at a glance: scientific and common names, the size of a plant, how much light it needs, what temperature it prefers, and whether it requires extra humidity. There is also an indication of how easy it is to grow and a page reference to the Encyclopedia of Houseplants.

Encyclopedia of Houseplants
Here you will find full descriptions of the plants featured in the color plates. Entries are arranged alphabetically by genus and cross-referenced to the color plates. If you are unfamiliar with scientific names, you can look up a common name in the index. Each description begins with the genus name, followed by the common and scientific family names. Pronunciation of the scientific name precedes a brief overview of the genus. The How to Grow section provides specific information on how much light, heat, humidity, water, and fertilizer the species pictured in the book need. It also tells you how and when to repot and propagate them. Next you will find descriptions of the plants included in the color plates. A black-and-white illustration next to a species description shows the overall shape of the plant or a particularly intricate feature of it.

This Guide

Gardening Essays

Written by experts, these essays explain every aspect of growing houseplants—how to choose plants, how to match their light and temperature requirements to conditions in your home, how to care for your plants day to day, and when and how to repot them. In the section on propagation, beginners will learn how to create new plants from old favorites. The essay on orchids shows you how to raise these exotic plants in your home.

Ideas for decorating with houseplants are presented, as well as valuable advice on what to look for—and avoid—when buying plants. If one of your plants looks unhealthy, the pests and problems chart will help you identify the difficulty and solve it. Finally, any technical terms you may encounter are defined in the glossary.

Using the Plant Chart

The chart beginning on page 42 helps you narrow the range of choices at a glance. Suppose you are looking for a hanging plant to add interest to a corner of your kitchen. There is no window nearby, but the overhead fluorescent lights are on most of the day. Check the hanging plant section of the chart for those that tolerate medium light. There are five plants that will do well in medium light, one of which—*Pilea nummularifolia*—has special needs. You can eliminate it because you want something that is easy to grow. That leaves four plants: *Chlorophytum comosum, Cissus antartica, Philodendron scandens,* and *Tolmeia menziesii.* Turn to the color plates for these four plants, then read their descriptions in the Encyclopedia. Now choose the one that appeals to you most.

Using the Color Plates to Choose Your Plants

When you decide to buy a houseplant, you should have in mind the particular space it will occupy in your home. Is there a large open area that needs filling in? A windowsill to be dressed up? Would you like to grow plants with bright flowers or lush green foliage? Suppose you decide on a series of small foliage plants to be placed in identical pots lined up on your kitchen windowsill. Turn to the small foliage plants and choose those that appeal to you and would look nice together. The captions will tell you quickly which will thrive in the space; for more information, turn to the descriptions.

Identifying the Plants You Have

More than a few of us have houseplants whose names we don't know. Perhaps they were bought on impulse or received as gifts. Not knowing their names makes caring for them a trial-and-error effort at best. Because the color plates are arranged by shape, you can look for your plants among other, similar plants. You may see, for example, that the lacy-leaved foliage plant you were given for your birthday is *Asplenium bulbiferum.* Now you can read about it in the Encyclopedia of Houseplants and give it the care it needs.

Basic Botany

Houseplants are no different botanically from plants growing in your garden or in the wild. Many houseplants are native to tropical or semitropical regions of the world, but the only characteristic they all share is their ability to thrive indoors. Houseplants belong to many different families, and it is often convenient to refer to them collectively, especially in instructions on how to grow them. The groups you'll find mentioned most often are described below.

Bromeliads
The family Bromeliaceae, also called the pineapple family, includes over a thousand plants native to tropical America, where they grow on trees, rocks, or sand dunes. Aechmeas, cryptanthus, and vriesias are a few of the bromeliads grown indoors. Most bromeliads are epiphytes, or air plants, and they have spiky leaves arranged in a rosette like that on top of a pineapple. In some, a stalk rises from the center of the rosette, bearing small flowers surrounded by dramatic, colorful bracts. Most bromeliads grow best in warm temperatures with high humidity, light soils, and bright light. Water them by pouring water into the cup formed by the rosette.

Gesneriads
African violets, gloxinias, streptocarpus, and several other popular flowering houseplants are members of the large, tropical family Gesneriaceae. Gesneriads are easy to propagate, and many cultivars have been created for frequent bloom and increased hardiness. Most gesneriads need extra humidity, light fertilizing, and bright light but no direct sun.

Cacti and Succulents
Members of the family Cactaceae are spiny desert plants, many from the dry regions of the southwest and Mexico. Cacti come under the larger heading of succulents, which includes plants that store water or have adapted to the lack of it without special storage organs. The fleshy stems of cacti store water that the plant can draw on in times of drought. Some other succulents have no storage capacity, but their reduced leaf area prevents the loss of moisture through pores. Examples of this type of succulent are yuccas and agaves. Cacti like sandy soils and sunlight; other succulents may have different requirements.

Palms
Members of the family Palmaceae are divided into two groups—those with feather-shaped, or pinnately compound, leaves and those with fan-shaped, or palmately compound, leaves. The palms grown as houseplants are dwarf species or immature versions of the tall, stately palms of tropical regions. Palms like average temperatures and medium to bright light with no direct sun. They are long-lived and generally very well suited to indoor life.

Ferns

Although ferns are not a single family but a group of families, they all have similar growth habits, no flowers, and reproduce by spores rather than seeds. Most have feathery leaves, called fronds. Ferns have differing needs, but most require extra humidity. Propagation by spores is not easy for the home grower, but many ferns can be increased by dividing their root masses.

Scientific Names

Many houseplants are referred to by their common names, but it is safer to know their scientific names to avoid confusion. Common names may vary from region to region, but scientific names are the same worldwide. Some plants have common names derived from their scientific names—*Dracaena* is one example—but many, like gloxinia—*Sinningia*—do not.

The scientific name of a plant has two parts. The first is the generic name, which tells us the genus to which the plant belongs. Within each of these groups, or genera, there are many members. The second part of a scientific name is the specific epithet; it indicates one member, or species, within the genus. The generic name is always capitalized, while the specific epithet is rarely capitalized. Both names are printed in italics.

Forms and Varieties

Below the level of species, plants are classified as forms and varieties. A form is a small but frequently occurring variation in a population, such as a white-flowered plant in a normally purple-flowered species. Variety is a term for a plant of greater variation within a species. It may have a different leaf shape or growth habit. A varietal name follows the species name and, like it, is written in italics. The term variety is often used more generally, however, to indicate any variation in plant groups, including those produced by horticulturists.

Hybrids

Many houseplants are hybrids—crosses between different species and sometimes between plants in different genera. Hybridization is relatively rare in nature, but horticulturists can produce hybrids more ornamental or hardy than their parents. The symbol × in a scientific name tells you that the plant is a hybrid.

Cultivars

An individual of a cultivated hybrid group is commonly called a cultivar. It is usually given a name in single quotation marks after the genus or species name—for example, *Columnea* 'California Gold' or *Jasminum sambac* 'Maid of Orleans'. This name is selected as a sort of trademark, and it assures you that the plant you buy will have the same characteristics as all others with that cultivar name.

Choosing Your

Living, growing plants are a unique source of beauty and pleasure; they enhance the indoor environment and lift the spirits of the people who live there, too. But the fact that a plant can be grown in somebody's house doesn't mean it can grow in yours, and a plant that wilts and dies, or limps along looking dreary, isn't going to bring joy to anyone. If you think you aren't "good" with plants, it may be that you simply haven't selected plants that are suited to you. It's important to look beyond the appearance of a plant in a shop; how it will thrive in your home is what counts.

The environmental factors that are most important in dictating your selection of plants are light, temperature, and humidity. These are discussed in detail below. In addition, for quick reference, the captions accompanying the color pictures give the plants' requirements.

Still, environment isn't everything; your own interests and lifestyle matter too. For some people, the best plant is the one that sits still, looks pretty, and makes very few demands. Others enjoy the process of taking care of plants, of gardening indoors. Still others enjoy the challenge of making a difficult plant succeed.

Temporary Houseplants
In recent years, a new kind of houseplant has appeared on the market. These are flowering plants brought into perfect bloom commercially, sold to be enjoyed for a few weeks or months, and then discarded. Many of them are annuals, which cannot be brought into bloom a second time; others are perennials that are difficult or impossible to grow outside of a commercial greenhouse. These plants offer a wonderful way to fill your home with flowers when you don't have the environmental conditions or the personal inclination to grow flowering plants. They are certainly far less expensive and much longer-lasting than cut flowers. Since even these "temporary" plants can be made to last longer and grow better with a little care, instructions on their maintenance appears in the How to Grow sections.

Light
More than any other single factor, light will determine your choice of plants. If all your windows face north or are obscured by evergreen trees or the shadows of tall buildings, you should not try cacti or succulents. Consider buying plant lights if you want to grow flowering plants. In a room flooded with bright light and sunshine, your range of choices will be much wider. Keep in mind, however, that sun—or even very intense bright light without sun—can be harmful to many foliage plants.

Sun
You will find the light requirements of each plant in this book in the caption next to its photograph. The term "sun" is used for

Plants

plants that need at least four hours of direct sun a day, summer and winter. They should be placed near a window facing east, west, or south.

Bright Light
This is the brightest light you can have without direct sun. You will find it on a north windowsill or about five to six feet back from a sunny window. You may find it under a skylight or in a room that has a great deal of unobstructed glass. This is the most desirable light for many foliage plants and for those flowering plants that don't need full sun to bloom.

Bright Light; Some Sun
This refers to sun that is filtered through a curtain or to winter sun. Plants that grow well in bright light will do as well—probably better—here.

Medium Light
A few feet back from a sunless window is where you will find medium light. To the side of a window, the intensity of light decreases dramatically. You will also find medium light in offices, kitchens, and other rooms where ceiling fluorescent lights are kept on all day. Many foliage plants do well in this light.

Low Light
Low light is loosely described as "bright enough to read by." Relatively few plants can grow here, so choose carefully and consider investing in artificial lighting if this is the best light you have.

Plant Lights
With fluorescent lights turned on for 14 to 16 hours a day, you can grow flowering plants in a cellar or a closet as well as a living room. The usual light arrangement is a pair of fluorescent tubes placed over a tray of potted plants. There is a wide variety of these light set-ups on the market, and to some extent your choice is a matter of esthetics. Bare bulbs are fine in the cellar, but in the living room you want something more attractive. You can buy lights with their own valence or install bulbs under a shelf.

Ordinary cool white fluorescent bulbs are perfectly satisfactory for foliage plants, but the light they cast is unattractively cold. A better choice is a combination of one warm white and one cool white bulb, which will satisfy the needs of both foliage and flowering plants. So-called "grow" lights give off a pinkish light, which intensifies the color of flowers.

In addition to the fluorescents, you can buy individual plant bulbs that screw into an ordinary socket. These are a good choice if you want to light up a plant in a dark corner but, unlike fluorescents, are not a complete substitute for natural light. Whatever kind of

Choosing Your Plants To supply extra humidity, group small plants together on a tray of water and pebbles. Be sure the water level is below the bottom of the pots and the tray is as wide as the spread of the plants.

artificial lighting you choose, make sure to light the top of the plant, not the bottom, since plants grow toward the light.

Under fluorescent lights, foliage plants need about 12 to 14 hours of light a day. Place the lights 12 to 24 inches above the tops of the leaves. Flowering plants usually need 16 to 18 hours of light, and the lights should be no farther than 6 to 12 inches from the tops of the plants. If lights are too close, the plants will show the typical signs of too much sun or light—pale leaves, browned leaf tips and edges, and distorted stems and flowers. If the lights are too far away, flowers and leaves will stretch toward the bulbs.

If you plan to go into light gardening seriously, or want to grow certain orchids, bromeliads, cacti, or other light-sensitive plants, you should investigate the complete range of plant lights now available and select the kind suited to the needs of your plants.

Finally, it is possible to increase the light in your room to some extent by turning on ordinary incandescent lamps. Their bulbs give off heat, so do not place them too close to your plants. They are also much more expensive to use than fluorescent lights.

Temperature

With a few exceptions, houseplants are quite adaptable when it comes to temperature. Most of them can live happily in the average home. A few have more stringent requirements; these are noted in the captions and in more detail in the back of the book. In the captions, average temperature refers to 65 to 75° F during the day and 5 to 10° F cooler at night; cool to below 65° F by day and 5 to 10° F cooler at night; and warm to above 75° F during the day and above 70° F at night.

Most plants prefer cooler temperatures in winter than in summer but do not require the change. Some plants *must* have it. Plants that require temperatures of 40 to 50° F in winter are probably not for you unless you have an unheated porch. At the other end of the scale, plants that need very warm temperatures are best suited to a greenhouse.

Humidity

Humidity refers to the moisture plants get from the air rather than from the soil. With the exception of cacti, succulents, and a few other desert plants, most growing things need more humidity than they'll find in a heated or air-conditioned house. It is not unusual for the humidity in a heated room to be as low as 5 to 10 percent, which is exceedingly unhealthy to both people and plants. Most houseplants need 50 to 60 percent humidity in order to thrive. The distress sign to watch for is browning of leaf tips or edges.

Many hardy houseplants can adapt to dry conditions; in other cases, you can supply extra humidity rather easily. Some plants, however, need so much moisture in the air that your wallpaper would peel and your furniture grow mushrooms if you were to try to

Choosing Your Plants

accommodate them. If they are to be grown indoors, these plants must be placed in a greenhouse or a terrarium. The captions in the color section of this book tell you if a plant requires more than the average amount of humidity found in most homes.

In any house or apartment there are some rooms better suited than others to growing plants that need extra humidity. The kitchen and bath—if they are well lighted—are particularly good rooms for hanging baskets of ferns or other moisture lovers. Try hanging a moss-lined basket of ferns over the kitchen sink for a handsome effect. The kitchen sink is one of the few places in the home where this type of planter will work, because watering it can be a messy job.

Supplying Extra Humidity

The usual recommendation for creating extra humidity is to mist your plants once or twice a day. This is fine, if you have the patience and if your plants aren't located where a fine mist of water will harm furniture and walls. Any bottle that delivers a fine vapor or spray can serve as a mister. The pretty little brass containers sold for the purpose are more likely to clog than an ordinary spray bottle such as you use to dampen the ironing. Don't mist African violets or other fuzzy-leaved plants; this will cause water spots.

Small plants that need extra humidity are best grouped together on a tray of damp pebbles. Be sure the tray is as wide as the plants' spread and the water level in the tray is below the bottom of the pots—the purpose is to moisturize the air, not the soil. Grouping plants together, even if you don't put them on a tray, also helps maintain a humid environment. The leaves expire moisture, which is trapped by the neighboring leaves to create a microclimate around the plants.

This set-up can be altered slightly for single large plants. Put a brick or a block of wood in an oversized saucer and fill the saucer with about an inch of water. Set the pot on the block, making sure that the water-level is below the bottom of the pot.

As complement to any of these methods, you should consider buying a room humidifier to improve the atmosphere. The new cool vapor humidifiers are particularly effective and can raise the humidity by as much as 30 percent.

After so many warnings about the need to provide plants with adequate humidity, it must also be said that on occasion plants can suffer from too much humidity. This is more likely to occur in warm, damp weather than in winter, but poor air circulation at any time can cause the gray mold or mildew that is a symptom of too much humidity. If you see mold, remove the affected leaves and isolate the plant from its neighbors. Increase the air circulation by using a fan, or consider moving your plants to a spot where the air is less stagnant.

Plant Care

Providing a suitable indoor environment for your plants is only the first step to growing them successfully. Next comes maintenance—watering, feeding, and grooming them so they will continue to thrive. The guidelines given here are general; read the descriptions in the encyclopedia section to learn about the particular needs of certain types of plants.

When to Water

More plants die from too much water than from any other cause. A dry plant can ask for water by letting its leaves droop. An overwatered plant doesn't send out warnings; it sits around looking fine while its roots are invisibly rotting away, and then one day it just keels over. At that point it is probably too late to save it. Because plant roots need oxygen as well as water, it is a good general rule to let the soil dry out *a little bit* between waterings. Experience is the best teacher here. Does the soil look dry? Is it dry to the touch? It should not be so dry that it feels powdery. Have the leaves lost their firmness? That is a sign that you've waited too long. The best test is to lift the pot, if it is small enough. If it feels light, the plant needs water.

Because growing houseplants is not an exact science, the watering instructions in this book include such phrases as "moderately moist" or "somewhat dry." Very few people are willing to test each pot with a hydrometer or to poke a finger deep into the soil, and that isn't necessary. Common sense, a little practice, and the understanding that it is usually better to err on the too-dry side will soon take the mystery out of watering. Meanwhile, here are some general rules:

1. The warmer the room, the more often your plants will need water.
2. Plants in sun or bright light need more frequent watering than plants in medium or low light.
3. Small pots dry out faster than large ones, clay faster than plastic.
4. Water is likely to run right through a potbound plant without thoroughly wetting the soil. If the pot is too large for the root ball, the excess soil will retain too much water and the roots will drown. Repot your plant if either of these problems exists.

How to Water

Always use room temperature water and apply it thoroughly—until the water seeps through the drainage holes at the bottom of the pot. If this happens almost immediately, it may be because the soil is extremely porous—like African violet soil—or because the plant is potbound. In these cases, let the pot sit in the saucer of water for no more than 15 minutes, or until the water is absorbed. Never let it remain standing in water.

Even plants that like dry conditions should be watered thoroughly when they need water. Watering just a little each time will moisten only the top of the soil, while the bottom remains dry as a desert. The easiest and most satisfactory way to water houseplants is from the top, using a can with a long, narrow spout. If you are afraid of water-spotting furry leaves, you can let the pot absorb water from the bottom, making sure to empty the saucer after the soil is thoroughly moist. Plants that are always watered this way should be flushed from the top periodically, or fertilizer salts will remain on the surface of the soil and burn the plant.

The best way to water hanging baskets is to take them to the sink or tub, where you can do a thorough job without worrying about spotting the floor. Immerse the root masses of ferns, and other plants growing in moss baskets or on bark, in a sink of water. All plants, including African violets, benefit from periodic gentle showers with room-temperature water, so long as the water isn't alkaline.

Resuscitating a Plant
If a plant has dried out, submerge its pot in water above the rim. Hold it under the water until it gets heavy enough to stand upright. Let the pot stay underwater until bubbles stop rising through the soil. Then let it drain—make sure it doesn't stand in the receding water.

Saving Overwatered Plants
An overwatered plant is usually a hopeless case if it has already wilted, but it's still worth a try to save it. Turn the plant out of the pot. If the roots are still intact, gently lift the plant out of the sodden soil and throw the soil away. Repot the plant in a pot just large enough to hold the roots comfortably. Use fresh soil, and water it just enough to settle the roots; don't water again until the soil is dry to the touch. If possible, cut off some top growth to compensate for the damaged roots.

About Fertilizer
To provide nutrients that your plants need for best growth, use any complete all-purpose houseplant fertilizer. A complete fertilizer contains nitrogen, phosphorus, and potassium, in amounts described on the package. The first number in the formula refers to the percentage of nitrogen, the second to the percentage of phosphorus, and the third to the percentage of potassium.

All-purpose fertilizers usually have equal numbers—for example, 20-20-20—or a higher middle number—like 5-10-5 or 3-6-3. It is the relationship between the numbers, not their individual values, that counts; a liquid fertilizer usually has smaller numbers only because it has already been diluted.

There is such a bewildering array of specially formulated fertilizers on the market that you may get discouraged just trying to read their

To resuscitate a plant that has dried out, hold its pot underwater until it gets heavy enough to stand upright. When bubbles stop rising from the soil, remove the pot and let it drain thoroughly.

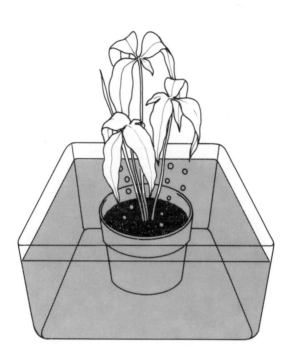

Plant Care

labels. Unless you specialize in cacti or orchids, it isn't necessary to buy specialty products. If a specific formula is recommended for certain plants, the How to Grow instructions in this book will describe it.

The easiest fertilizer to use is a liquid one, which must be further diluted according to the manufacturer's directions. A dry fertilizer, to be dissolved in water, is just as good for your plants. Long-acting fertilizers can cause problems and are not recommended here.

When to Fertilize

The feeding schedules suggested for each plant in the Encyclopedia are the optimum for plants growing under ideal conditions. If your plant is existing on the low edge of its light requirements, or if you don't want a foliage plant to grow too large, feed it less frequently. Flowering plants may not bloom unless fed according to schedule. Some general rules:

1. Dilute your fertilizer to a weaker strength than that recommended by the manufacturer. Never try to make up for a missed feeding by using a stronger solution. After overwatering, overfeeding is the largest cause of houseplant death.
2. Don't feed a newly purchased foliage plant for at least six months, because it will have been given long-acting plant food in the nursery. Feed flowering plants according to the normal schedule.
3. Plants growing in soil can manage with less fertilizer than plants growing in a soilless potting mix. If you don't know what kind of mix your plant is growing in, see the section on potting (p. 30).
4. Don't feed a plant when the soil is bone dry; wet it first.
5. Above all, remember that fertilizer is food—not medicine—and should never be given to a plant that is resting or ailing. If the roots are not healthy and growing, they can't absorb the fertilizer. It will remain in the soil, building up to a lethal concentration.

Pinching and Pruning

You pinch or prune plants in order to keep them shapely, force them to branch, or make them more compact. Soft new growth can be pinched off between your thumb and first finger to force a single-stemmed seedling of a coleus, for example, to branch out and become shrubby. Pinching is also used to keep long vining plants like the Wandering Jews full instead of long and lanky. If you want to keep a jade plant shapely, simply pinch off the newest leaves wherever the stems seem to be growing out of bounds. It is best to pinch just above a node—where a leaf is attached to the stem. Keeping plants pinched back conserves energy that is otherwise wasted on long, ungainly stems.

Pruning serves the same purpose as pinching but is used when plant stems are too hard or woody to be pinched off sharply. Use small pruning shears for these plants.

Grooming

When it comes to caring for houseplants, there is no bigger payoff
for a small effort than in grooming. A yellowing leaf will never turn
green again; a faded flower will never revive. Cut or pinch them
right off and see how much better the whole plant looks. Neatly
trim brown tips off of leaves. Pick fallen leaves off the surface of the
soil—for sanitary as well as esthetic reasons. Unless your plant is too
big, carry it to the sink or bathtub for a refreshing shower. Gently
wipe off large leaves with a soft, damp cloth or sponge. As well as
making the leaves look dull, dirt blocks their pores so that the plant
can't take in air and moisture. Don't apply commercial leaf "shiners"
or milk or mineral oil to the leaves—they just attract more dirt.

A Summer Outdoors

With the exception of the gesneriads and other fuzzy-leaved plants
that can't stand water-spotting, most plants are refreshed and
invigorated by a summer out of doors. Even delicate ones appreciate
a porch vacation—remember to water these by hand, since rainfall
and sprinklers won't reach them.

Outdoor light is far more intense than even the brightest light
shining on a windowsill, so start your plants in the shade and move
them gradually into brighter sunlight. Most cacti and succulents can
stand full sun; other flowering plants are better off in dappled light.
Place foliage plants in light or heavy shade, depending on their
indoor needs. Keep all plants out of drying winds, and if you keep
them under a tree, make sure that they are in a spot where rain
reaches the soil. Hanging plants will dry out very quickly outdoors,
so hang them where they can receive daily waterings.

Don't put plants out until all danger of frost has passed, and bring
them in if you get an unexpectedly cold night. Move your plants
back inside at the end of summer while the weather is still warm so
they can readjust to indoor life before the heat is turned on.

Before you bring any plants inside—especially those that have been
sitting on the ground—look them over carefully. Wash and inspect
the foliage to be sure it is free of insects and insect larvae. Turn the
plants out of their pots to check that no creatures have crawled in
through the drainage holes. Return the plants to their pots—this is
not a good time to repot because most plants are just entering their
slow-growth or dormancy period and will not recover easily.

Vacation Care

If you have a house full of plants with different requirements for
water and you plan to be away for ten days or longer, the most
practical way to tide them over is to rely on a kind friend or a plant
sitter. Group the plants together, if possible, and leave notes with
clear instructions.

For shorter vacations, remember that your plants don't need you as
much as you may think they do. Water them well before you go;

Plant Care

A wick watering system works by capillary action and gravity. Place one end of a wick deep into a jar of water and the other into the soil. Make sure the pots are standing at a level below the water surface. You can attach 4 or 5 plants to a large, full reservoir while you are on vacation.

this is one time when it is safe to leave a little water in the saucers of those plants that need to be kept moist. But leave just a little bit—you don't want the pot to sit in water the whole time you are gone. Plants that should be allowed to dry out a little between waterings rarely need extra water in the saucer.

To prevent plants from drying out quickly, turn down the heat and put the pots where they won't get any direct sun. In summer a closed-up house may be impossible to keep cool; a shady spot outdoors is an alternative.

If you have a manageable number of plants, you might invest in a wick watering system. This involves wicks drawing water from a reservoir into separate pots through their drainage holes. You can also buy your own nylon wicks and connect four or five plants to each container of water. Be sure there is sufficient water for the number of plants connected to each reservoir.

There are also capillary mats on which you can set plants in plastic pots. Hang one end of the mat in the water in the kitchen sink while the other end rests on the drain board. Capillary action makes the whole mat wet, and the plants absorb water through the drainage holes. This method does not work well with clay pots because they are too thick to allow the potting mix to touch the mat.

Another alternative is a plastic-bag greenhouse. Attach the bag firmly to the rim of each watered pot and hold it away from the leaves with three or four sticks pushed into the soil. Keep your plants out of the sun.

You can make a larger "greenhouse" by putting your plants in the bathtub and taping plastic to the walls and the side of the tub. If your bathroom has no window, you can use a lamp with a timer attached to provide a certain number of hours of light each day.

When to Say Goodbye

Very few houseplants live forever, to be handed down from generation to generation. Some are annuals, or best treated as annuals, and thrown away after a few months or a year. Most flourish for some number of years in between those extremes, but sooner or later they lose their looks and should be discarded. This is almost unbearable for some people, who insist on caring for a distorted African violet that puts forth one small blossom a year or a foliage plant that is more stem than leaves. It's not only a waste of time to care for these pathetic specimens—their presence affects the overall appearance of your collection. If you want to keep their memories alive, take cuttings before you throw away the parent plants.

Potting Plants

Because a houseplant is a prisoner of its pot, it is important that you choose the right type and size and learn to recognize signs that a change is needed. The type of plant, its growth habit, and its water and soil requirements will all affect how it should be potted.

Choosing Pots

Plants are usually sold in plastic pots because plastic is cheaper and lighter than clay. Small plastic pots are likely to be square—a space-saving shape for the grower but an unnatural shape for a plant. Unglazed clay and plastic pots each have advantages and drawbacks for plants and their owners. Unglazed clay pots are porous, so plants potted up in clay will need water more often than those in plastic pots, but they are less likely to get waterlogged. A plant that must be kept constantly moist is probably better off in a plastic pot, while a cactus or succulent will be healthier in a clay pot. The weight of clay makes it a better choice for a tall plant, which might be top-heavy in a plastic container.

Clay is easily stained by mineral salts left by fertilizer or trace elements in water, and it is hard to clean without using bleach and a stiff brush. Clay is also more likely to chip and break than plastic. Choose plastic pots if you travel a lot and leave your plants behind. Not only does it help retain water, but a plastic pot will even absorb water if placed on a piece of wet matting, as clay will not. (See the section on vacation care, page 23.)

Glazed clay pots—always with a drainage hole—are an attractive alternative if you don't like the look of plastic and don't want to water as frequently as may be necessary with unglazed clay. Although no plant should be put directly into a pot without a drainage hole, or holes, there is no reason not to put a utilitarian pot inside an attractive outer container—a cachepot, a jardiniere, a decorative wooden tub, or a basket. Just be sure when you water that the water doesn't sit in the bottom.

No matter which container you choose—unglazed clay, plastic, glazed clay, or an outer decorative pot—remember that the pot should enhance the plant, not dominate it. Unglazed clay, a natural earthy material, is suited to any plant but particularly to cacti and other desert dwellers. Dark green is the most suitable color for plastic—avoid bright colors altogether. Glazed clay is most attractive in black or an earth tone. As a general rule, decorative jardinieres should be of very simple design.

To protect furniture and floors, set porous pots and those with drainage holes on matching saucers. Unglazed clay saucers are useless as protectors, but you can buy waterproof saucers of a synthetic material that look exactly like the real thing.

To Clean Pots

Whatever kind of pot you decide on, make sure that it is scrupulously clean before you use it. A stiff brush and hot soapy water is usually enough to clean a plastic pot. Clay is more difficult. If this kind of cleaning doesn't remove the stains and ground-in dirt, soak the pot in bleach, diluted according to the directions on the bottle. If you want to sterilize clay or plastic pots that may have contained diseased plants, run them through the dishwasher or put them in a pan and pour boiling water over them.

Before using an unglazed clay pot, soak it in water so that the dry clay doesn't draw water from the soil.

When to Repot

Some plants can live for years in the same pot; others need to be repotted yearly. And some plants, especially flowering ones, perform best when they are potbound—when their roots are cramped in the pot. In general, the plant that you buy in a two-inch pot from the nursery will need repotting soon after you bring it home, while a large, mature plant growing in a big pot or tub will need repotting only every few years, if then. Specific tips on repotting individual plants appear in the How to Grow instructions.

Since you can't see its roots, how can you tell when a plant needs repotting? Here are some of the symptoms that indicate it is time for a larger pot:

1. Roots showing through the drainage holes of the pot or rising to the top of the soil
2. Water running immediately out of the drainage hole
3. Leaves turning yellow
4. New leaves growing smaller and farther apart than normal

The only way to be absolutely sure a plant needs repotting is to knock it out of its pot and look at the roots. This is easy to do with a small pot, but you can manage it with a large one, too. In both cases, it helps to water the plant a day or two before you perform the operation.

To remove a plant from a small pot, place your hand across the top of the pot. Tap the bottom of the pot sharply with a trowel. The plant will almost always slip out, but if it doesn't, don't tug on the stem. Instead, take a sharp knife and run it around the inside of the pot.

A very large pot is best handled by two people. Lay the pot on its side, wrap a piece of protective toweling around the rim, and then tap the pot all around the edge with any blunt instrument. Let one person pull the pot away from the roots while the other holds the plant. Again, if it doesn't come loose, use a sharp knife to cut between the pot and the root ball.

The plant needs repotting if the soil is encased in a mesh of roots or if long roots are wound around and around the outside of the root ball. If it turns out the plant does not have these symptoms, simply set it back in its pot, water it, and leave it alone.

Potting Plants

A plant needs repotting
if its roots encase the soil
and wind around the
root ball. Pull out
some of the circling
roots before potting.

To repot, put 1 or 2 inches of gravel in a pot 1 inch larger than the old one.

Set the plant at the same level as it was in the old pot. Fill around the sides to within 1 inch of the rim, tamping the soil down firmly.

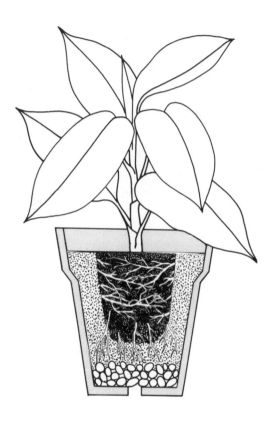

How to Repot a Plant

Potting plants is a messy business best done outside. If you must do it indoors, the kitchen is the best place. You'll do a better job and do it more easily if you don't have to worry about being neat. Put plenty of newspaper on the counter and pour your potting soil or soil mixes into a large pan. A roasting pan works very well—use the turkey roaster size if you are doing a big job.

Select a clean pot that is one size larger than the pot the plant is growing in. In practice, move plants to one-inch larger pots until you reach the ten-inch size. After that, move them to two-inch larger pots.

Before you repot your plant, inspect the roots carefully, cutting away any that are damaged or unhealthy. Gently remove any small stones or pot shards used for drainage, and unwind long lengths of roots that may be wound around the root ball. If the root ball is encased in large white roots, prune them to stimulate new growth that will penetrate the fresh soil. To prune roots, take a sharp knife and make three or four cuts, about an inch wide, from the top of the root ball to the bottom.

In the bottom of pots over six inches wide, put an inch or two of gravel or pebbles before you add new soil. Plants in pots six inches wide or smaller do not need this extra drainage material. Set plants in their new pots at the same level from the rim as they were in the old. For convenient watering, always leave at least an inch between the top of the soil and the rim of the pot.

Set the plant on a layer of new soil and start filling around the sides, gently but firmly tamping down the soil with your fingers or a flat stick. It is very important to settle this new soil firmly around the root ball, or water will just run down the sides and out the drainage holes. To be sure you have pressed down hard enough, water the pot and firm the soil again, adding more if necessary.

If a plant has outgrown its pot but you don't want to put it in a larger one, you can cut a slice off of each side of its root ball and then replace it as above. If it is the kind of plant that can be pruned from the top, cut off some of the top growth to compensate for the lost roots. Another way to treat an oversized root ball is to divide the roots to make two or more smaller plants (see Propagation, page 32).

Soils and Soilless Potting Mixes

Although soil is not the same thing as dirt, even the best garden soil contains too much bacteria for potted plants. It would have to be sterilized in the oven—a smelly process—and then improved with various amendments. It is much easier to buy potting soil formulated for houseplants. In the How to Grow sections of the Encyclopedia you will find recommendations for the proper soil mix to use for particular plants. Occasionally you will be advised to add peat moss or sand to a prepared mix for improved drainage.

Most foliage plants—and many of the flowering ones, too—can be potted in an all-purpose soil mix. The commercial ones are quite variable in texture. The one to choose is coarse and crumbly, not fine and silty, since the latter types tend to compact and do not hold water well.

Some plants do well in a soilless mix. This is a scientifically formulated medium—often called the Cornell Mix—that contains peat moss, vermiculite, and perlite, in addition to fertilizer and other necessary trace elements. Soilless mixes are light and easy to use; the plants you buy in the nursery are often potted up in this kind of mix. If you use a soilless mix, be conscientious about the fertilizing schedule, because once the built-in fertilizer is used up, the mix is virtually inert. Unlike soil, it contains no nutritive elements of its own.

African violet mix is recommended for many other plants as well as the gesneriads. It is more porous and slightly more acidic than an all-purpose mix, and it holds moisture well. Cactus soil mixes are sandier, grittier, and less acidic than ordinary potting mixtures. Most—although not all—orchids and bromeliads are epiphytes, obtaining their nutrients from air and water rather than from soil. These plants are grown in various mixtures of bark or fern fiber, or in unshredded sphagnum moss. (See Orchids, page 432.)

Bromeliads, which are less temperamental than orchids, may be potted in a soilless mix or even in porous potting soil.

Propagation

Sooner or later, the gardener who owns a few houseplants gets involved, often unwittingly, in propagating new ones. You cut off the tip of an extra-long vine and put it in water instead of throwing it out. In a few weeks, the stem has rooted. Or a leaf from your jade plant drops onto the soil in the pot, and before you know it, a new little jade plant is on its way. Not all houseplants can be propagated so readily, but a surprising number can. In the growing information at the back of the book you will find the best methods to use for individual plants.

Plants reproduce themselves in two ways—sexually and vegetatively. Sexual reproduction is through seeds; the resulting plants may or may not be identical to the parent. Houseplants, most of which are perennials or shrubs or trees, are rarely grown from seeds. Not only are the seeds often very slow to germinate, but the seedlings that are finally produced literally take years to grow to an attractive or marketable size. Moreover, the new plants may not have the same attributes that made the parents so desirable.

Vegetative reproduction involves using some part, or parts, of the original plant to make new plants. These new plants are not offspring of the parent but younger versions of the same plant. They are clones, identical in every way to the plant from which they were made. Furthermore, they are not "born" as seedlings but as mature plants.

Division

Plants that have multiple stems or grow in clumps are easy to propagate by division. This is also a useful way to solve the problem of plants growing too large for the pots you want to keep them in. To divide a large spathiphyllum or an African violet that has developed several clumps, knock it out of its pot and gently pull the roots and tops apart. You now have two or more separate plants. Repot these divisions, making sure each has both roots and leaves, in a pot one to two inches wider than the new plant.

Plants with tough root balls—asparagus ferns or Boston Fern, for example—can also be divided, but in these cases you will have to slice through the roots with a sharp knife. Although there are no hard-and-fast rules, you can usually divide a large plant into three or four pieces. To rejuvenate the plants and make sure that the new divisions grow luxuriantly, it is a good idea to cut off all the top growth before you begin. These are fast-growing plants that will easily renew themselves. Put them into pots three or four inches larger than the root ball.

Plantlets and Offsets

Spider Plants, epicias, Strawberry Begonias, and some other houseplants produce little replicas of themselves at the ends of long stems or, in the case of the Piggyback Plant, on the surface of the leaves. If these plantlets have roots, simply cut them off and plant

To propagate from
plantlets, pin the
plantlet down with
a paper clip to the
soil in a small pot.
After it has rooted,
cut the connecting
stolon.

Propagation

Offsets are small plants growing beside the parent. Remove the whole plant from the pot, preserving as many roots as you can. Use a sharp knife to cut the offset away, making sure it has roots attached, and plant it in a new pot.

them in potting soil or a soilless mix. If the plantlet doesn't have roots, leave it attached to the parent plant and pin it down with a paper clip to the soil in a new little pot. After it has rooted, cut the umbilical cord. Ferns that send out runners, like the Boston Fern, can also be propagated in this manner.

Bromeliads, cacti, African violets, and many other plants produce new little plants right next to the parent plant. These are called offsets and are treated much like the plantlets. Cut them away from the plant with a sharp knife, making sure that the plantlet has some roots attached. You can do the same thing with plants that grow from rhizomes, like the davallias. Be sure that each piece of rhizome has roots.

Cuttings

Most commercial growers take cuttings to propagate because they can make a great many plants from a single one. Cuttings can be made from virtually any part of a plant—roots, stems, leaves or parts of leaves, and even thick canes. No matter what part is used, the resulting plant will be an exact duplicate of the parent. Since not all plants reproduce satisfactorily from any part of their anatomy, check the encyclopedia instructions on propagation to learn what kind of cutting works best.

Cuttings have to grow their own roots, so they should not be put directly into ordinary potting soil. A few can root in water, which is easy but not particularly desirable. Water-bred roots don't make the transition to soil very well. If you do root plants in water, don't let the roots grow longer than an inch or two before you move the plant to soil or a soilless mixture.

To root plants you can use perlite, builder's sand, vermiculite, a combination of peat moss and builder's sand, or any mixture of these materials. Plastic flower pots and plastic bags to create a humid atmosphere are all the equipment you need. Hormone rooting powder, though usually not essential, will speed things along; buy it at your garden center and use it according to the manufacturer's directions.

Stem Cuttings

The most commonly used type of cuttings are stem—also called tip—cuttings. They are best taken from firm but not woody growth, usually in spring or summer, when plants are actively growing. The cuttings should be three to six inches long and have at least two but no more than six nodes. Nodes are the little bumps in the stem where leaves emerge. Remove all the leaves but two or three of the top ones, and if you're propagating a flowering plant, be sure to remove the flower buds. It's important that all the plant's energy go into producing roots.

Dampen the rooting material and make a hole in it with a pencil so that you don't have to force the stem in. If you are using a rooting

Propagation

hormone, dip the stem end into the powder and then insert it in the pot. Firm the cutting in the rooting material and mist it with water. Settle the plastic bag over the pot, making sure that it is held away from the plant with sticks or other supports. Put the bagged plant in a bright place out of the sunlight. After a few weeks—or sooner, if you see new top growth—check the cutting by tugging gently at it. If it comes out with a light tug, replant it in the rooting medium. If it resists your tug, it is probably ready to be moved out of its plastic house and into a pot of real soil.

Leaf Cuttings

African violets and other fleshy-leaved plants are easy to propagate by leaf cuttings. Take a healthy, medium-sized leaf with its stem, which should be cut to one inch. Insert the stem at a 45-degree angle into the rooting material and wait. There is no need, usually, to cover these pots with plastic, but keep them well watered. If the leaf is very large, cut part of it off. When little plants appear at the base of the stem, separate them gently and pot them up, cutting off the parent leaf. Some succulents and other plants without leaf stems can be rooted by putting the cut end of a leaf into rooting medium.

Cane Cuttings

To root plants with thick stems, like dracaenas, aucubas, and dieffenbachias, cut the stem into as many two-inch lengths as you can, making sure that each length has one or two nodes. The stem pieces may be set upright in the rooting medium—but be sure you have planted what was the bottom part when the stem was originally growing—or you can half-bury the cutting in the rooting medium horizontally, making sure that the leaf node is facing upward.

Air Layering

Large plants like rubber trees and dracaenas tend to grow into ungainly specimens with tufts of leaves at the top of their long trunks. Air layering is a dramatic, but actually easy, way to root such plants.
To air layer a plant, take a sharp knife and make an upwardly slanting cut where you want the new roots to grow. Don't cut more than a third of the way through the stem. Hold the cut open with a toothpick and dust the surface of the cut with a hormone rooting powder. Take a handful of sphagnum moss—not peat moss—and dampen it. Wrap the damp moss around the stem, covering the place where it is cut, and then wrap the moss in clear plastic, securing it with string or tape above and below the moss.
Care for the plant in the normal way. In a few months, when the plastic cover is filled with roots, remove it and cut the stem off below the roots. Put your "new" plant, moss and all, into its own pot using the soil mix recommended for the species.

Stem cuttings should be 3–6 inches long with 2–6 nodes. Cut just below a leaf joint and remove all but the top leaves.

Make a hole in the rooting medium with a pencil and insert cuttings.

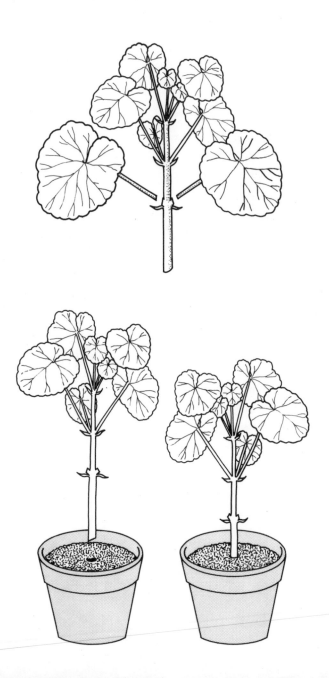

Propagation

Plants with long thick stems can be propagated in two ways. Air layering involves cutting ⅓ of the way into the stem, then wrapping a damp wad of sphagnum moss covered with clear plastic around the cut. When roots fill the bag, cut the stem off below the new roots, remove the plastic, and plant.

To propagate by cane cuttings, cut the stem into 2-inch lengths, making sure each has one or two nodes. Set the pieces upright in rooting medium, or half-bury them horizontally. Leaves will grow from exposed nodes and roots from buried ones.

Propagation

Cuttings can be made from almost any plant part. A leaf cutting should have a 1-inch stem. Insert it at a 45° angle in rooting medium. When little plants appear, separate and pot them, cutting off the parent leaf.

Seeds

Houseplants rarely form seeds indoors, but you can buy seeds of cacti and some other kinds of plants. Shallow flower pots, called pans, filled with any of the soil mixes recommended for cuttings, are handy for starting seeds. Sow the seeds according to the directions on the package, then set the pan in a bowl of lukewarm water to moisten the mix without disturbing the seeds. Let the excess water drain out and cover the pan with a plastic bag. Put it in a warm, bright place but never in the sun.

The first two leaves to emerge are the so-called seed leaves. The next two are the true leaves. After the first two or four true leaves emerge, carefully prick the seedling out of the soil with the tip of a pencil and, holding it by a leaf—not the fragile stem—pot it up in the mixture recommended for the species.

Plant Chart

	Page Numbers	Under 1 ft.
Hanging Plants		
Aeschynanthus radicans	86	
Begonia × semperflorens-cultorum	80	☐
Ceropegia woodii	87	
Chlorophytum comosum	85	
Cissus antarctica	76	
Cissus discolor	81	
Hedera helix	77, 78, 79	
Hoya carnosa	80	
Pellionia daveauana	82	
Philodendron scandens	76	
Pilea nummulariifolia	86	
Plectranthus australis 'Purple Majesty'	81	
Senecio macroglossus 'Variegatum'	79	
Senecio rowleyanus	87	
Setcreasea pallida 'Purple Heart'	83	
Tolmiea menziesii	77	☐
Tradescantia fluminensis	82, 85	
Zebrina pendula	83, 84	
Small Foliage Plants		
Acalypha wilkesiana	116	
Aglaonema commutatum	98	
Aglaonema costatum	91	☐
Anthurium crystallinum	104	
Aphelandra squarrosa 'Louisae'	109	☐
Begonia boweri	102	☐
Begonia × erythrophylla	106	☐
Begonia masoniana	100	
Begonia × rex-cultorum	110–12, 115	
Caladium × hortulanum	109, 112–13	
Calathea makoyana	99	
Calathea picturata	97	

1-3 ft.	Over 3 ft.	Trailing	Sun	Bright Light	Bright, some sun	Medium Light	Low Light	Warm Temperature	Avg. Temperature	Cool Temperature	Easy	Difficult	Fairly Easy	Special Needs
■	▨	□	■	▨	□	■	▨	□	■	▨	□	■	▨	□
		□			□			□						□
			■					■		□				
		□	■					■		□				
■				▨	□	■		■						
		□		■	□	■	▨	■	▨	□				
		□		■				□				■		□
		□		▨				■	▨	□				
		□		■		□		■		□				
		□		■				■		□				
		□		■		■		■		□				
		□		■		■		□					▨	□
		□		■				■		□				
		□		■				■		□				
		□				□		■	▨	□				
		□	■					■		□				
			▨	□	■									
		□			□			■		□				
		□			□			■		□				
	▨				□			□						□
■						■	▨	■		□				
						■	▨	■		□				
■				□			□	■				■		□
				▨			□	■				■		□
				□				■		□				
				□				■		□				
■				▨				■		□				
■				▨			□						▨	□
■				▨			□					■		□
■						■		■	▨	□				
■						■		■	▨	□				

Plant Chart

	Page Numbers	Under 1 ft.
Small Foliage Plants continued		
Calathea roseopicta	104	☐
Calathea vittata	103	
Calathea zebrina	100	
Coleus × *hybridus* 'Lacey Leaf'	96	
Coleus × *hybridus* 'Reasoners' Fancy Leaf'	95	
Coleus × *hybridus* 'Red Lace Leaf'	113	
Coleus × *hybridus* 'Wizard Mixture'	114	
Cordyline terminalis	116	
Cyanotis kewensis	110	
Dieffenbachia amoena	97	
Dieffenbachia 'Camille'	96	
Dracaena surculosa	91	
Epipremnum aureum	92, 93	
Episcia cupreata	108	
Ficus benjamina	90	
Fittonia verschaffeltii argyroneura	107	
Gynura aurantiaca	117	
Iresine herbstii	117	
Maranta leuconeura	101	☐
Maranta leuconeura kerchoviana	101	☐
Monstera obliqua	92	
Osmanthus fragrans	90	
Pelargonium hortorum hybrids	94	
Peperomia argyreia	105	☐
Peperomia caperata	107	☐
Peperomia obtusifolia	93	☐
Peperomia scandens 'Variegata'	95	
Pilea cadierei	99	☐
Pilea involucrata	102	☐
Pilea spruceana 'Norfolk'	108	☐
Plectranthus coleoides 'Marginatus'	94	

1-3 ft.	Over 3 ft.	Trailing	Sun	Bright Light	Bright, some sun	Medium Light	Low Light	Warm Temperature	Avg. Temperature	Cool Temperature	Easy	Difficult	Fairly Easy	Special Needs
■	▨	□	■	▨	□	■	▨	□	■	▨	□	■	▨	□
						■			■	▨	□			
■						■			■	▨	□			
■						■			■	▨	□			
■					□				■		□			
■					□				■		□			
■					□				■		□			
■					□				■		□			
■				■					■				▨	□
		□	■						■					□
	▨			■					■		□			
	▨			■					■		□			
■				■		■			■		□			
		□		■	□	■	■		■		□			
		□		■				□					▨	□
	▨			■	□	■			■		□			
		□		■	□	■		□						□
		□	■					□	■		□			
■					□				■		□			
					□				■	▨	□			
						■			■	▨	□			
		□		■					■		□			
■					□					▨	□			
	▨			■					■		□			
				■	□	■			■		□			
				■	□	■			■		□			
				■	□	■			■		□			
		□		■	□	■			■		□			
				■		■		□			□			□
				■				□			□			□
				■				□					▨	□
		□		■					■		□			

Plant Chart

	Page Numbers	Under 1 ft.
Small Foliage Plants continued		
Saxifraga stolonifera	106	☐
Syngonium podophyllum	103	
Xanthosoma lindenii	105	
Orchids		
Angraecum sesquipedale	136, 137	
Ansellia africana	132, 133	
Asocentrum curvifolium	122, 123	☐
Aspasia epidendroides	140, 141	☐
Brassavola nodosa	134, 135	
Brassia gireoudiana	134, 135	☐
Broughtonia negrilensis × *sanguinea*	146, 147	☐
Bulbophyllum blumei	126, 127	☐
Cattleya violacea	148, 149	
Cattleya walkerana	148, 149	☐
Cymbidium Gainesville × Dan Carpenter	130, 131	
Dendrobium primulinum	146, 147	☐
Dendrobium Tangerine × Mushroom Pink	130, 131	☐
Epidendrum cordigera	150, 151	
Epidendrum radicans	124, 125	
Laelia anceps	150, 151	
Laeliocattleya Park Ridge	142, 143	
Lycaste cruenta	128, 129	
Masdevallia Marguerite 'Selby'	126, 127	☐
Miltonia flavescens	136, 137	☐
Odontioda Memoria Len Page	142, 143	
Odontoglossum bilobum	140, 141	
Oncidium Equitant hybrids	120, 121	☐
Oncidium maculatum	132, 133	
Oncidium viperinum	128, 129	☐
Paphiopedilum Maudiae	138, 139	☐
Phalaenopsis Carnival Queen × Zauberot	144, 145	

1–3 ft.	Over 3 ft.	Trailing	Sun	Bright Light	Bright, some sun	Medium Light	Low Light	Warm Temperature	Avg. Temperature	Cool Temperature	Easy	Difficult	Fairly Easy	Special Needs
■	▦	□	■	▦	□	■	▦	□	■	▦	□	■	▦	□
						□				▦	□			
		□		▦					■			□		
■				▦				□						□
■						□		□	■					□
■						□		□	■					□
			■					□	■					□
				▦				□	■					□
■			■	▦	□			□	■					□
				▦				□	■					□
						□		□	■					□
				▦				□						□
■						□		□	■					□
						□		□	■					□
		□				□			■	▦				□
						□			■					□
						□	□							□
■						□		□	■					□
		□	■					□	■					□
	▦					□			■					□
■						□			■					□
■						□			■	▦				□
				▦					■	▦				□
						□	□		■					□
		□				□				▦				□
■						□			■	▦				□
						□			■					□
■						□			■					□
						□			■					□
						□		□	■					□
■						□		□	■					□

Plant Chart

	Page Numbers	Under 1 ft.
		☐
Orchids continued		
Phalaenopsis stuartiana	138, 139	☐
Sophrolaeliocattleya Jewel Box	122, 123	☐
Sophronitis cernua	124, 125	☐
Vanda sanderana	144, 145	
Bromeliads and Flowers		
Abutilon hybridum	180	
Acalypha hispida	183	
Aechmea chantinii	158	☐
Aechmea fasciata	159	
Allamanda cathartica	193	
Anthurium scherzeranum	155	
Begonia coccinea	179	
Begonia 'Di-Erna'	178	
Begonia × *erythrophylla*	169	☐
Begonia × *hiemalis*	162	
Begonia 'Lana'	179	
Begonia × *semperflorens-cultorum*	169, 186	☐
Billbergia 'Theodore L. Mead'	178	
Bougainvillea 'Barbara Karst'	197	
Bougainvillea glabra 'Sanderana Variegata'	198	
Browallia speciosa	174	
Calceolaria herbeohybrida	162	☐
Camellia japonica	192	
Capsicum annuum	194	
Carissa grandiflora	191	
Clerodendrum thomsoniae	193	
Clivia miniata	155	
Columnea 'California Gold'	185	
Crossandra infundibuliformis	188	
Cuphea ignea	182	
Cyclamen persicum	168	☐

1-3 ft.	Over 3 ft.	Trailing	Sun	Bright Light	Bright, some sun	Medium Light	Low Light	Warm Temperature	Avg. Temperature	Cool Temperature	Easy	Difficult	Fairly Easy	Special Needs
■	▥	□	■	▥	□	■	▥	□	■	▥	□	■	▥	□
					□			□	■					□
					□				■					□
				▥					■	▥				□
	▥		■					□						□
	■				□				■	▥			▥	
	▥				□			□						□
					□			□	■		□			□
■					□			□	■		□			□
		□			□			□	■					□
■				▥				□	■			■		□
■					□				■	□				
■					□				■	□				
					□				■	□				
■					□				■				▥	
■					□				■					□
			■						■	□				
■					□			□	■	□				□
		□	■					□						□
		□	■					□						□
				□		□			■	▥				□
				▥					■	▥				□
	▥			□						▥		■		□
■				▥					■					□
■			■						■	□				
	▥			▥				□						□
■				▥					■	□				
		□		▥					■				■	□
■					□	■		□				■		□
■					□				■	□				
				▥						▥				□

Plant Chart

	Page Numbers	Under 1 ft.
Bromeliads and Flowers continued		
Euphorbia milli	170, 197	
Euphorbia pulcherrima	199	
Exacum affine	175	
Fuchsia × hybrida	176, 177	☐
Gardenia jasminoides	189	
Gesneria cuneifolia	182	☐
Guzmania 'Cherry'	156	
Guzmania lingulata	156	☐
Hibiscus rosa-sinensis	188	
Impatiens hybrid	198	
Impatiens wallerana	170, 171	
Ixora coccinea	187	
Jasminum nitidum	190	
Jasminum polyanthum	192	
Jasminum sambac 'Maid of Orleans'	190	
Justicia brandegeana	184	
Kalanchoe blossfeldiana	187	☐
Kohleria 'Dark Velvet'	181	☐
Lantana camara	185, 189	☐
Nematanthus 'Castanet'	184	☐
Nematanthus 'Tropicana'	183	☐
Neoregelia carolinae 'Meyendorffii Flandria'	161	☐
Neoregelia carolinae 'Tricolor'	161	☐
Nerium oleander	196	
Nidularium billbergioides	157	☐
Nidularium 'Ra Ru' × 'Sao Paulo'	157	
Pelargonium Cascade hybrids	172, 173	
Pelargonium domesticum hybrids	172	
Pelargonium hortorum hybrids	199	
Pelargonium peltatum hybrids	173	
Pelargonium tomentosum	180	

1–3 ft.	Over 3 ft.	Trailing	Sun	Bright Light	Bright, some sun	Medium Light	Low Light	Warm Temperature	Avg. Temperature	Cool Temperature	Easy	Difficult	Fairly Easy	Special Needs
■	▨	□	■	▨	□	■	▨	□	■	▨	□	■	▨	□
■			■						■		□			
■				▨					■	▨				□
■				▨					■					□
			■							▨				□
■			■						■	▨		■		□
				▨			□					■		□
■					□		□	■		□				□
					□		□	■		□				□
	▨		■						■					□
■					□			■		□				
■			▨					■		□				
	▨		■				□					■		□
	□				□		□	■					▨	
	□				□				▨				▨	
	□				□		□	■					▨	
■					□			■		□				
			▨					■						□
					□			■				■		□
					□			■	▨				▨	□
			▨					■					▨	□
			▨					■					▨	□
					□		□	■		□				
					□		□	■		□				
	▨		■					■		□				
				▨	□	■	□	■		□				
■				▨	□	■	□	■		□				
		□	▨					■		□				
■			■					■		□				
	▨		■					■		□				
		□	■					■		□				
■				▨				■		□				

Plant Chart

	Page Numbers	Under 1 ft.
Bromeliads and Flowers continued		
Plectranthus australis	176	
Plumbago auriculata	195	
Saintpaulia 'Jelly Bean'	168	☐
Saintpaulia Optimara hybrids	166, 167	☐
Saintpaulia 'Pendula'	174	
Sinningia concinna	163	☐
Sinningia hybrid	181	☐
Sinningia speciosa	163	☐
Spathiphyllum 'Mauna Loa'	154	
Spathiphyllum wallisii	154	☐
Streptocarpus 'Constant Nymph'	165	☐
Streptocarpus 'Good Hope'	175	☐
Streptocarpus 'John Innes' hybrids	164, 165	☐
Streptocarpus 'Wiesmoor' hybrids	164	☐
Thunbergia alata	194	
Thunbergia erecta	195	
Tillandsia cyanea	160	☐
Tillandsia didisticha	160	☐
Trachelospermum jasminoides	191	
Vriesea ensiformis	159	
Vriesea splendens	158	
Showy Foliage Plants		
Acorus gramineus 'Variegatus'	226	☐
Aeonium arboreum	212	
Ananas comosus 'Variegatus'	237	
Araucaria bidwillii	221	
Araucaria heterophylla	221	
Ardisia crenata	216	
Aspidistra elatior	225, 228	
Aucuba japonica 'Variegata'	214	
Beaucarnea recurvata	236	

1–3 ft.	Over 3 ft.	Trailing	Sun	Bright Light	Bright, some sun	Medium Light	Low Light	Warm Temperature	Avg. Temperature	Cool Temperature	Easy	Difficult	Fairly Easy	Special Needs
■	▨	□	■	▨	□	■	▨	□	■	▨	□	■	▨	□
		□		▨					■		□			
	▨		■						■	▨			▨	
				▨			□				□			□
				▨			□				□			□
		□		▨			□						■	□
				▨			□						■	
				▨			□							
				▨			□			□				
■						■		■		□				
					▨			■		□				
				▨				■					▨	□
				▨				■					▨	□
				▨				■					▨	□
				▨				■					▨	□
		□	■					■	▨	□				
	▨		■					■	▨	□				
					□		□	■		□				
					□		□	■		□				
	▨		■					■		□				
■					□		□	■		□				
■					□		□	■		□				
				▨	□	■		■		□				
■			■					■		□				
■			■				□					■		□
■						■		■		□				
	▨					■		■		□				
■					□				■			■		□
■							□	■		□				
■				▨				■	▨	□				
■				▨	□	■		■		□				

	Page Numbers	Under 1 ft.
Showy Foliage Plants continued		
Begonia maculata 'Wightii'	204	
Begonia 'Medora'	208	☐
Brassaia actinophylla	213	
Caryota mitis	229	
Chamaedorea elegans	230, 231	
Chamaerops humilis	233	
Chrysalidocarpus lutescens	232	
Cissus rhombifolia	207	
Citrus × citrofortunella mitis	218	
Citrus limon 'Meyer'	218	
Codiaem variegatum pictum	204, 223–4	
Coffea arabica	217	
Cycas revoluta	230	
Cyperus alternifolius	233	
Dieffenbachia maculata	203	
Dizygotheca elegantissima	222	
Dracaena deremensis 'Warneckii'	227	
Dracaena fragrans 'Massangeana'	226	
Dracaena marginata	236	
Dracaena sanderana	224	
Evonymus japonica 'Mediopicta'	215	
Fatshedera lizei	207	
Fatsia japonica	210	
Ficus benjamina	216	
Ficus deltoidea	219	
Ficus elastica	205	
Ficus 'Elegante'	219	
Ficus lyrata	205	
Ficus pumila	208	
Grevillea robusta	222	
Heptapleurum arboricola	211	

1-3 ft.	Over 3 ft.	Trailing	Sun	Bright Light	Bright, some sun	Medium Light	Low Light	Warm Temperature	Avg. Temperature	Cool Temperature	Easy	Difficult	Fairly Easy	Special Needs
■	▦	□	■	▦	□	■	▦	□	■	▦	□	■	▦	□
■					□				■		□			
					□				■		□			
▦					□				■		□			□
	▦			■		■			■		□			
■				▦	□	■			■		□			
	▦				□				■		□			
	▦		■				□		■					□
		□		▦	□	■	▦		■		□			
	▦		■						■				▦	
	▦		■						■				▦	
■			■				□		■				▦	□
	▦		■						■		□			
■				▦					■		□			
■						■			■		□			
	▦			▦					■		□			
	▦			▦					■				▦	
	▦			▦		■			■		□			
	▦			▦		■			■		□			
	▦			▦		■			■		□			
■				▦		■			■		□			
	▦				□			■	▦				▦	
	▦			▦	□	■			■		□			
	▦			▦	□					▦	□			
	▦			▦	□	■			■		□			
■				▦	□	■			■		□			
	▦			▦	□	■			■		□			
	▦			▦	□	■			■		□			
	▦			▦	□	■			■		□			
		□		▦	□	■	▦		■					□
	▦				□			■	▦		□			
	▦				□				■		□			□

	Page Numbers	Under 1 ft.
		☐
Showy Foliage Plants continued		
Howea belmoreana	232	
Hypoestes phyllostachya	214	
Livistonia chinensis	234	
Monstera deliciosa	211	
Osmanthus heterophyllus 'Variegatus'	215	
Pandanus veitchii	237	
Passiflora caerulea	209	
Passiflora coccinea	209	
Philodendron bipennifolium	206	
Philodendron erubescens	206	
Philodendron selloum	210	
Phoenix roebelenii	231	
Pittosporum tobira	212	
Pleomele reflexa	225, 228	
Podocarpus macrophyllus	223	
Polyscias balfouriana	202, 203	
Polyscias fruticosa	220	
Polyscias paniculata 'Variegata'	217	
Punica granatum 'Nana'	220	
Rhapis excelsa	229	
Rhoeo spathacea	227	☐
Schefflera arboricola	213	
Washingtonia filifera	234	
Yucca aloifolia	235	
Yucca elephantipes	235	
Lacy Leaves		
Adiantum capillus-veneris	251	☐
Adiantum raddianum	251	
Asparagus densiflorus 'Myers'	245	
Asparagus densiflorus 'Sprengeri'	245	
Asparagus setaceus	247	

1–3 ft.	Over 3 ft.	Trailing	Sun	Bright Light	Bright, some sun	Medium Light	Low Light	Warm Temperature	Avg. Temperature	Cool Temperature	Easy	Difficult	Fairly Easy	Special Needs
■	▨	□	■	▨	□	■	▨	□	■	▨	□	■	▨	□
	▨			▨	□	■			■		□			
	▨				□				■		□			
	▨			▨	□	■			■		□			
	▨			▨	□		□		■		□			
■					□					▨	□			
■							□							□
	▨		■				□					■		
		□	■				□					■		
	▨			▨		■			■		□			
	▨			▨		■			■		□			
	▨			▨		■			■		□			
	▨				□				■		□			
	▨		■						■	▨	□			
	▨			▨			□		■		□			
	▨			▨					■	▨	□			
	▨			▨			□				□			□
	▨			▨			□				□			□
	▨			▨			□				□			□
■			■						■	▨			■	
	▨			▨					■		□			
					□				■		□			
	▨				□				■		□			
	▨				□				■		□			
	▨			▨	□	■			■		□			
	▨			▨	□	■			■		□			
						■			■					□
■						■			■					□
■				▨					■		□			
		□	■						■		□			
■				▨					■		□			

	Page Numbers	Under 1 ft.
Lacy Leaves continued		
Asplenium bulbiferum	250	
Asplenium nidus	242, 243	
Blechnum gibbum	244	
Cyrtomium falcatum	240	
Davallia fejeensis	250	
Davallia trichomanoides	247	
Hatiora salicornioides	246	
Malpighia coccigera	253	☐
Nephrolepis cordifolia	244	
Nephrolepis exaltata 'Bostoniensis'	248	
Oplismenus hirtellus 'Variegatus'	252	☐
Pellaea rotundifolia	252	☐
Philodendron pinnatilobum 'Fernleaf'	246	
Philodendron 'Pluto'	243	
Phyllitis scolipendrium 'Crispum'	242	
Pilea microphylla	253	☐
Platycerium bifurcatum	240	
Polypodium aureum	241	
Pteris cretica 'Alexandrae'	241	
Pteris ensiformis 'Victoriae'	249	
Rumohra adiantiformis	248	
Selaginella willdenovii	249	
Succulents and Others		
Aechmea lueddemanniana	273	
Aeonium arboreum	286	
Aeonium tabuliforme	285	☐
Agave leopoldii	281	☐
Agave victoriae-reginae	281	☐
Aloe barbadensis	280	
Aloe variegata	278	☐
Aporocactus flagelliformis	266	

1-3 ft.	Over 3 ft.	Trailing	Sun	Bright Light	Bright, some sun	Medium Light	Low Light	Warm Temperature	Avg. Temperature	Cool Temperature	Easy	Difficult	Fairly Easy	Special Needs
■	▦	□	■	▦	□	■	▦	□	■	▦	□	■	▦	□
■						■			■		□			□
■						■			■		□			□
■					□	■			■				▦	□
■				□				■	▦	□				
■						■			■		□			
■						■			■		□			
	□			▦					■					□
		■							■		□			
■				□		■			■		□			
■				▦		■			■		□			
					□				■		□			
						■			■	▦			▦	□
	□			▦		■			■		□			
■				▦		■			■		□			
■						■			■		□			
				▦			□					■	□
■				▦					■			■		□
■						■			■		□			
■				▦					■				■	
■				▦					■				■	
■						■		□	■		□			□
	□					■	▦	□				■		□
■					□			□	■		□			□
■		■						□	■		□			
		■						□	■		□			
		■							■		□			
		■							■		□			
■				▦					■		□			
				▦					■		□			
	□	■							■		□			

Plant Chart

	Page Numbers	Under 1 ft.
Succulents and Others continued		
Cephalocereus senilis	261	☐
Chamaecereus sylvestri	266	
Cleistocactus strausii	263	
Columnea hirta	269	
Crassula argentea	287	
Crassula falcata	283	☐
Crassula lycopodioides	265	☐
Crassula rupestris	284	
Cryptanthus acaulis	276	☐
Cryptanthus bivittatus	274	☐
Cryptanthus 'Starlite'	275	☐
Cryptanthus zonatus	275	☐
Dyckia fosterana	282	☐
Echeveria 'Black Prince'	286	☐
Echeveria elegans	268	☐
Echeveria runyonii	285	☐
Echinocactus grusonii	257	☐
Echinocactus horizonthalonius	257	☐
Echinocereus pectinatus	262	☐
Echinopsis multiplex	256	☐
Epiphyllum 'Ackermannii'	271	
Euphorbia tirucalli	272	
Gasteria liliputana	278	☐
Gymnocalycium mihanovichii	256	☐
Haworthia fasciata	279	☐
Haworthia margaritifera	279	☐
Hoya carnosa 'Krinkle Kurl'	267	
Kalanchoe pumila	283	☐
Kalanchoe tomentosa	282	☐
Lithops lesliei	284	☐
Lobivia arachnacantha	262	☐

1–3 ft.	Over 3 ft.	Trailing	Sun	Bright Light	Bright, some sun	Medium Light	Low Light	Warm Temperature	Avg. Temperature	Cool Temperature	Easy	Difficult	Fairly Easy	Special Needs
■	▨	□	■	▨	□	■	▨	□	■	▨	□	■	▨	□
			■						■	□				
		□	■						■	□				
■			■						■	□				
		□			▨				■				▨	□
	▨					□			■	▨	□			
						□			■	□				
						□			■	□				
		□				□			■	□				
						□	□		■	□				□
						□	□		■	□				□
						□	□		■	□				□
						□	□		■	□				□
		■							■	□				
		■							■	□				
		■							■	□				
		■							■	□				
		■							■	□				
		■							■	□				
		■							■	□				
		■							■	□				
	□			▨					■					□
▨				▨					■	□				
				▨	□	■			■	□				
		■							■	□				
				▨	□	■			■	□				
				▨	□	■			■	□				
	□					□			■	□				
						□			■	□				
						□			■	□				
		■							■	□				
		■							■	□				

Plant Chart

	Page Numbers	Under 1 ft.
Succulents and Others continued		
Lobivia leucomalla	258	☐
Mammillaria bocasana	260, 261	☐
Mammillaria camptotricha	258	☐
Mammillaria guelzowiana	259	☐
Mammillaria hahniana	260	☐
Opuntia microdasys	263	
Opuntia subulata	265	
Pachyphytum oviferum	268	☐
Portulacaria afra	287	
Rebutia kupperana	259	☐
Rhipsalidopsis gaertneri	270	
Rhipsalis baccifera	272	
Rhipsalis crispata	271	
Rhipsalis rhombea	269	
Sansevieria trifasciata 'Hahnii'	276, 277	☐
Sansevieria trifasciata 'Laurentii'	277	
Schlumbergera bridgesii	270	☐
Sedum morganianum	267	
Stapelia hirsuta	264	☐
Stapelia leendertziae	280	☐
Stapelia variegata	264	☐
Tillandsia caput-medusae	273	☐

1–3 ft.	Over 3 ft.	Trailing	Sun	Bright Light	Bright, some sun	Medium Light	Low Light	Warm Temperature	Avg. Temperature	Cool Temperature	Easy	Difficult	Fairly Easy	Special Needs
■	■	□	■	■	□	■	■	□	■	■	□	■	■	□
			■						■		□			
			■						■		□			
			■						■		□			
			■						■		□			
			■						■		□			
■			■						■		□			
	■		■						■		□			
			■						■		□			
	■				□				■	■	□			
			■						■		□			
		□		■		■			■					□
		□		■					■					□
		□		■					■					□
		□		■					■					□
				■	□	■	■		■		□			
■				■	□	■			■		□			
				■		■			■					□
		□			□				■		□			
				■					■		□			
				■					■		□			
				■					■		□			
					□		□		■		□			

The plates on the following pages are
divided into seven groups: hanging plants;
small foliage plants; orchids; bromeliads
and flowers; showy foliage plants; lacy
leaves; and succulents and others.

Visual Key
Preceding the color plates is the Visual Key,
which shows the kinds of plants in each
group. The hanging plants include climbers
like senecio and philodendron, as well as
cascading types like the Spider Plant.
Color-splashed coleus, crinkly peperomias,
and other small foliage plants of striking
shape, color, or texture appear next, followed
by orchids, with their exotic blooms.
Flowering plants—bushy begonias, bright
gloxinias, elegant spathe flowers, and
more—appear along with bromeliads grown
for their brightly-colored bracts or leaves.
The fifth section includes dramatic foliage
plants such as rubber trees, palms, and
dracaenas. Ferns appear in the next group,
along with other plants that have interesting
foliage. The last group includes spiny cacti
with surprisingly delicate blossoms, fleshy
succulents like aloes and jades, and such
spiky plants as the star-shaped cryptanthus.

Visual Key

Hanging Plants

Climbing, trailing, and cascading plants usually grown in hanging containers are shown here. Some plants in other groups may also be grown this way.

Small Foliage Plants

These plants usually grow to less than 3 ft. tall and have leaves of striking color, shape, or texture. Attractive young forms of some larger plants are also included.

Orchids

Here are orchids with flowers ranging from small and delicate to large and flamboyant. A view of an entire plant is shown along with a detail of its flowers.

Pages 74–87

Pages 88–117

Pages 118–151

Bromeliads and Flowers

This group includes a wide variety of plants grown for their colorful flowers, bracts, or leaves. Some bloom continuously; others seasonally.

Showy Foliage Plants

Small trees and other foliage plants of dramatic shape or size are featured here.

Pages 152–199

Pages 200–237

Lacy Leaves   This group includes
true ferns and other
plants prized for
their foliage.

**Succulents and
Others**   Cacti and other
water-storing plants
are shown here,
along with some
nonsucculents of
similar habit.

73

Pages 238–253

Pages 254–287

Hanging Plants

Philodendron
scandens

Heart-leaf
Philodendron
Vine
Bright to medium
light
Average temperature
Easy to grow
p. 399

Cissus antarctica

Kangaroo Vine
Bright to low light;
some sun
Average to cool
temperature
Easy to grow
p. 328

Tolmiea menziesii

Piggyback Plant
Vine
Bright to medium
light
Average to cool
temperature
Easy to grow
p. 424

Hedera helix
'Ripples'

English Ivy
Vine
Bright light
Average to cool
temperature
Easy to grow
p. 366

Hedera helix
hybrid

English Ivy Vine
Bright light
Average to cool
temperature
Easy to grow
p. 366

Hedera helix
'Harald'

English Ivy
Vine
Bright light
Average to cool
temperature
Easy to grow
p. 366

Senecio macroglossus
'Variegatum'

Variegated Wax Vine
Bright light
Average temperature
Easy to grow
p. 416

Hedera helix
hybrid

Variegated English Ivy
Vine
Bright light
Average to cool
temperature
Easy to grow
p. 366

Begonia × semperflorens-cultorum 'Charm'

Wax Begonia
Plant height:
6 to 12 in.
Sun
Average temperature
Easy to grow
p. 310

Hoya carnosa

Wax Plant
Vine
Bright light; some sun
Average temperature
Easy to grow
p. 369

Plectranthus australis
'Purple Majesty'

Swedish Ivy
Vine
Bright light
Average temperature
Easy to grow
p. 403

Cissus discolor

Trailing Begonia
Vine
Bright light
Warm temperature
Extra humidity
Difficult to grow
p. 328

Tradescantia fluminensis 'Quicksilver'

Wandering Jew
Trailing plant
Bright light; some sun
Average temperature
Easy to grow
p. 425

Pellionia daveauana

Trailing Watermelon
Begonia
Creeper
Bright light
Average temperature
Easy to grow
p. 396

Setcreasea pallida 'Purple Heart'

Purple-heart
Trailing plant
Sun
Average temperature
Easy to grow
p. 417

Zebrina pendula 'Purposii'

Wandering Jew
Trailing plant
Bright light; some sun
Average temperature
Easy to grow
p. 429

Zebrina pendula

Wandering Jew
Trailing plant
Bright light; some sun
Average temperature
Easy to grow
p. 429

Zebrina pendula
'Quadricolor'

Wandering Jew
Trailing plant
Bright light; some sun
Average temperature
Easy to grow
p. 429

Tradescantia fluminensis 'Variegata'

Wandering Jew
Trailing plant
Bright light; some sun
Average temperature
Easy to grow
p. 425

Chlorophytum comosum

Spider Plant
Trailing Plant
Bright to medium
light
Average temperature
Easy to grow
p. 327

Pilea
nummulariifolia

Creeping Charlie
Creeper
Bright to medium
light
Warm temperature
Extra humidity
Fairly easy to grow
p. 401

Aeschynanthus
radicans

Lipstick Plant
Trailing plant
Bright light; some sun
Warm temperature
Extra humidity
Special needs
p. 294

Senecio rowleyanus

String-of-beads
Vine
Bright light; some sun
Average temperature
Easy to grow
p. 416

Ceropegia woodii

Hearts-on-a-string
Vine
Sun
Average temperature
Easy to grow
p. 324

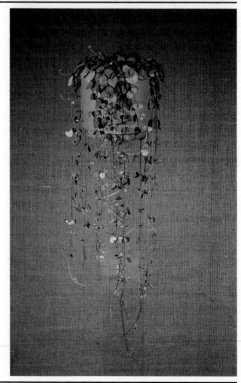

Small Foliage

Plants

Ficus benjamina 'Variegata'

Weeping Fig
Plant height:
2 to 18 ft.
Bright to medium
light
Average temperature
Easy to grow
p. 359

Osmanthus fragrans

Sweet Olive
Plant height: 1 to 2 ft.
Bright light; some sun
Cool temperature
Easy to grow
p. 390

Dracaena surculosa

*Gold-dust Plant
Plant height:
1½ to 2 ft.
Bright to medium
light
Average temperature
Easy to grow
p. 347*

Aglaonema costatum

*Spotted Evergreen
Plant height: to 10 in.
Medium to low light
Average temperature
Easy to grow
p. 296*

Epipremnum aureum

Pothos
Vine
Bright to low light
Average temperature
Easy to grow
p. 353

Monstera obliqua

Monstera
Climber
Bright light
Warm to average
temperature
Easy to grow
p. 383

Peperomia
obtusifolia

Baby Rubber Plant
Plant height:
6 to 8 in.
Bright to medium
light
Average temperature
Easy to grow
p. 396

Epipremnum
aureum
'Marble Queen'

Pothos
Vine
Bright to low light
Average temperature
Easy to grow
p. 353

**Plectranthus
coleoides
'Marginatus'**

*Prostrate Coleus
Vine
Bright light
Average temperature
Easy to grow
p. 404*

**Pelargonium ×
hortorum
'Mrs. Parker'**

*Zonal Geranium
Plant height: 3 to 4 ft.
Sun
Average temperature
Easy to grow
p. 394*

Peperomia scandens
'Variegata'

Philodendron
Peperomia
Vine
Bright to medium
light
Average temperature
Easy to grow
p. 396

Coleus × hybridus
'Reasoner's Fancy
Leaf'

Painted Nettle
Plant height: to 3 ft.
Bright light; some sun
Average temperature
Easy to grow
p. 333

Coleus × hybridus 'Lacey Leaf'

Painted Nettle
Plant height: to 3 ft.
Bright light; some sun
Average temperature
Easy to grow
p. 333

Dieffenbachia 'Camille'

Dumb Cane
Plant height: 3 to 4 ft.
Bright light
Average temperature
Easy to grow
p. 345

Calathea picturata

Calathea
Plant height: to 2 ft.
Medium light
Average temperature
Easy to grow
p. 318

Dieffenbachia amoena

Dumb Cane
Plant height: 5 to 6 ft.
Bright light
Average temperature
Easy to grow
p. 345

***Aglaonema
commutatum*
'Treubii'**

*Chinese Evergreen
Plant height: 1 to 2 ft.
Medium to low light
Average temperature
Easy to grow
p. 296*

***Aglaonema
commutatum***

*Chinese Evergreen
Plant height: 1 to 2 ft.
Medium to low light
Average temperature
Easy to grow
p. 296*

Pilea cadierei

Aluminum Plant
Plant height: to 12 in.
Bright to medium
light
Warm temperature
Extra humidity
Easy to grow
p. 401

Calathea makoyana

Peacock Plant
Plant height: to 2 ft.
Medium light
Average temperature
Easy to grow
p. 318

Calathea zebrina

Zebra Plant
Plant height: to 15 in.
Medium light
Average temperature
Easy to grow
p. 318

Begonia masoniana

Iron-Cross Begonia
Plant height:
12 to 16 in.
Bright light
Average temperature
Easy to grow
p. 310

Maranta leuconeura kerchoviana

Prayer Plant
Plant height: to 12 in.
Medium light
Average temperature
Easy to grow
p. 380

Maranta leuconeura

Prayer Plant
Plant height: to 12 in.
Medium light
Average temperature
Easy to grow
p. 380

Begonia boweri

Eyelash Begonia
Plant height: 6 to 8 in.
Bright light; some sun
Average temperature
Easy to grow
p. 309

Pilea involucrata

Panamiga
Plant height: 6 to 8 in.
Bright light
Warm temperature
Extra humidity
Easy to grow
p. 401

Calathea vittata

Calathea
Plant height: to 3 ft.
Medium light
Average temperature
Easy to grow
p. 318

Syngonium podophyllum

Arrowhead Vine
Bright light
Average temperature
Easy to grow
p. 422

Anthurium crystallinum

Crystal Anthurium
Plant height: to 3 ft.
Bright light
Warm to average
temperature
Extra humidity
Difficult to grow
p. 300

Calathea roseopicta

Calathea
Plant height: to 8 in.
Medium light
Average temperature
Easy to grow
p. 318

Xanthosoma lindenii

Indian Kale
Plant height:
12 to 18 in.
Bright light
Warm temperature
Extra humidity
Special needs
p. 428

Peperomia argyreia

Watermelon Peperomia
Plant height:
6 to 12 in.
Bright to medium light
Average temperature
Easy to grow
p. 396

Begonia × erythrophylla

Beefsteak Begonia
Plant height: to 9 in.
Bright light; some sun
Average temperature
Easy to grow
p. 309

Saxifraga stolonifera

Mother-of-thousands
Plant height: to 9 in.
Bright light; some sun
Cool temperature
Easy to grow
p. 414

Peperomia caperata

Emerald Ripple
Peperomia
Plant height: to 6 in.
Bright to medium
light
Average temperature
Easy to grow
p. 396

Fittonia
verschaffeltii
argyroneura

Mosaic Plant
Trailing plant
Bright to medium
light
Warm temperature
Extra humidity
Special needs
p. 360

Pilea spruceana 'Norfolk'

Angelwings
Plant height: 6 to 8 in.
Bright light
Warm temperature
Extra humidity
Fairly easy to grow
p. 401

Episcia cupreata

Flame Violet
Trailing plant
Bright light
Warm temperature
Extra humidity
Fairly easy to grow
p. 354

*Aphelandra
squarrosa*
'Louisae'

*Zebra Plant
Plant height: 12 in.
Bright light
Warm to average
temperature
Extra humidity
Difficult to grow
p. 300*

Caladium ×
hortulanum
'Candidum'

*Fancy-leaved Caladium
Plant height: to 2 ft.
Bright light
Warm temperature
Extra humidity
Difficult to grow
p. 317*

Cyanotis kewensis

Teddy-bear Plant
Trailing plant
Sun
Average temperature
Extra humidity
Special needs
p. 338

Begonia × rex-cultorum

Rex Begonia
Plant height:
12 to 15 in.
Bright light
Warm temperature
Extra humidity
Fairly easy to grow
p. 310

Begonia × rex-cultorum

*Rex Begonia
Plant height:
12 to 15 in.
Bright light
Warm temperature
Extra humidity
Fairly easy to grow
p. 310*

Begonia × rex-cultorum

*Rex Begonia
Plant height:
12 to 15 in.
Bright light
Warm temperature
Extra humidity
Fairly easy to grow
p. 310*

Begonia ×
rex-cultorum

Rex Begonia
Plant height:
12 to 15 in.
Bright light
Warm temperature
Extra humidity
Fairly easy to grow
p. 310

Caladium ×
hortulanum
'Crimson Glow'

Fancy-leaved Caladium
Plant height: to 2 ft.
Bright light
Warm temperature
Extra humidity
Difficult to grow
p. 317

Coleus × hybridus 'Red Lace Leaf'

Painted Nettle
Plant height: to 3 ft.
Bright light; some sun
Average temperature
Easy to grow
p. 333

Caladium × hortulanum 'Rosalie'

Fancy-leaved Caladium
Plant height: to 2 ft.
Bright light
Warm temperature
Extra humidity
Difficult to grow
p. 317

Coleus × *hybridus*
'Wizard Mixture'

Painted Nettle
Plant height: to 3 ft.
Bright light; some sun
Average temperature
Easy to grow
p. 333

Coleus × *hybridus*

Painted Nettle
Plant height: to 3 ft.
Bright light; some sun
Average temperature
Easy to grow
p. 333

**Begonia ×
rex-cultorum**

*Rex Begonia
Plant height:
12 to 15 in.
Bright light
Warm temperature
Extra humidity
Fairly easy to grow
p. 310*

**Begonia ×
rex-cultorum**

*Rex Begonia
Plant height:
12 to 15 in.
Bright light
Warm temperature
Extra humidity
Fairly easy to grow
p. 310*

116

Cordyline terminalis

Ti Plant
Plant height: to 2 ft.
Bright light
Average temperature
Extra humidity
Fairly easy to grow
p. 334

Acalypha wilkesiana

Jacob's-coat
Plant height: to 6 ft., but best kept lower
Bright light; some sun
Warm temperature
Extra humidity
Special needs
p. 291

Iresine herbstii

Beef Plant
Plant height: to 2 ft.,
but best kept lower
Bright light; some sun
Average temperature
Easy to grow
p. 371

Gynura aurantiaca

Purple Velvet Plant
Trailing plant
Sun
Warm to average
temperature
Easy to grow
p. 365

Orchids

Oncidium
**William Thurston
'Orchidglade'**

*Equitant Hybrid
Oncidium
Plant height: 1 to 6 in.
Bright light; some sun
Average temperature
Extra humidity
Special needs
p. 388*

Oncidium
**Golden Sunset ×
Orglade's Rose
Claret**

*Equitant Hybrid
Oncidium
Plant height: 1 to 6 in.
Bright light; some sun
Average temperature
Extra humidity
Special needs
p. 388*

Oncidium
William Thurston
'Orchidglade'

Flowers: to 1 in. wide
p. 388

Oncidium
Golden Sunset ×
Orglade's Rose
Claret

Flowers: to 1 in. wide
p. 388

Sophrolaeliocattleya 'Jewel Box'

Plant height:
10 to 12 in.
Bright light; some sun
Average temperature
Extra humidity
Special needs
p. 323

Ascocentrum curvifolium

Plant height: 4 to 8 in.
Sun
Warm to average
temperature
Extra humidity
Special needs
p. 303

**Sophrolaeliocattleya
'Jewel Box'**

Flowers:
2 to 4 in. wide
p. 323

**Ascocentrum
curvifolium**

Flowers: to ½ in. wide
p. 303

Epidendrum radicans

Stems 3 to 5 ft. long
Sun
Warm to average
temperature
Extra humidity
Special needs
p. 351

Sophronitis cernua

Plant height: 1 in.
Bright light
Average to cool
temperature
Extra humidity
Special needs
p. 419

Epidendrum radicans

Flowers:
1 to 1½ in. wide
p. 351

Sophronitis cernua

Flowers: to 1 in. wide
p. 419

Masdevallia Marguerite 'Selby'

Plant height:
10 to 12 in.
Bright light
Average to cool
temperature
Extra humidity
Special needs
p. 381

Bulbophyllum blumei

Plant height: 6 to 8 in.
Bright light
Warm temperature
Extra humidity
Special needs
p. 316

Masdevallia Marguerite 'Selby'

Flowers:
3½ to 4 in. long
p. 381

Bulbophyllum blumei

Flowers:
1 to 2 in. wide
p. 316

Oncidium viperinum

Plant height:
8 to 12 in.
Bright light; some sun
Average temperature
Extra humidity
Special needs
p. 389

Lycaste cruenta

Plant height:
10 to 15 in.
Bright light; some sun
Average to cool
temperature
Extra humidity
Special needs
p. 378

Oncidium viperinum

Flowers:
1 to 2 in. wide
p. 389

Lycaste cruenta

Flowers:
3 to 4 in. wide
p. 378

Cymbidium
Gainesville ×
Dan Carpenter

Stems 2 to 3 ft.
Bright light; some sun
Average to cool
temperature
Extra humidity
Special needs
p. 341

Dendrobium
Tangerine ×
Mushroom Pink

Plant height:
10 to 12 in.
Bright light; some sun
Warm temperature
Extra humidity
Special needs
p. 344

Cymbidium
Gainesville ×
Dan Carpenter

Flowers:
3½ to 4 in. wide
p. 341

Dendrobium
Tangerine ×
Mushroom Pink

Flowers:
1 to 2 in. wide
p. 344

Oncidium maculatum

Dancing Dolls
Plant height:
1½ to 2 ft.
Bright light; some sun
Average temperature
Extra humidity
Special needs
p. 389

Ansellia africana

Leopard Orchid
Plant height: 1 to 2 ft.
Bright light; some sun
Warm to average
temperature
Extra humidity
Special needs
p. 299

Oncidium maculatum

Flowers:
1 to 2 in. wide
p. 389

Ansellia africana

Flowers:
1 to 1½ in. wide
p. 299

Brassavola nodosa

Lady of the Night
Plant height:
10 to 15 in.
Bright light; full sun
in winter
Warm to average
temperature
Extra humidity
Special needs
p. 313

Brassia gireoudiana

Spider Orchid
Plant height:
6 to 15 in.
Bright light
Warm to average
temperature
Extra humidity
Special needs
p. 314

Brassavola nodosa

Flowers:
2 to 3 in. wide
p. 313

Brassia gireoudiana

Flowers:
10 to 12 in. wide
p. 314

Miltonia flavescens

Plant height:
10 to 12 in.
Bright light; some sun
Warm to average
temperature
Extra humidity
Special needs
p. 382

Angraecum
sesquipedale

Darwin Orchid
Plant height: 1 to 2 ft.
Bright light; some sun
Warm to average
temperature
Extra humidity
Special needs
p. 298

Miltonia flavescens

Flowers: to 3 in. wide
p. 382

**Angraecum
sesquipedale**

*Flowers:
6 to 10 in. wide*
p. 298

Paphiopedilum Maudiae

Lady Slipper Orchid
Plant height: 6 to
8 in.
Bright light; some sun
Warm to average
temperature
Extra humidity
Special needs
p. 392

Phalaenopsis stuartiana

Moth Orchid
Plant height:
8 to 10 in.
Bright light; some sun
Average to warm
temperature
Extra humidity
Special needs
p. 398

Paphiopedilum
Maudiae

Flowers:
10 to 15 in. long
p. 392

Phalaenopsis
stuartiana

Flowers: to 2 in. wide
p. 398

Odontoglossum bilobum

Plant height: 1 to 2 ft.
Bright light; some sun
Average to cool
temperature
Extra humidity
Special needs
p. 387

Aspasia epidendroides

Plant height: 6 to 8 in.
Bright light
Warm to average
temperature
Extra humidity
Special needs
p. 305

Odontoglossum bilobum

Flowers:
1½ to 2 in. wide
p. 387

Aspasia epidendroides

Flowers:
1 to 2 in. wide
p. 305

Laeliocattleya
Park Ridge

Plant height:
12 to 15 in.
Bright light; some sun
Average temperature
Extra humidity
Special needs
p. 322

Odontioda
Memoria Len Page

Stems 2 to 3 ft. long
Bright light; some sun
Cool temperature
Extra humidity
Special needs
p. 387

Laeliocattleya
Park Ridge

Flowers: 6 in. wide
p. 322

Odontioda
Memoria Len Page

Flowers:
to 3½ in. wide
p. 387

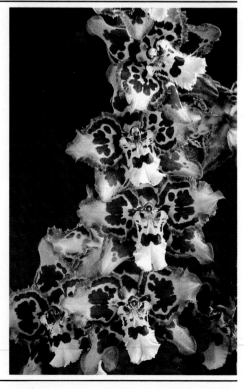

Vanda sanderana

Plant height: 2 to 4 ft.
Sun
Warm temperature
Extra humidity
Special needs
p. 426

Phalaenopsis
Carnival Queen ×
Zauberot

Plant height: 1 to 3 ft.
Bright light; some sun
Warm to average
temperature
Extra humidity
Special needs
p. 398

Vanda sanderana

Flowers:
3 to 4 in. wide
p. 426

Phalaenopsis
Carnival Queen ×
Zauberot

Flowers:
2½ to 3 in. wide
p. 398

Broughtonia negrilensis × sanguinea

Plant height: 6 to 8 in.
Bright light; some sun
Warm to average
temperature
Extra humidity
Special needs
p. 315

Dendrobium primulinum

Plant height:
10 to 12 in.
Bright light; some sun
Average temperature
Extra humidity
Special needs
p. 344

**Broughtonia
negrilensis ×
sanguinea**

Flowers:
1 to 2 in. wide
p. 315

**Dendrobium
primulinum**

Flowers:
1 to 2 in. wide
p. 344

Cattleya walkerana

Plant height: 6 to 8 in.
Bright light; some sun
Warm to average
temperature
Extra humidity
Special needs
p. 323

Cattleya violacea

Plant height:
14 to 16 in.
Bright light; some sun
Warm to average
temperature
Extra humidity
Special needs
p. 323

Cattleya walkerana

Flowers:
3 to 4 in. wide
p. 323

Cattleya violacea

Flowers:
4 to 5 in. wide
p. 323

Laelia anceps

Plant height: 2 to 4 ft.
Bright light; some sun
Average temperature
Extra humidity
Special needs
p. 374

Epidendrum cordigera

Spice Orchid
Plant height:
8 to 15 in.
Bright light; some sun
Warm to average
temperature
Extra humidity
Special needs
p. 351

Laelia anceps

Flowers:
2 to 4 in. wide
p. 374

Epidendrum cordigera

Flowers:
1 to 2 in. wide
p. 351

Bromeliads &

Flowers

Spathiphyllum 'Mauna Loa'

Spathe Flower
Plant height: to 2 ft.
Medium light
Average temperature
Easy to grow
p. 420

Spathiphyllum wallisii

Spathe Flower
Plant height: to 12 in.
Medium light
Average temperature
Easy to grow
p. 420

Anthurium scherzeranum

Flamingo Flower
Plant height: 1 ft.
Bright light
Warm to average
temperature
Extra humidity
Difficult to grow
p. 300

Clivia miniata

Kaffir Lily
Plant size:
to 2 ft. by 3 ft.
Bright light
Average temperature
Easy to grow
p. 331

Guzmania lingulata

Guzmania
Plant height: to 12 in.
Bright light; some sun
Warm to average
temperature
Extra humidity
Easy to grow
p. 364

Guzmania
'Cherry'

Guzmania
Plant height: to 18 in.
Bright light; some sun
Warm to average
temperature
Easy to grow
p. 364

**Nidularium
'Ra Ru' ×
'Sao Paulo'**

*Nidularium
Plant height:
12 to 18 in.
Bright to medium
light
Warm to average
temperature
Easy to grow
p. 386*

**Nidularium
billbergioides**

*Nidularium
Plant height: to 9 in.
Bright to medium
light
Warm to average
temperature
Easy to grow
p. 386*

Aechmea chantinii

Aechmea
Plant height: to 12 in.
Bright light; some sun
Warm to average
temperature
Extra humidity
Easy to grow
p. 293

Vriesea splendens

Flaming Sword
Plant height: 2 to 3 ft.
Bright light; some sun
Warm to average
temperature
Easy to grow
p. 427

Aechmea fasciata

Living Vase Plant
Plant height: 2 to 3 ft.
Bright light; some sun
Warm to average
temperature
Extra humidity
Easy to grow
p. 293

Vriesea ensiformis

Vriesea
Plant height: to 3 ft.
Bright light; some sun
Warm to average
temperature
Easy to grow
p. 427

Tillandsia cyanea

Tillandsia
Plant height: to 10 in.
Bright light; some sun
Warm to average
temperature
Easy to grow
p. 423

Tillandsia
didisticha

Tillandsia
Plant height:
10 to 12 in.
Bright light; some sun
Warm to average
temperature
Easy to grow
p. 423

Neoregelia carolinae 'Tricolor'

Blushing Bromeliad
Plant size:
to 1 ft. by 2½ ft.
Bright light; some sun
Warm to average
temperature
Easy to grow
p. 384

Neoregelia carolinae 'Meyendorffii Flandria'

Blushing Bromeliad
Plant size:
to 1 ft. by 2½ ft.
Bright light; some sun
Warm to average
temperature
Easy to grow
p. 384

Calceolaria herbeohybrida

Slipper Plant
Plant height:
6 to 12 in.
Bright light
Average to cool
temperature
Treat as an annual
p. 319

Begonia × hiemalis

Rieger Begonia
Plant height:
12 to 18 in.
Bright light; some sun
Average temperature
Fairly easy to grow
p. 309

Sinningia speciosa 'Kiss of Fire'

Florist Gloxinia
Plant height: to 12 in.
Bright light
Warm temperature
Easy to grow
p. 418

Sinningia concinna

Sinningia
Plant height: to 6 in.
Bright light
Warm temperature
Fairly easy to grow
p. 418

Streptocarpus 'Wiesmoor' hybrid

Cape Primrose
Plant height:
6 to 12 in.
Bright light
Average temperature
Extra humidity
Fairly easy to grow
p. 422

Streptocarpus 'John Innes' hybrid

Cape Primrose
Plant height:
6 to 12 in.
Bright light
Average temperature
Extra humidity
Fairly easy to grow
p. 422

Streptocarpus 'Constant Nymph'

Cape Primrose
Plant height:
6 to 12 in.
Bright light
Average temperature
Extra humidity
Fairly easy to grow
p. 421

Streptocarpus 'John Innes' hybrid

Cape Primrose
Plant height:
6 to 12 in.
Bright light
Average temperature
Extra humidity
Fairly easy to grow
p. 422

Saintpaulia
'Alabama'

Optimara Hybrid
African Violet
Plant size:
6 in. by 12 in.
Bright light
Warm temperature
Extra humidity
Easy to grow
p. 412

Saintpaulia
'New Mexico'

Optimara Hybrid
African Violet
Plant size:
6 in. by 12 in.
Bright light
Warm temperature
Extra humidity
Easy to grow
p. 412

Saintpaulia
'Hawaii'

Optimara Hybrid
African Violet
Plant size:
6 in. by 12 in.
Bright light
Warm temperature
Extra humidity
Easy to grow
p. 412

Saintpaulia
'Wisconsin'

Optimara Hybrid
African Violet
Plant size:
6 in. by 12 in.
Bright light
Warm temperature
Extra humidity
Easy to grow
p. 412

Cyclamen persicum 'Shell Pink'

Cyclamen
Plant height:
10 to 12 in.
Bright light
Cool temperature
Treat as an annual
p. 340

Saintpaulia 'Jelly Bean'

Miniature African
Violet
Plant size:
3 in. by 6 in.
Bright light
Warm temperature
Extra humidity
Easy to grow
p. 412

Begonia ×
semperflorens-cultorum

Wax Begonia
Plant height:
_6 to 12 in._
Sun
Average temperature
Easy to grow
_p. 310_

Begonia ×
erythrophylla

Beefsteak Begonia
Plant height: to 9 in.
Bright light; some sun
Average temperature
Easy to grow
_p. 309_

Impatiens wallerana 'Super Elfin Blush'

Busy Lizzy
Plant height:
12 to 15 in.
Bright light
Average temperature
Easy to grow
p. 370

Euphorbia milii

Dwarf Crown-of-thorns
Plant height: to 12 in.
Sun
Average temperature
Easy to grow
p. 355

Impatiens wallerana 'Twinkles'

*Busy Lizzy
Plant height:
12 to 15 in.
Bright light
Average temperature
Easy to grow
p. 370*

Impatiens wallerana hybrid

*Busy Lizzy
Plant height:
12 to 15 in.
Bright light
Average temperature
Easy to grow
p. 370*

Pelargonium
'Sofie-Cascade'

Cascade Hybrid
Geranium
Hanging plant
Bright light
Average temperature
Easy to grow
p. 394

Pelargonium
peltatum
hybrid

Ivy Geranium
Trailing plant
Sun
Average temperature
Easy to grow
p. 394

Pelargonium
hybrid

Cascade Hybrid
Geranium
Hanging plant
Bright light
Average temperature
Easy to grow
p. 394

Pelargonium
peltatum
hybrid

Ivy Geranium
Trailing plant
Sun
Average temperature
Easy to grow
p. 394

Browallia speciosa

Bush Violet
Stems 1½ to 2 ft. long
Bright light; some sun
Average to cool
temperature
Treat as an annual
p. 316

Saintpaulia 'Pendula'

Trailing African
Violet
Trailing plant
Bright light
Warm temperature
Extra humidity
Fairly easy to grow
p. 412

Streptocarpus 'Good Hope'

Cape Primrose
Plant height:
6 to 12 in.
Bright light
Average temperature
Extra humidity
Fairly easy to grow
p. 421

Exacum affine

Persian Violet
Plant height: to 2 ft.,
but best kept lower
Bright light
Average temperature
Treat as an annual
p. 356

Plectranthus australis

Swedish Ivy
Vine
Bright light
Average temperature
Easy to grow
p. 403

Fuchsia × hybrida

Lady's Ear-drop
Plant height: 6 to 8 in.
Sun
Cool temperature
Special needs
p. 361

**Fuchsia ×
hybrida**

*Lady's Ear-drop
Plant height: 6 to 8 in.
Sun
Cool temperature
Special needs
p. 361*

**Fuchsia ×
hybrida**

*Lady's Ear-drop
Plant height: 6 to 8 in.
Sun
Cool temperature
Special needs
p. 361*

Billbergia
'Theodore L. Mead'

Billbergia
Plant size:
to 3 ft. wide
Bright light; some sun
Warm to average
temperature
Extra humidity
Easy to grow
p. 311

Begonia
'Di-Erna'

Begonia
Plant height: to 3 ft.
Bright light; some sun
Average temperature
Easy to grow
p. 309

Begonia 'Lana'

Superba Hybrid
Begonia
Plant height: to 3 ft.
Bright light; some sun
Average temperature
Special needs
p. 309

Begonia coccinea

Angel-wing Begonia
Plant height: to 3 ft.
Bright light; some sun
Average temperature
Easy to grow
p. 309

Pelargonium tomentosum

Peppermint Geranium
Plant height: to 3 ft.
Bright light
Average temperature
Easy to grow
p. 394

Abutilon hybridum

Chinese Lantern
Plant height: to 5 ft.
Bright light; some sun
Average to cool
temperature
Fairly easy to grow
p. 290

Sinningia hybrid

Miniature Hybrid
Sinningia
Plant height: 3 in.
Bright light
Warm temperature
p. 418

Kohleria
'Dark Velvet'

Tree Gloxinia
Plant height: to 12 in.
Bright light; some sun
Average temperature
Extra humidity
Difficult to grow
p. 373

Gesneria cuneifolia

Gesneria
Plant height: to 6 in.
Bright light
Warm temperature
Extra humidity
Difficult to grow
p. 363

Cuphea ignea

Cigar Flower
Plant height: to 2 ft.
Bright light; some sun
Average temperature
Easy to grow
p. 337

Acalypha hispida

Chenille Plant
Plant height: to 6 ft.,
but best kept lower
Bright light; some sun
Warm temperature
Extra humidity
Special needs
p. 291

Nematanthus 'Tropicana'

Nematanthus
Plant height:
10 to 12 in.
Bright light
Average temperature
Extra humidity
Fairly easy to grow
p. 384

Nematanthus
'Castanet'

Nematanthus
Plant height:
10 to 12 in.
Bright light
Average temperature
Extra humidity
Fairly easy to grow
p. 383

Justicia
brandegeana

Shrimp Plant
Plant height: to 2 ft.,
but best kept lower
Bright light; some sun
Average temperature
Easy to grow
p. 372

Columnea
'California Gold'

Goldfish Plant
Vine
Bright light
Average temperature
Extra humidity
Fairly easy to grow
p. 334

Lantana camara
hybrid

Yellow Sage
Plant height: best kept
to 12 in.
Bright light; some sun
Average to cool
temperature
Extra humidity
Fairly easy to grow
p. 375

Begonia × semperflorens-cultorum

Wax Begonia
Plant height:
6 to 12 in.
Sun
Average temperature
Easy to grow
p. 310

Begonia × semperflorens-cultorum

Wax Begonia
Plant height:
6 to 12 in.
Sun
Average temperature
Easy to grow
p. 310

Ixora coccinea

Flame-of-the-woods
Plant height: to 4 ft.
Sun
Warm temperature
Extra humidity
Difficult to grow
p. 371

Kalanchoe blossfeldiana

Kalanchoe
Plant height:
6 to 12 in.
Bright light
Average temperature
Treat as an annual
p. 373

Hibiscus
rosa-sinensis

Chinese Hibiscus
Plant height: to 6 ft.,
but best kept lower
Sun
Average temperature
Special needs
p. 367

Crossandra
infundibuliformis

Firecracker Flower
Plant height: to 2 ft.
Medium light; some
sun
Warm temperature
Extra humidity
Difficult to grow
p. 336

Gardenia
jasminoides

Gardenia
Plant height: to 2 ft.
Sun
Average to cool
temperature
Extra humidity
Difficult to grow
p. 362

Lantana camara
hybrid

Yellow Sage
Plant height: best kept
to 12 in.
Bright light; some sun
Average to cool
temperature
Extra humidity
Fairly easy to grow
p. 375

Jasminum sambac
'Maid of Orleans'

Arabian Jasmine
Climber
Bright light; some sun
Warm to average
temperature
Fairly easy to grow
p. 372

Jasminum nitidum

Angel-wing Jasmine
Vine
Bright light; some sun
Warm to average
temperature
Fairly easy to grow
p. 372

Trachelospermum jasminoides

Star Jasmine
Plant height: to 8 ft.,
but best kept lower
Sun
Average temperature
Easy to grow
p. 425

Carissa grandiflora

Natal Plum
Plant height: to
2 ½ ft.
Sun
Average temperature
Easy to grow
p. 320

Jasminum polyanthum

Winter Jasmine
Climber
Bright light; some sun
Cool temperature
Fairly easy to grow
p. 372

Camellia japonica

Camellia
Plant height: 3 to 4 ft.
Bright light
Cool temperature
Extra humidity
Difficult to grow
p. 319

Clerodendrum thomsoniae

Bleeding Glory-bower
Plant height: to 10 ft.,
but best kept lower
Bright light
Warm temperature
Extra humidity
Special needs
p. 330

Allamanda cathartica

Golden Trumpet
Vine
Bright light; some sun
Warm to average
temperature
Extra humidity
p. 296

Thunbergia alata

Black-eyed Susan Vine
Sun
Average to cool
temperature
Easy to grow
p. 423

Capsicum annuum

Christmas Pepper
Plant height:
12 to 15 in.
Bright light
Average temperature
Treat as an annual
p. 320

Plumbago auriculata

Cape Leadwort
Plant height: to 4 ft.
Sun
Average to cool temperature
Fairly easy to grow
p. 405

Thunbergia erecta

King's Mantle
Plant height: to 6 ft.
Sun
Average to cool temperature
Easy to grow
p. 423

Nerium oleander
hybrid

Dwarf Oleander
Plant height: 3 to 4 ft.
Sun
Average temperature
Easy to grow
p. 386

Nerium oleander

Common Oleander
Plant height: to 6 ft.
Sun
Average temperature
Easy to grow
p. 386

Euphorbia milii

Crown-of-thorns
Plant height: to 3 ft.
Sun
Average temperature
Easy to grow
p. 355

Bougainvillea 'Barbara Karst'

Paper Flower
Vine
Sun
Warm temperature
Special needs
p. 312

***Bougainvillea
glabra***
'Sanderana
Variegata'

*Paper Flower
Vine
Sun
Warm temperature
Special needs
p. 312*

Impatiens
hybrid

*New Guinea Hybrid
Impatiens
Plant height:
10 to 16 in.
Bright light; some sun
Average temperature
Easy to grow
p. 370*

Pelargonium × hortorum

Zonal Geranium
Plant height: 3 to 4 ft.
Sun
Average temperature
Easy to grow
p. 394

Euphorbia pulcherrima

Poinsettia
Plant height: to 2 ft.
Bright light
Average to cool
temperature
Treat as an annual
p. 355

Showy Foliage

Plants

Polyscias
balfouriana

Balfour Aralia
Plant height: 3 to 4 ft.
Bright to medium
light
Warm temperature
Extra humidity
Easy to grow
p. 406

Polyscias
balfouriana
'Marginata'

Balfour Aralia
Plant height: 3 to 4 ft.
Bright light
Warm temperature
Extra humidity
Easy to grow
p. 406

Polyscias balfouriana 'Pennockii'

Balfour Aralia
Plant height: 3 to 4 ft.
Bright light
Warm temperature
Extra humidity
Easy to grow
p. 406

Dieffenbachia maculata

Spotted Dumb Cane
Plant height: 4 to 5 ft.
Bright light
Average temperature
Easy to grow
p. 345

Codiaeum variegatum pictum

Croton
Plant height: to 3 ft.
Sun
Warm to average temperature
Extra humidity
Fairly easy to grow
p. 331

Begonia maculata '*Wightii*'

Polka Dot Begonia
Plant height: to 3 ft.
Bright light; some sun
Average temperature
Easy to grow
p. 310

Ficus elastica

Rubber Plant
Plant height: to 6 ft.
Bright to medium
light
Average temperature
Easy to grow
p. 359

Ficus lyrata

Fiddle-leaf Fig
Plant height: to 6 ft.
Bright to medium
light
Average temperature
Easy to grow
p. 359

Philodendron erubescens

Red-leaf Philodendron
Plant height: to 6 ft.
Bright to medium light
Average temperature
Easy to grow
p. 399

Philodendron bipennifolium

Panda Plant
Plant height: to 6 ft.
Bright to medium light
Average temperature
Easy to grow
p. 398

Fatshedera lizei

Aralia Ivy
Plant height: 3 to 4 ft.
Bright to medium light
Average temperature
Easy to grow
p. 357

Cissus rhombifolia 'Ellen Danica'

Grape Ivy
Vine
Bright to low light
Average temperature
Easy to grow
p. 328

Ficus pumila

Creeping Fig
Vine
Medium to low light
Average temperature
Extra humidity
Special needs
p. 360

Begonia
'Medora'

Troutleaf Begonia
Plant height: to 12 in.
Bright light; some sun
Average temperature
Easy to grow
p. 310

Passiflora coccinea

Red Passionflower
Vine
Sun
Warm temperature
Difficult to grow
p. 393

Passiflora caerulea

Blue Passionflower
Plant height: to 20 ft.
Sun
Warm temperature
Difficult to grow
p. 393

Fatsia japonica

Japanese Fatsia
Plant height: to 5 ft.,
but best kept lower
Bright light
Cool temperature
Easy to grow
p. 358

Philodendron selloum

Philodendron
Plant height: to 6 ft.
Bright to medium
light
Average temperature
Easy to grow
p. 399

Monstera deliciosa

Swiss-cheese Plant
Plant height: to 6 ft.
Bright light
Warm to average
temperature
Easy to grow
p. 383

Heptapleurum arboricola

Dwarf Schefflera
Plant height: 4 to 6 ft.
Bright light; some sun
Average temperature
Extra humidity
Easy to grow
p. 367

Aeonium arboreum

Aeonium
Plant height: to 3 ft.
Sun
Average temperature
Easy to grow
p. 294

Pittosporum tobira

Japanese Pittosporum
Plant height: 3 to 4 ft.
Sun
Average to cool
temperature
Easy to grow
p. 402

Brassaia
actinophylla

Schefflera
Plant height: to 8 ft.
Bright light; some sun
Average temperature
Extra humidity
Easy to grow
p. 312

Schefflera arboricola

Australian Umbrella
Tree
Plant height: to 6 ft.
Bright light; some sun
Average temperature
Easy to grow
p. 414

Aucuba japonica 'Variegata'

Gold-dust Tree
Plant height: to 3 ft.
Bright light
Average to cool
temperature
Easy to grow
p. 307

Hypoestes phyllostachya

Polka-dot Plant
Plant height: to 3 ft.,
but best kept lower
Bright light; some sun
Average temperature
Easy to grow
p. 369

Euonymus japonica
'Mediopicta'

Spindle Tree
Plant height: to 4 ft.
Bright light; some sun
Average to cool
temperature
Fairly easy to grow
p. 354

Osmanthus
heterophyllus
'Variegatus'

False Holly
Plant height: to 3 ft.
Bright light; some sun
Cool temperature
Easy to grow
p. 390

Ardisia crenata

Coralberry
Plant height: to 3 ft.
Bright light; some sun
Cool temperature
Extra humidity
Difficult to grow
p. 302

Ficus benjamina

Weeping Fig
Plant height:
2 to 18 ft.
Bright to medium
light
Average temperature
Easy to grow
p. 359

Coffea arabica

Coffee Plant
Plant height: 3 to 4 ft.
Sun
Average temperature
Easy to grow
p. 332

Polyscias paniculata 'Variegata'

Aralia
Plant height: 3 to 4 ft.
Bright light
Warm temperature
Extra humidity
Easy to grow
p. 406

Citrus limon 'Meyer'

Meyer Lemon
Plant height: to 4 ft.
Sun
Average temperature
Fairly easy to grow
p. 329

Citrus × citrofortunella mitis

Calamondin Orange
Plant height: to 4 ft.
Sun
Average temperature
Fairly easy to grow
p. 329

Ficus deltoidea

Mistletoe Fig
Plant height: to 3 ft.
Bright to medium
light
Average temperature
Easy to grow
p. 359

Ficus 'Elegante'

Hybrid Fig
Plant height: 3 to 4 ft.
Bright to medium
light
Average temperature
Easy to grow
p. 359

Punica granatum 'Nana'

Dwarf Pomegranate
Plant height: to 3 ft.
Sun
Average to cool
temperature
Fairly easy to grow
p. 408

Polyscias fruticosa

Ming Aralia
Plant height: 3 to 4 ft.
Bright light
Warm temperature
Extra humidity
Easy to grow
p. 406

Araucaria bidwillii

Monkey Puzzle Tree
Plant height: 2 to 3 ft.
Medium light
Average temperature
Easy to grow
p. 301

Araucaria heterophylla

Norfolk Island Pine
Plant height: to 6 ft.
Medium light
Average temperature
Easy to grow
p. 302

Grevillea robusta

Silk Oak
Plant height: to 6 ft.
Bright light; some sun
Average to cool
temperature
Easy to grow
p. 363

Dizygotheca elegantissima

False Aralia
Plant height: to 6 ft.
Bright light
Average temperature
Fairly easy to grow
p. 346

Podocarpus macrophyllus

Southern Yew
Plant height:
6 to 10 ft.
Bright light
Average to cool
temperature
Easy to grow
p. 405

Codiaeum variegatum pictum 'Punctatum Aureum'

Croton
Plant height: to 3 ft.
Sun
Warm to average
temperature
Extra humidity
Fairly easy to grow
p. 331

Codiaeum variegatum pictum 'Fascination'

Croton
Plant height: to 3 ft.
Sun
Warm to average temperature
Extra humidity
Fairly easy to grow
p. 331

Dracaena sanderana

Belgian Evergreen
Plant height: to 3 ft.
Bright to medium light
Average temperature
Easy to grow
p. 347

Pleomele reflexa 'Variegata'

Song of India
Plant height: to 4 ft.
Bright light
Warm to average
temperature
Easy to grow
p. 404

Aspidistra elatior variegata

Cast-iron Plant
Plant height: to 3 ft.
Bright to medium
light
Average temperature
Easy to grow
p. 306

Acorus gramineus 'Variegatus'

Japanese Sweet Flag
Plant height:
8 to 12 in.
Bright to medium
light
Average temperature
Easy to grow
p. 292

Dracaena fragrans 'Massangeana'

Corn Plant
Plant height:
best kept to 5 ft.
Bright to medium
light
Average temperature
Easy to grow
p. 347

Dracaena deremensis 'Warneckii'

Striped Dracaena
Plant height: to 15 ft.,
but best kept lower
Bright to medium
light
Average temperature
Easy to grow
p. 347

Rhoeo spathacea

Moses-in-the-cradle
Plant height: to 12 in.
Bright light; some sun
Average temperature
Easy to grow
p. 411

Aspidistra elatior

Cast-iron Plant
Plant height: to 3 ft.
Low light
Average temperature
Easy to grow
p. 306

Pleomele reflexa

Pleomele
Plant height: to 4 ft.
Bright light
Warm to average
temperature
Easy to grow
p. 404

Caryota mitis

Burmese Fishtail Palm
Plant height: to 8 ft.
Bright to medium
light
Average temperature
Easy to grow
p. 321

Rhapis excelsa

Bamboo Palm
Plant height: to 5 ft.
Bright light
Average temperature
Easy to grow
p. 409

Cycas revoluta

Sago Palm
Plant height: to 3 ft.
Bright light
Average temperature
Easy to grow
p. 339

Chamaedorea
elegans
'Bella'

Parlor Palm
Plant height: 2 to 3 ft.
Bright to medium
light
Average temperature
Easy to grow
p. 325

Chamaedorea elegans

Parlor Palm
Plant height: to 3 ft.
Bright to medium light
Average temperature
Easy to grow
p. 325

Phoenix roebelenii

Miniature Date Palm
Plant height: to 4 ft.
Bright light; some sun
Average temperature
Easy to grow
p. 400

Chrysalidocarpus lutescens

Areca Palm
Plant height: to 5 ft.
Sun
Warm to average
temperature
Extra humidity
Special needs
p. 327

Howea belmoreana

Sentry Palm
Plant height: to 8 ft.
Bright to medium
light
Average temperature
Easy to grow
p. 368

Cyperus alternifolius

Umbrella Plant
Plant height: 2 to 4 ft.
Medium light
Average temperature
Easy to grow
p. 341

Chamaerops humilis

European Fan Palm
Plant height: to 4 ft.
Bright light; some sun
Average temperature
Easy to grow
p. 326

Washingtonia filifera

Desert Fan
Plant height: 3 to 4 ft.
Bright light; some sun
Average temperature
Easy to grow
p. 427

Livistona chinensis

Chinese Fan Palm
Plant height: 5 to 6 ft.
Bright to medium
light
Average temperature
Easy to grow
p. 376

Yucca aloifolia

Spanish-Bayonet
Plant height: to 4 ft.
Bright to medium
light
Average temperature
Easy to grow
p. 428

Yucca elephantipes

Spineless Yucca
Plant height: to 6 ft.
Bright to medium
light
Average temperature
Easy to grow
p. 428

Dracaena marginata

Dragon Tree
Plant height: to 8 ft.
Bright to medium
light
Average temperature
Easy to grow
p. 347

Beaucarnea recurvata

Ponytail
Plant height: to 3 ft.
Bright to medium
light
Average temperature
Easy to grow
p. 308

Pandanus veitchii

Screw Pine
Plant height: 2 to 3 ft.
Bright light
Warm temperature
Extra humidity
Special needs
p. 391

Ananas comosus 'Variegatus'

Variegated Pineapple
Plant height: to 3 ft.
Sun
Warm temperature
Extra humidity
Difficult to grow
p. 297

Lacy Leaves

Cyrtomium falcatum

Holly Fern
Plant height: 1 to 2 ft.
Bright light
Average to cool
temperature
Easy to grow
p. 342

Platycerium bifurcatum

Staghorn Fern
Plant height: 1 to 3 ft.
Bright light
Average temperature
Extra humidity
Difficult to grow
p. 403

**Pteris cretica
'Alexandrae'**

*Cretan Brake
Plant height: to 18 in.
Bright light
Average temperature
Fairly easy to grow
p. 407*

Polypodium aureum

*Rabbit's-foot Fern
Plant height: to 2 ft.
Medium light
Average temperature
Easy to grow
p. 406*

Asplenium nidus

Bird's-nest Fern
Plant height: to 18 in.
Medium light
Average temperature
Extra humidity
Easy to grow
p. 307

Phyllitis scolopendrium 'Crispum'

Hart's-tongue Fern
Plant height: to 18 in.
Medium light
Average temperature
Easy to grow
p. 400

Asplenium nidus
'Antiquum'

Bird's-nest Fern
Plant height: to 18 in.
Medium light
Average temperature
Extra humidity
Easy to grow
p. 307

Philodendron
'Pluto'

Philodendron
Plant height: to 2 ft.
Bright to medium light
Average temperature
Easy to grow
p. 399

Nephrolepis cordifolia

Sword Fern
Plant height: to 2 ft.
Bright to medium light
Average temperature
Easy to grow
p. 385

Blechnum gibbum

Blechnum
Plant height: to 3 ft.
Bright to medium light
Average temperature
Extra humidity
Fairly easy to grow
p. 311

**Asparagus
densiflorus
'Myers'**

*Foxtail Asparagus
Fern
Plant height: 1 to 2 ft.
Bright light
Average temperature
Easy to grow
p. 304*

**Asparagus
densiflorus
'Sprengeri'**

*Emerald Feather
Stems to 3 ft. long
Bright light
Average temperature
Easy to grow
p. 304*

Philodendron pinnatilobum 'Fernleaf'

Fernleaf Philodendron
Vine
Bright to medium
light
Average temperature
Easy to grow
p. 399

Hatiora salicornioides

Drunkard's Dream
Stems to 6 ft. long
Bright light
Average temperature
Extra humidity
Special needs
p. 365

Davallia trichomanoides

Squirrel's-foot Fern
Plant height: to 18 in.
Medium light
Average temperature
Easy to grow
p. 343

Asparagus setaceus

Asparagus Fern
Plant height: to 2 ft.
Bright light
Average temperature
Easy to grow
p. 304

Nephrolepis exaltata bostoniensis

Boston Fern
Plant height: to 3 ft.
Bright to medium
light
Average temperature
Easy to grow
p. 385

Rumohra adiantiformis

Leather Fern
Plant height: to 3 ft.
Medium light
Warm to average
temperature
Extra humidity
Easy to grow
p. 411

Selaginella willdenovii

Peacock Fern
Climber
Medium to low light
Warm temperature
Extra humidity
Difficult to grow
p. 416

Pteris ensiformis 'Victoriae'

Victoria Brake
Plant height: to 20 in.
Bright light
Average temperature
Fairly easy to grow
p. 408

Asplenium bulbiferum

Hen-and-chickens Fern
Plant height: to 2 ft.
Medium light
Average temperature
Extra humidity
Easy to grow
p. 307

Davallia fejeensis

Rabbit's-foot Fern
Plant height: to 2 ft.
Medium light
Average temperature
Easy to grow
p. 343

**Adiantum
capillus-veneris**

*Venus-hair
Plant height: to 12 in.
Medium light
Average temperature
Extra humidity
Special needs
p. 292*

**Adiantum
raddianum**

*Delta Maidenhair
Plant height: to 18 in.
Medium light
Average temperature
Extra humidity
Special needs
p. 292*

Pellaea rotundifolia

Button Fern
Plant height: to 12 in.
Medium light
Average to cool
temperature
Extra humidity
Fairly easy to grow
p. 395

Oplismenus hirtellus
'Variegatus'

Basket Grass
Plant height: to 12 in.
Bright light; some sun
Average temperature
Easy to grow
p. 389

Pilea microphylla

Artillery Plant
Plant height: to 12 in.
Bright light
Warm temperature
Extra humidity
Fairly easy to grow
p. 401

Malpighia coccigera

Miniature Holly
Plant height: to 12 in.
Sun
Average temperature
Easy to grow
p. 379

Succulents and

Others

Gymnocalycium mihanovichii

Chin Cactus
Plant height: to 3 in.
Sun
Warm temperature
Easy to grow
p. 364

Echinopsis multiplex

Barrel Cactus
Plant height: to 8 in.
Sun
Average temperature
Easy to grow
p. 350

Echinocactus horizonthalonius

Eagle Claws
Plant size:
to 12 in. by 6 in.
Sun
Average temperature
Easy to grow
p. 349

Echinocactus grusonii

Barrel Cactus
Plant size:
10 to 12 in. wide
Sun
Average temperature
Easy to grow
p. 349

Lobivia leucomalla

Cob Cactus
Plant height: 1 to 2 in.
Sun
Average temperature
Easy to grow
p. 377

Mammillaria camptotricha

Bird's-nest Cactus
Plant height: to 4 in.
Sun
Average temperature
Easy to grow
p. 379

Mammillaria guelzowiana

Strawberry Cactus
Plant height: to 2 ½ in.
Sun
Average temperature
Easy to grow
p. 379

Rebutia kupperana

Scarlet Crown Cactus
Plant height: to 3 in.
Sun
Average temperature
Easy to grow
p. 408

Mammillaria hahniana

Old-woman Cactus
Plant height:
8 to 10 in.
Sun
Average temperature
Easy to grow
p. 379

Mammillaria bocasana

Snowball Cacti
Plant height: 4 to 6 in.
Sun
Average temperature
Easy to grow
p. 379

Mammillaria bocasana

Snowball Cactus
Plant height: 4 to 6 in.
Sun
Average temperature
Easy to grow
p. 379

Cephalocereus senilis

Old-man Cactus
Plant height: to 12 in.
Sun
Average temperature
Easy to grow
p. 324

Lobivia
arachnacantha

Cob Cactus
Plant height: to 3 in.
Sun
Average temperature
Easy to grow
p. 377

Echinocereus
pectinatus

Rainbow Cactus
Plant height: to 12 in.
Sun
Average temperature
Easy to grow
p. 350

Cleistocactus strausii

Silver Torch
Plant height: 5 to 6 ft.
Sun
Average temperature
Easy to grow
p. 330

Opuntia microdasys

Rabbit-ears
Plant height: to 3 ft.
Sun
Average temperature
Easy to grow
p. 390

Stapelia hirsuta

Hairy Toad Plant
Plant height: 8 in.
Bright light
Average temperature
Easy to grow
p. 420

Stapelia variegata

Toad Plant
Plant height: to 6 in.
Bright light
Average temperature
Easy to grow
p. 421

Opuntia subulata

Eve's-pin Cactus
Plant height: to 6 ft.
Sun
Average temperature
Easy to grow
p. 390

Crassula lycopodioides

Rattail
Plant height: to 8 in.
Bright light; some sun
Average temperature
Easy to grow
p. 335

Chamaecereus sylvestri

Peanut Cactus
Stems to 6 in. long
Sun
Average temperature
Easy to grow
p. 325

Aporocactus flagelliformis

Rattail Cactus
Stems to 3 ft. long
Sun
Average temperature
Easy to grow
p. 301

Hoya carnosa 'Krinkle Kurl'

Hindu-rope
Vine
Bright light; some sun
Average temperature
Easy to grow
p. 369

Sedum morganianum

Burro's Tail
Trailing plant
Bright light; some sun
Average temperature
Easy to grow
p. 415

Echeveria elegans

Mexican Gem
Plant size:
to 4 in. wide
Sun
Average temperature
Easy to grow
p. 349

Pachyphytum oviferum

Moonstones
Plant height: to 3 in.
Sun
Average temperature
Easy to grow
p. 391

Columnea hirta

Goldfish Plant
Vine
Bright light
Average temperature
Extra humidity
Fairly easy to grow
p. 334

Rhipsalis rhombea

Rhipsalis
Trailing plant
Bright light
Average temperature
Extra humidity
Special needs
p. 410

Rhipsalidopsis gaertneri

Easter Cactus
Stems to 1½ in. long
Bright to medium light
Average temperature
Special needs
p. 409

Schlumbergera bridgesii

Christmas Cactus
Branches to 12 in. long
Bright to medium
light
Average temperature
Special needs
p. 415

Epiphyllum 'Ackermannii'

Red Orchid Cactus
Stems to 3 ft. long
Bright light
Average temperature
Special needs
p. 352

Rhipsalis crispata

Wickerware Cactus
Trailing plant
Bright light
Average temperature
Extra humidity
Special needs
p. 410

Rhipsalis baccifera

Mistletoe Cactus
Trailing plant
Bright light
Average temperature
Extra humidity
Special needs
p. 410

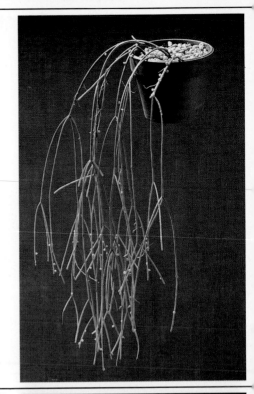

Euphorbia tirucalli

Milkbush
Plant height: to 6 ft.
Bright light
Average temperature
Easy to grow
p. 356

Tillandsia
caput-medusae

Tillandsia
Plant height: to 10 in.
Bright light; some sun
Warm to average
temperature
Easy to grow
p. 423

Aechmea
lueddemanniana

Aechmea
Plant height: to 2 ft.
Bright light; some sun
Warm to average
temperature
Extra humidity
Easy to grow
p. 293

Cryptanthus bivittatus

Earth-Star
Leaves 3 to 4 in. long
Bright light; some sun
Warm to average
temperature
Extra humidity
Easy to grow
p. 337

Cryptanthus bivittatus 'Pink Starlight'

Earth-Star
Leaves 3 to 4 in. long
Bright light; some sun
Warm to average
temperature
Extra humidity
Easy to grow
p. 337

Cryptanthus 'Starlite'

Earth-Star
Leaves to 4 in. long
Bright light; some sun
Warm to average
temperature
Extra humidity
Easy to grow
p. 337

Cryptanthus zonatus

Zebra Plant
Leaves to 9 in. long
Bright light; some sun
Warm to average
temperature
Extra humidity
Easy to grow
p. 337

Sansevieria trifasciata 'Hahnii'

Bird's-nest Sansevieria
Plant height: to 6 in.
Bright to medium light
Average temperature
Easy to grow
p. 413

Cryptanthus acaulis

Starfish Plant
Leaves to 6 in. long
Bright light; some sun
Warm to average temperature
Extra humidity
Easy to grow
p. 337

Sansevieria
trifasciata
'Laurentii'

Snake Plant
Plant height: to 18 in.
Bright to medium
light
Average temperature
Easy to grow
p. 413

Sansevieria
trifasciata
'Golden Hahnii'

Bird's-nest Sansevieria
Plant height: to 6 in.
Bright to medium
light
Average temperature
Easy to grow
p. 413

Aloe variegata

Kaniedood Aloe
Plant height: to 12 in.
Bright light
Average temperature
Easy to grow
p. 297

Gasteria liliputana

Dutch-wings
Plant height: 2 to 4 in.
Bright to medium
light
Average temperature
Easy to grow
p. 362

Haworthia margaritifera

Pearl Plant
Plant size:
to 3 in. by 6 in.
Bright to medium
light
Average temperature
Easy to grow
p. 366

Haworthia fasciata

Zebra Haworthia
Plant size:
to 2 in. by 4 in.
Bright to medium
light
Average temperature
Easy to grow
p. 366

Aloe barbadensis

Barbados Aloe
Plant height: to 2 ft.
Bright light
Average temperature
Easy to grow
p. 297

Stapelia leendertziae

Stapelia
Plant height: to 4 in.
Bright light
Average temperature
Easy to grow
p. 420

Agave leopoldii

Agave
Plant height: 10 in.
Sun
Average temperature
Easy to grow
p. 295

Agave victoriae-reginae

Century Plant
Plant height: to 10 in.
Sun
Average temperature
Easy to grow
p. 295

Dyckia fosterana

Dyckia
Plant height: to 12 in.
Sun
Average temperature
Easy to grow
p. 348

Kalanchoe tomentosa

Pussy Ears
Plant height: to 10 in.
Bright light; some sun
Average temperature
Easy to grow
p. 373

Crassula falcata

Propeller Plant
Plant height: to 12 in.
Bright light; some sun
Average temperature
Easy to grow
p. 335

Kalanchoe pumila

Kalanchoe
Plant height: to 12 in.
Bright light; some sun
Average temperature
Easy to grow
p. 373

Crassula rupestris

Buttons-on-a-string
Vine
Bright light; some sun
Average temperature
Easy to grow
p. 336

Lithops lesliei

Living Stones
Plant height: to 1 in.
Sun
Average temperature
Easy to grow
p. 376

Echeveria runyonii

Hen-and-chickens
Plant height: to 4 in.
Sun
Average temperature
Easy to grow
p. 349

Aeonium
tabuliforme

Aeonium
Plant height: to 1 in.
Sun
Warm to average
temperature
Easy to grow
p. 294

Echeveria
'Black Prince'

Hen-and-chickens
Plant height: to 3 in.
Sun
Average temperature
Easy to grow
p. 348

Aeonium arboreum
'Black Rose'

Aeonium
Plant height: to 3 ft.
Sun
Warm to average
temperature
Easy to grow
p. 294

Crassula argentea

Jade Plant
Plant height: to 4 ft.
Bright light; some sun
Average to cool
temperature
Easy to grow
p. 335

Portulacaria afra

Elephant Bush
Plant height: 3 to 4 ft.
Bright light; some sun
Average to cool
temperature
Easy to grow
p. 407

Abutilon
Mallow family
Malvaceae

A-bū′ti-lon. This old-fashioned plant belongs to the same family as the hollyhocks. Frequent hybridization has resulted in new varieties that are much larger and more diverse than the original plant. Once known as parlor maple, today the genus is usually called flowering maple.

How to Grow
To ensure flowering, give these plants direct sun and room temperatures that differ by 10° F (12° C) day to night. They are fast-growing plants that need to be kept constantly moist and fed once a month. Repot them, using all-purpose potting soil, whenever they need it. Propagate by taking tip cuttings at any time. A well-adjusted abutilon will flower all year, although less vigorously in winter. Use that time to prune it.

hybridum p. 180
Chinese Lantern. Grows to 5 ft. (1.5 m) high. The flowers in this group of hybrids come in white, yellow, salmon, or purple. Other interesting abutilons include *A. pictum* 'Thompsoni', with salmon flowers; and *A. megapotamicum* 'Variegata', a good basket plant that has mottled leaves and red and yellow flowers.

Acalypha
Spurge family
Euphorbiaceae

A-ka-lee′fa, or A-ka-ly′fa. A genus of fast-growing, shrubby plants that includes two excellent indoor species: one prized for its flowers, the other for its colorful foliage.

How to Grow
Warmth, humidity, bright light, and some sunshine are essential for these plants. Acalyphas can stand temperatures to 80° F (26.5° C) in summer; never let temperature drop below 60° F (15.5° C) in winter. They need high humidity year round. Place them on trays of moistened pebbles and mist daily in spring when growth starts, but never mist *A. hispada* when it is in flower. In spring

and summer, water freely and fertilize every 2 weeks. In winter, water just enough to keep the soil from drying out. Propagate by taking tip or side cuttings in early spring. Root them in a warm room with bright light but no direct sun. After the cuttings have rooted, place them in 4-inch pots filled with all-purpose soil. If a parent plant becomes too large, discard it.

hispida p. 183
Chenille Plant; Red-hot Cattail; Philippine Medusa. This showy, somewhat demanding plant is prized for its 12- to 18-in. (30- to 45-cm) tassels of bright red flowers that look like lengths of chenille. The cultivar 'Alba' has white flowers. The Chenille Plant grows almost too quickly; it may reach 6 ft. (1.8 m) but is most attractive when small. To keep it under control, cut it back severely in early spring.

wilkesiana p. 116
Jacob's-coat; Copperleaf; Match-me-if-you-can; Fire-dragon; Beefsteak Plant. To 6 ft. (1.8 m), but best when small. Unlike *A. hispida,* the leaves of this species are the plant's glory. They are bronzy green, mottled with red, copper, or purple. Cultivars display an even greater variety. Among the best are 'Godseffiana', which has green leaves with white margins; 'Macrophylla', with large, reddish-brown leaves; 'Marginata', with leaf margins in red and other colors; and 'Musaica', with red and orange markings.

Acorus
Arum family
Araceae

Ak'or-us. There are only two species of *Acorus.* One of them, *A. gramineus,* is a pretty, grasslike plant that is easy to grow indoors.

How to Grow
Since these are marsh plants, they need plenty of water. Unlike almost all other houseplants, these flourish when they stand in a saucer of water—you can even grow them in water without any soil. Give your plant bright or medium light and grow it in any indoor temperature. Never let the soil

dry out. Fertilize twice a year, and repot whenever necessary, using an all-purpose soil mix. Propagate by division.

gramineus 'Variegatus' *p. 226*
Japanese Sweet Flag. The white stripes that run along its green leaves make this the most decorative of the sweet flags. It grows to a height of 12 in. (30 cm). A dwarf version, *A. g. pusillus,* grows no more than 6 in. (15 cm) high.

Adiantum
Polypody family
Polypodiaceae

A-dee-an'tum. Of all the ferns, the delicate, elegant *Adiantum,* or maidenhair, is the most admired. Unfortunately, it is also the most difficult to grow, since it will thrive only in the humid conditions of a greenhouse. Small plants do well in terrariums.

How to Grow
Medium to bright light and normal room temperatures suit maidenhair ferns, but you must provide them with a great deal of humidity. Try standing them on a large tray of pebbles in the company of other moisture-loving plants; in a group, the plants generate more humidity than they do standing alone. Keep the soil evenly moist from spring to fall. In winter, let it dry out slightly between waterings. Be careful not to overfertilize; apply half-strength fertilizer once in the spring and once in the summer. Repot in late winter or early spring, just before the ferns start their new growth. To retain moisture, use a potting mixture that is high in organic matter; equal parts of all-purpose potting soil and peat moss make a good mix. Propagate by division when you repot your plant.

capillus-veneris *p. 251*
Venus-hair. This species grows to 12 in. (30 cm) high. It has pretty, light green, fan-shaped leaves.

raddianum *p. 251*
Delta Maidenhair. This fern grows to about 18 in. (45 cm) and is the most tolerant of home conditions. *A. tenerum* 'Wrightii' is

similar but somewhat bigger. Its leaves are
pink at first, then green.

Aechmea
Bromeliad family
Bromeliaceae

Eek'mee-a. Aechmeas are South American
epiphytes, several of which are excellent and
popular indoor plants.

How to Grow
Like most bromeliads, aechmeas need bright
light with some sun, warm temperatures and
extra humidity, which is best supplied by
standing the pot on a tray of moistened
pebbles and misting the leaves several times
a week. Water the soil moderately, letting it
dry out a bit between waterings, but keep
the central cup of the rosette filled with
water at all times. Use only soft water or
rainwater, since lime deposits will stain the
leaves. Once in a while, turn the plant
upside down to drain the stale water and
then refill the cup. Every 2 weeks, pour
half-strength fertilizer over the leaves and
into the cup. Aechmeas don't send up flower
stalks until they are a few years old. The
flowers bloom briefly, but the dramatic
bracts that surround them remain colorful
for as long as 6 months.
Although the plant will die gradually after
flowering, it sends up new offsets. Detach
these carefully with a knife and plant them
in the same size pot as the one the parent
plant grew in, using a soilless potting mix.

chantinii p. 158
These plants have yellow flowers and
orange-red bracts. 'Pink Goddess' has bright
pink bracts; 'Red Goddess', red bracts. They
will grow to 12 in. (30 cm) high.

fasciata p. 159
Living Vase Plant; Urn Plant. This plant is
large: It grows to 2 to 3 ft. (60 to 90 cm).
Its big, spiny, silver-and-green leaves arch
outward from a central cup. The blue
flowers are encased in a bright pink rosette.

lueddemanniana p. 273
This species, native to Mexico and
Honduras, has green leaves that turn bronze
in the sun. It grows to 2 ft. (60 cm) high.
The flower has rose petals and green sepals.

Aeonium
Orpine family
Crassulaceae

Ee-o'ni-um. These fine succulents are distinguished by their beautiful rosettes of leaves, which are held at the ends of the branches. They vary in color from light green to almost black or variegated.

How to Grow
See *Crassula*. Although bright light will suffice for plants that have plain leaves, the cultivars with colorful leaves need full sun.

arboreum p. 212, 286
This plant can reach heights of 3 ft. (90 cm). It has glossy green leaves. The cultivars 'Black Rose' and 'Schwartzkopf' have nearly black foliage. 'Atropurpureum' has purple leaves.

tabuliforme p. 285
Unlike the other aeoniums, this plant looks almost stemless. It is only 1 in. (2.5 cm) high and has a single flat rosette, 6 to 12 in. (15 to 30 cm) wide, that rests on the soil.

Aeschynanthus
Gesneriad family
Gesneriaceae

Eyes-ki-nan'thus. Several species of *Aeschynanthus* are grown indoors in hanging baskets. They usually bloom in spring and summer, but some cultivars flower throughout the year.

How to Grow
Aeschynanthus is difficult to distinguish from its close relative *Columnea* and has the same cultural requirements. Watch for aphids, which are attracted to the plant's new leaves.

radicans p. 86
Lipstick Plant. This species bears bright red flowers that grow in pairs. Each is streaked with white and has a purple calyx. *A. pulcher* is a similar species.

Agave
Agave family
Agavaceae

A-gah'vee. In the wild, century plants don't actually take 100 years to bloom—15 is more like it—but they rarely flower indoors. Although several *Agave* species are sold as houseplants, *A. victoriae-reginae* is by far the best one.

How to Grow
An agave is not a cactus, but you should be careful of the sharp leaf tips when you handle the plant. Grow it in the brightest spot you have, preferably in full sun. Normal room temperatures are suitable. During warm weather, water it when the soil feels dry; in winter, let it get so dry that the plant looks almost shriveled before you water. Fertilize once a year in spring or summer. Agaves do well when they are potbound. If you want to repot one, use gloves, cactus soil, and a pot one size larger.

leopoldii *p. 281*
This species is probably actually a hybrid of *A. filifera* and *A. schidigera*. Its light green leaves are thinner than *A. victoriae-reginae*'s. They have white stripes on the edges, from which threadlike fibers curl.

victoriae-reginae *p. 281*
This, the most popular agave, has blue-green leaves edged with white. The plant grows in a tight rosette about 10 in. (25 cm) tall and 16 in. (40.5 cm) wide.

Aglaonema
Arum family
Araceae

Ag-la-o-nee'ma. This is one of the easiest to grow of all plants in conditions of medium to low light.

How to Grow
Water moderately and allow the soil to dry out slightly between waterings. Fertilize once a month except during the winter. If the plant is growing in low light, be stingy with the fertilizer. Propagate by division of the rootstock or by cuttings, which can be stuck right into the parent's pot.

commutatum *p. 98*
This species has long, dark green leaves
blotched with pale green or white markings.
It grows to 1 to 2 ft. (30 to 60 cm) high.
'Treubii' has light green leaves with creamier
markings.

costatum *p. 91*
More compact than other members of genus
Aglaonema, this plant grows to 10 in.
(25 cm). Its leaves are numerous and
crowded; each has a white midrib and is
tapered at both ends.

Allamanda
Dogbane family
Apocynaceae

Al-la-man′da. Allamandas are profusely
blooming woody vines from South America.
The species most commonly grown indoors
is *A. cathartica,* known as Golden Trumpet.

How to Grow
Place allamandas near a window that gets
about 4 hours of sun a day. Provide plenty
of humidity and average to warm
temperatures. When plants are actively
growing, water frequently and feed twice
a month. Cut down on both water and
fertilizer from late fall to spring. Propagate
by tip cuttings in spring. Spring is also a
good time to move your plant to a larger
pot. Golden Trumpet does grow quickly.

cathartica *p. 193*
Golden Trumpet. The funnel-shaped yellow
flowers of this vine contrast boldly with its
dark green leaves. 'Grandiflora' is a compact
variety.

Aloe
Lily family
Liliaceae

A′low; a-low′. In the days of the Roman
Empire, aloes were grown as pot plants.
Then as now, their juices were used as a
soothing ointment for burns. Today's best
houseplants are the small species such as
A. barbadensis, Barbados Aloe, and
A. variegata.

How to Grow

Aloes are succulents and have similar cultural needs to *Agave,* although they are much more tolerant of indoor light. Unlike agaves, however, aloes are propagated by planting the shoots that grow at the base of the parent plant.

barbadensis p. 280

Barbados Aloe; Medicinal Aloe. This plant is a major source of the drug aloe. Juice from the leaves, which grow to 2 ft. (60 cm), quickly soothes burns. Also known as *A. vera.*

variegata p. 278

Kaniedood Aloe; Partridge-breast Aloe; Pheasant's-wing Aloe. With its heavily striped leaves, this plant is the most popular aloe. In late winter, it may produce a 12- in. (30-cm) stalk bearing pink flowers.

Ananas
Bromeliad family
Bromeliaceae

A-na'nas. The decorative pineapple bromeliads grown indoors belong to the same genus as our edible pineapple, *A. comosus.*

How to Grow

Pineapples need a good deal of sun all year long to develop their colorful pink fruit. They also need warmth and high humidity. Water them moderately, but keep the rosette full at all times. Fertilize every 2 weeks throughout the year. For more on the care and propagation of bromeliads, see *Aechmea.*

comosus 'Variegatus' p. 237

Variegated Pineapple. This cultivar of the edible pineapple grows to 3 ft. (90 cm) and has spiny pink, green, and ivory leaves. When the plant is about 3 years old, if conditions have been right, a flower stalk will develop, and then a small pineapple.

Angraecum
Orchid family
Orchidaceae

An-gree′kum. Most of the popular orchids in the genus *Angraecum* come from Madagascar and nearby East Africa. Spectacular waxy white flowers with long tails and a pleasing night perfume are exciting characteristics of all the species. Many bloom in the winter when long-lasting, fragrant orchids are especially welcome.

How to Grow
The tall-growing orchids in this genus, such as *A. sesquipedale,* thrive in containers with a coarse mix of bark, gravel, and charcoal. Recently some new hybrids have been created from dwarf species. These smaller types do well positioned on a mound of cork bark or unmilled sphagnum above a well-drained mix of hardwood charcoal, gravel, and cork or fir bark. In nature, some species live on mossy tree branches, while others are found in full sun on rocky hills.
Leaf substance is a clue to light requirements. Thin-leaved sorts need diffuse light; thick, waxy-leaved species accept stronger sun. The species that are native to mountain areas can tolerate nights in the 50s (10 to 15° C); the popular hybrids and the species described here thrive with night temperatures of 60 to 68° F (15.5 to 20.0° C).

sesquipedale *pp. 136, 137*
Darwin Orchid. A 1- to 2-ft. (30- to 60-cm) plant with flowers 6 to 10 in. (15 to 25 cm) wide on spikes from 10 to 15 in. (25 to 38 cm) long. It often blooms during the winter holidays. The flowers last 2 to 3 weeks and have a pleasant fragrance at night.

Ansellia
Orchid family
Orchidaceae

An-sel′ee-a. Two species in this genus, *A. africana* and the very similar *A. gigantea,* are called leopard orchids because of their brown-spotted yellow flowers. These easy-to-grow epiphytes have bright flowers on durable sprays, which are sometimes as much as 2 to 3 ft. (60 to 90 cm) long.

How to Grow

In their native East African habitat, ansellias live on tree branches, where they get very bright light and excellent air circulation. The plants are so tall, even in cultivation, that they will not fit in light boxes and are best grown in greenhouses or bright windows. Each cigar-shaped pseudobulb has thin leaves along the top portion. These usually drop off a year or so after growth is complete. When new growth begins at the base of last year's stem, increase watering and fertilizer. While new pseudobulbs are forming, provide warm temperatures and allow the potting mix to dry out only slightly between waterings. When the growing cycle is complete, ansellias need a break from watering and fertilizer. Begin watering when flower stems start to grow again. Repot every 3 to 4 years when new growth appears. Heavy clay pots are most practical for tall, mature clumps. Plant them in a mixture of tree fern, charcoal, and bark.

africana pp. 132, 133

This species and the related *A. gigantea* both have sprays of yellow flowers, usually with brown spots. Commercial growers may offer select clones noted for clear color, the absence of spots, or especially dark spots. Some forms give off a pleasant honey fragrance when the flowers are warmed by the sun, yet ansellias are grown mainly for their abundance of flowers, each 1 to 1½ in. (2.5 to 4.0 cm) wide. They grow 1 to 2 ft. (30 to 60 cm) high.

Anthurium
Arum family
Araceae

An-thoor'i-um. Anthuriums are beautiful plants but difficult to grow. They require a great deal of humidity and are suited to a greenhouse, a plant room, or any other place that is constantly humid.

How to Grow

Summer and winter, anthuriums thrive in temperatures of 80 to 85° F (26.5 to 29.5° C) by day and 65 to 70° F (18.5 to 21.0° C) at night, with a great deal of humidity. Grow them in bright light but not in direct sun. Keep the soil constantly moist and fertilize them every 2 weeks. In spring, repot using a mixture of coarse sphagnum moss and fir bark or equal parts of all-purpose potting soil, sphagnum moss, and sand. Propagate by division.

crystallinum p. 104
Crystal Anthurium. Although this anthurium doesn't have significant flowers, it is prized for its beautiful shimmering leaves, up to 21 in. (52.5 cm) long and 13 in. (32.5 cm) wide.

scherzeranum p. 155
Flamingo Flower. This species grows to 12 in. (30 cm) high. It has short stems and large leaves and flowers, making it particularly attractive to the home gardener. There are many cultivars to choose from.

Aphelandra
Acanthus family
Acanthaceae

A-fell-an'dra. The aphelandras grown indoors have bright yellow bracts that remain for several weeks after the small, yellow flowers have died back.

How to Grow
Bright light, temperatures above 65° F (18.5° C), and a good deal of humidity are essential to make these plants flower. They also need a winter rest period at temperatures between 55 and 60° F (13.0 and 15.5° C). Water them frequently during their active growth period and fertilize them every 2 weeks. During the rest period, let the soil dry out slightly between waterings. In the spring, cut the plant back drastically and then repot it in all-purpose potting soil. Propagate in spring by taking tip cuttings.

squarrosa 'Louisae' p. 109
Zebra Plant; Saffron Spike. This plant grows to a height of at least 12 in. (30 cm) and is one of the best of the compact cultivars. Others include 'Fritz Prinsler' and 'Leopoldii'.

Aporocactus
Cactus family
Cactaceae

A-pore-o-kak′tus. *Aporocactus* is a genus of long-stemmed desert cacti with bright pink or red flowers. They are easy to grow and quite striking in hanging baskets.

How to Grow
These cacti need full sun to flower. For most of the year, average room temperatures are fine, but in winter they should be kept at 60° F (15.5° C) or below. They should also be put outside in summer if possible. While the plants are in active growth, water them freely, keeping the soil constantly moist. In winter, water them just enough to keep them from drying out. Feed them every 2 weeks in spring and summer. Repot each spring, using a cactus soil mix. Propagate by taking tip cuttings or by planting seeds.

flagelliformis p. 266
Rattail Cactus. The flowering season for this cactus can last up to 2 months. The pink blossoms open during the day and close at night. Stems grow to 3 ft. (90 cm) long.

Araucaria
Araucaria family
Araucariaceae

Or-ro-cay′ri-a. This genus contains 2 popular houseplants, *A. bidwillii,* or Monkey Puzzle Tree, and *A. heterophylla,* the Norfolk Island Pine.

How to Grow
Average room temperatures and medium light suit these indoor trees. Be sure to turn your plant frequently so that it doesn't lean toward the light. Water freely in spring and summer, keeping the soil uniformly moist but not wet. In winter, let the soil dry out slightly between waterings. Fertilize every 2 weeks during the growing season. These are slow-growing plants and should need repotting only every 3 years or so. Use a standard all-purpose potting mixture. Propagation is by seed, which is not practical for the home grower.

bidwillii p. 221
Monkey Puzzle Tree. This plant grows to a

height of 2 to 3 ft. (60 to 90 cm) indoors.
Unlike its relative, the Norfolk Island Pine,
it has hard, shiny, pointed leaves. In the
wild, where it presumably looks more vicious
than it does indoors, the tree is said to
puzzle monkeys, who are unable to climb
over its spiked leaves—hence its common
name.

heterophylla p. 221

Norfolk Island Pine. To 6 ft. (1.8 m). A
large, well-grown Norfolk Island Pine is
probably the ultimate indoor tree. Few
people, however, have room to accommodate
an evergreen of 6 ft. (1.8 m) with broadly
spreading branches. Fortunately, a small
araucaria is also a beautiful plant if it is lush
and symmetrical. When you buy your plant,
look it over very carefully to be sure that
there are 4 branches on each tier and that
the tiers are closely spaced on the trunk. If a
plant doesn't meet these standards, don't buy
it or you'll end up with a lopsided, spindly
tree. This plant was formerly known as
A. excelsa.

Ardisia
Myrsine family
Myrsinaceae

Ar-diz′i-a. The only ardisia to be grown
indoors is *A. crenata*. Its berries turn bright
red at Christmastime and remain into the
spring.

How to Grow
Ardisias prefer cool temperatures. Above
60° F (15.5° C) they need the kind of high
humidity that can best be supplied in a
greenhouse in order to keep the berries from
dropping. They also need bright light with
some direct sun. Keep the soil constantly
moist while your plants are in active growth,
and fertilize them every 2 weeks. Repot in
spring, using an all-purpose soil mix. Ardisias
are usually grown from seed, but this is
difficult for the home gardener. Stem or
shoot cuttings taken before they have
matured can be rooted.

crenata p. 216

Coralberry; Spiceberry. This 3-ft. (90-cm)
shrub has pink to white flowers followed by
extremely long-lasting berries.

Ascocentrum
Orchid family
Orchidaceae

As-ko-sen'trum. These delightful dwarf Asian epiphytes are perfect orchids for a bright window or sunny greenhouse. The plants have stiff, shiny leaves arranged like a fan. Flowers are only ½ to 1 in. (1.3 to 2.5 cm) across, but they appear tightly packed on upright to gently arching spikes, making a magnificent show of red, yellow, and orange.

How to Grow
Ascocentrums thrive in small clay pots; they need perfect drainage. Tree fern, hardwood charcoal, redwood bark, and cork are suitable potting materials. Under the humid conditions of a greenhouse or a sunroom, mature plants grow well on chunks of tree fern or in teak baskets. Since these orchids have no pseudobulbs, the roots should always be exposed to moisture. Ascocentrums may stop producing new leaves during cooler winter months; discontinue fertilizing and water less frequently. Average to warm temperatures are best.

curvifolium pp. 122, 123
This species grows 4 to 8 in. (10 to 20 cm) high and comes in a variety of forms, most with orange flowers. A few select clones and strains have yellow flowers. In recent years *A. curvifolium* has been hybridized with the genus *Vanda*. These charming, well-known crosses are called *Ascocenda*. They often have much shorter and more compact growth than the tall vandas, but come in more varied colors than *Ascocentrum* species. *Ascocenda* Yip Sum Wah and *Ascocenda* Meda Arnold have spikes of 1 to 2 in. (2.5 to 5.0 cm), and orange to orange-red flowers.

Asparagus
Lily family
Liliaceae

As-pa'ra-gus. None of the three popular houseplants in this genus is a fern, despite the feathery foliage that inspired their common names. Instead, they are close relatives of the edible asparagus. *A. setaceus*

grows upright; the two cultivars of
A. densiflorus are grown in hanging baskets.

How to Grow
Asparagus ferns grow best in full sun but
will tolerate bright, indirect light. Average
or cool room temperatures are fine. Keep the
soil evenly moist and feed the plants once
every 2 weeks during spring and summer or
every 3 or 4 months all year.
The *A. densiflorus* cultivars have fast-growing
roots, which can fill a pot within months,
using up all the nutrients in the soil and
making it impossible to keep them
adequately watered. As a result, a plant turns
yellow, sheds its thousands of tiny needlelike
leaves, and looks shabby. To prevent this
damage, divide your plant before its huge
succulent roots come to the surface or even
break the pot.
To divide an asparagus fern, turn it out of
its pot, cut off the top foliage (wear thick
gloves—the stems are prickly), and then slice
your plant into 3- to 4-in. (7.5- to 10.0-cm)
sections with a kitchen knife. Plant each
section in a 6-inch (15-cm) pot filled to
about 2 in. (5 cm) from the top with an
all-purpose potting mixture. This allows
room for watering and for the roots to push
up the soil.

densiflorus 'Myers' *p. 245*
Foxtail Asparagus Fern. This cultivar has
arching stems, 1 to 2 ft. (30 to 60 cm) long,
so heavily covered with tiny needlelike leaves
that they look as bushy as a fox's tail.
Because the stems are held much more stiffly
than those of 'Sprengeri', they look better in
a pot or planter than in a graceful hanging
basket.

densiflorus 'Sprengeri' *p. 245*
Emerald Feather; Asparagus Fern. The long,
graceful branches of this hanging plant can
reach 3 ft. (90 cm). In a bright, cool room,
tiny pink flowers are followed by bright red
berries. There is no more glorious hanging
plant if you heed the warnings in the How
to Grow section and don't let it get too big
for its pot.

setaceus *p. 247*
Asparagus Fern; Lacefern. This species, often
called *A. plumosus,* is the one that florists use
as a cut green, especially with long-stemmed

roses. It grows upright, to about 2 ft.
(60 cm); eventually, the plant may send out
a stem that can reach 4 ft. (120 cm) long. If
you don't want these long stems, simply cut
them off.

Aspasia
Orchid family
Orchidaceae

Ass-pay'-zee-ah. Steamy Panama is the
original home of this compact-growing
epiphyte. *Aspasia* flowers are waxy, long
lasting, and sweetly fragrant. Pure species
have flowers in shades of cream to yellow,
with brown or maroon markings. Plants can
produce spikes of 4 to 8 in. (10 to 20 cm)
from each side of the flat pseudobulbs, often
twice a year.

How to Grow
Aspasias do best with bright diffuse light,
moderate to warm temperatures, and high
humidity. These are good choices for light
gardens or small sunrooms. Pot in
well-drained plastic or clay containers with a
mixture of tree fern, hardwood charcoal, and
coarse, unmilled sphagnum moss. As new
growth appears, give one-quarter-strength
fertilizer with every other watering.
Although aspasia roots are rather fine, the
pseudobulbs store water, so let the potting
mix dry slightly between waterings.

epidendroides *pp. 140, 141*
This species has creamy white flowers
marked with lines of brownish lavender. It
will reach 6 to 8 in. (15 to 20 cm) high.
A. principissa has larger flowers, with a
broader, lighter-colored lip, yet some
taxonomists lump the two species together.
In recent years *Aspasia* has been crossed with
related genera, such as *Odontoglossum*, to
produce hybrids that will adapt to a wider
range of conditions than pure species of
either genus. *Aspoglossum* Copper Butte is
one good example, producing flowers with
much more purple coloration than plain
Aspasia and under warmer conditions than
pure *Odontoglossum* species can accept.

Aspidistra
Lily family
Liliaceae

As-pi-dis'tra. A genus prized for its ability to stand poor soil, low light, and minimal care. *A. elatior,* the most famous indoor plant of the Victorian era, got the popular name Cast-iron Plant for its ability to survive cold, dimly lit rooms, and the fumes of coal gas.

How to Grow
Water your plant somewhat sparingly and let the soil dry out slightly between waterings. If it receives low light, don't fertilize it more than once a year or so. In medium or bright light, fertilize monthly from spring to fall. Wash both surfaces of the leaves with tepid water every few weeks to keep spider-mites away. Propagate by division.

elatior pp. 225, 228
Cast-iron Plant. This slow-growing species will reach 3 ft. (90 cm) with reasonably good care. The variety *variegata* has green-and-white striped leaves that need medium to bright light to keep their color.

Asplenium
Polypody family
Polypodiaceae

As-plee'ni-um. Members of the genus *Asplenium* are known collectively as spleenworts. Two are interesting and fairly easy to grow, *A. nidus,* the Bird's-nest Fern, and *A. bulbiferum,* the Hen-and-chickens Fern.

How to Grow
Spleenworts need medium light, normal room temperatures, and, like all ferns, some extra humidity. Water them frequently during the warm months and never let the soil dry out; in winter, keep the soil barely moist. The foliage of the Bird's-nest Fern benefits from an occasional washing, but be careful not to rub the fronds or you may damage them. Feed your fern once a month from spring to fall, using half-strength fertilizer.
Repot in spring, but only when the root ball has clearly outgrown its present pot, using a soilless mix or a mixture of half potting soil and half peat moss.

A. nidus is propagated from spores, which is difficult, but propagating *A. bulbiferum* couldn't be easier. Simply pick off the little plantlets (the "chickens") that grow on the fronds and pot them in the soil mix you use for ferns. Keep them covered with a plastic bag until they root.

bulbiferum p. 250
Hen-and-chickens Fern; Mother Fern; Parsley Fern. The feathery foliage, 2 ft. (60 cm) long, is bowed over by the weight of the little bulbils, or plantlets, that sprout on the surface of the mother hen's fronds. *A. daucifolium* is a similar species with darker foliage.

nidus pp. 242, 243
Bird's-nest Fern. The pale green, wavy fronds can grow to more than 3 ft. (90 cm) but they are most likely to reach 12 to 18 in. (30 to 45 cm). 'Antiquum' has wavy-edged leaves. Keep the soil constantly moist. Low humidity will cause the tips of the shiny fronds to turn brown. If they do, cut them off and increase the humidity.

Aucuba
Dogwood family
Cornaceae

Aw-kew′ba. Aucubas are tough, handsome plants that can stand cold and drafts; outdoors, they even survive some freezing.

How to Grow
The plain-leaved aucubas will do well in medium or even low light. The cultivars with variegated leaves need bright light, with or without sun. Both types do well in cool temperatures. Keep the soil moist at all times and fertilize sparingly when the plant is actively growing. Aucubas like to be potbound, but they do grow vigorous roots, so you will have to repot them yearly, using an all-purpose soil mix. Propagate from tip cuttings, which root easily in water.

japonica 'Variegata' p. 214
Gold-dust Tree. Outdoors, these plants grow to be large bushes. In the house, they look best kept to 3 ft. (90 cm) in height by pruning at any time. Very few foliage plants that tolerate low light have such shiny, leathery leaves. The deep green leaves are

speckled with gold. Another cultivar, 'Crotonifolia', is more heavily spotted with cream or gold.

Beaucarnea
Agave family
Agavaceae

Bo-kar'nee-a. In spite of the 'beau' in their name, plants of this genus are more likely to be called interesting than beautiful. The only one grown indoors is *B. recurvata*.

How to Grow
These easy-going plants thrive in bright or medium light in average room temperatures. Water thoroughly and allow the soil to dry out a bit between waterings. Fertilize monthly from spring to fall. Ponytails prefer being potbound. Repot them every 3 or 4 years, using a cactus soil mix. Propagate by planting the offsets that occasionally appear at the base of the trunk.

recurvata p. 236
Ponytail; Elephant-foot Tree; Bottle Palm. Ponytails grow to 3 ft. (90 cm) high. When small, they look like onions sprouting topknots of long, thin ribbons. As they grow, their trunks stretch out at the top and thicken at the base.

Begonia
Begonia family
Begoniaceae

Bee-gō'ni-a. There are at least 1000 species of begonias and more than 10,000 recorded hybrids and cultivars. Some are prized for their flowers, others for their leaves, and some for both. Begonias are usually classified according to their root structure. Some are fibrous-rooted, as are most plants; some grow from creeping rhizomes; and some from tubers. Tuberous begonias, however, are not commonly grown indoors.

How to Grow
Begonias grown primarily for their flowers need several hours of sun a day; the fancy-leaved types, which may also flower, need only bright light. Average temperatures are fine. Begonias benefit from additional

humidity but cannot tolerate too much moisture around their roots or stems. Left standing in water, they can rot. Let the soil dry out a bit between waterings; fertilize very lightly every 2 weeks when the plants are actively growing.

Repot fibrous-rooted begonias in spring using a soilless mix or a mixture of half potting soil and half peat moss. Propagate by taking tip cuttings. Rhizomatous begonias should be repotted only when the rhizomes cover the top of the soil. They do best in shallow pots. To propagate, cut off the tips of the rhizomes and root them.

boweri p. 102

Eyelash Begonia. A rhizomatous begonia 6 to 8 in. (15 to 20 cm) tall. The green leaves of this plant are edged in black, with prominent white hairs, and the flowers are pink. Let the soil get slightly dry between waterings.

coccinea p. 179

Angel-wing Begonia. A fibrous-rooted begonia. To 3 ft. (90 cm) tall. This is a tall, canelike plant with dangling clusters of flowers.

'Di-Erna' p. 178

A fibrous-rooted begonia. This hybrid has canelike stems and dangling coral flowers. It will grow to 3 ft. (90 cm) high and is a profuse bloomer.

× *erythrophylla* pp. 106, 169

Beefsteak Begonia; Kidney Begonia. A rhizomatous begonia. To 9 in. (22.5 cm) tall. The shiny, round leaves are green on top and red underneath. There is also a spiral-leaved variety. This begonia is compact and easy to grow.

× *hiemalis* p. 162

Rieger Begonia; Begonia Elatior Hybrids; Winter-flowering Begonia. A fibrous-rooted begonia 12 to 18 in. (30 to 45 cm) tall. This recent introduction is a stunning plant, something of a cross between a wax begonia and one of the dramatic tuberous varieties. It is susceptible to mildew.

'Lana' p. 179

This fibrous-rooted begonia belongs to the Superba hybrid group, which was developed for tall, slender stems. It is about 3 ft. (90 cm) high, and its rose-red flowers bloom profusely. Prune back sharply in early spring to keep the plant full at the bottom.

maculata '**Wightii**' *p. 204*
A fibrous-rooted begonia. Sometimes called Polka Dot, this beautiful begonia has white flowers and silver-spotted leaves shaped like bat wings. It can grow as tall as 3 ft. (90 cm).

masoniana *p. 100*
Iron-cross Begonia. A rhizomatous begonia. 12 to 16 in. (30.0 to 40.5 cm) tall. The hairy leaves of this begonia are light green with a dark green cross in the center. Keep this plant out of the sun and never give it too much water.

'**Medora**' *p. 208*
Troutleaf Begonia. A fibrous-rooted, cane-stemmed type grown for its silver-spotted dark leaves and pink flowers. It grows to about 12 in. (30 cm) high.

× *rex-cultorum* *pp. 110, 111, 112, 115*
Rex Begonias. Rhizomatous begonias. These begonias are grown for their gorgeously colored and marked leaves. They grow 12 to 15 in. (30 to 38 cm) high; miniature varieties are 6 to 8 in. (15 to 20 cm) tall. They need a little more warmth and humidity than the other varieties, but they are well worth it.

× *semperflorens-cultorum* *pp. 80, 169, 186*
Wax Begonia; Bedding Begonia. A fibrous-rooted begonia 6 to 12 in. (15 to 30 cm) tall. This is the begonia commonly grown as a mass bedding plant in outdoor gardens. It will thrive indoors, in sun. 'Charm' is a variegated form with pink flowers.

Billbergia
Bromeliad family
Bromeliaceae

Bill-ber'ji-a. This group of South American epiphytes includes one of the easiest bromeliads to grow indoors.

How to Grow
See *Aechmea* for directions on growing and propagating bromeliads. When you increase

this one, be sure each offset is at least 4 in. (10 cm) high and has roots.

'Theodore L. Mead' *p. 178*
This hybrid of unknown parentage has soft green leaves and rose-colored bracts with blue-green flowers that hang gracefully.

Blechnum
Polypody family
Polypodiaceae

Bleck'num. Blechnums are mostly tropical ferns with stiffish fronds. They are easy to grow in the dry atmosphere of the home, yet, like any fern, they appreciate added humidity.

How to Grow
The ideal temperature for a blechnum is between 60 and 70° F (15.5 and 21.0° C), but 5 degrees more or less is tolerable. Give your plant extra humidity and medium to bright light, but no sun. Water freely; don't let the soil dry out, but don't let it stand in water, either. Feed once, or at the most twice, a year with half-strength fertilizer. Propagation is by spores—rarely practical for the home grower.

gibbum *p. 244*
This fern has stiff, shiny leaves that grow in a rosette to 3 ft. (90 cm) tall. A somewhat smaller form, with fewer and more erect fronds, is usually sold as *B. moorei,* although it is actually a variety of this species.

Bougainvillea
Four-o'clock family
Nyctaginaceae

Boo-gen-vill-ee′a. Bougainvilleas are shrubs or vines that grow in warm, dry places in full sunshine. A number of cultivars are available.

How to Grow
These plants do best in a warm greenhouse or a sunny room that remains warm in winter. They need at least half a day of sun. Let the soil dry out somewhat between waterings and feed them every 2 weeks while they are in active growth. After flowering,

prune them back, then water them sparingly, just enough to keep their leaves from wilting. Pinch the tips frequently to encourage bushiness. Repot in spring using an all-purpose soil mix. These plants can be propagated by stem or shoot cuttings taken before they mature. It is more difficult to grow them from seeds.

'Barbara Karst' *p. 197*
Paper Flower. The bright red bracts make this an especially striking specimen. Other cultivars come in shades of pink, yellow, orange, lavender, and white.

glabra 'Sanderana Variegata' *p. 198*
Paper Flower. The purple or magenta flowers of this bougainvillea may bloom almost continuously. This, one of several variegated cultivars, has white-edged leaves.

Brassaia
Ginseng family
Araliaceae

Brass´i-a. Only one plant in this genus of tropical trees is usually grown indoors. *B. actinophylla* is often sold as *Schefflera actinophylla,* the name by which it was formerly known. It is one of the most popular of the large indoor foliage plants.

How to Grow
Brassaias require bright light with some sun. Average room temperatures are satisfactory, but in rooms that are very warm and dry plants are subject to spider mites. To provide extra humidity, stand your plant on a tray of pebbles, use a room humidifier, or do both. Wash the leaves frequently with lukewarm water. If your plant is small, take it to the sink and give it a shower, being careful to wash the leaves' undersides, as well. Fertilize the tree monthly during the growing season and keep it bushy by pruning it back from time to time. Repot whenever necessary, using an all-purpose potting soil. Propagate by air layering.

actinophylla p. 213
Schefflera; Umbrella Tree; Australian Umbrella Tree. This sturdy indoor tree can reach 8 ft. (2.4 m) if the light is good and your ceilings are high. The large, glossy

leaves are composed of separate leaflets in the shape of an umbrella.

Brassavola
Orchid family
Orchidaceae

Brah-sa-vol´a. The most famous orchid in the genus *Brassavola* is called Lady of the Night because its flowers become deliciously fragrant after sunset. Its botanical name is *B. nodosa,* and it has a very adaptable, compact growth habit. Hybrids with *B. nodosa* have the same compact habit and starry flower shape but may lack the sweet perfume. Other popular species are called *Rhyncholaelia* by some botanists.

How to Grow
All of the brassavolas are epiphytes. They do best in well-drained mixtures of tree fern, coarse perlite, cork, charcoal, and bark. Some smaller species, such as *B. nodosa,* will succeed on slabs of cork, oak bark, or tree fern. For the most flowers provide bright light. Most of the popular species grow in tree tops where the sunlight is intense. In captivity, they prefer some shade during mid-day from spring to early fall. Fertilize with water-soluble fertilizers every other watering as new growths begin. *B. nodosa* usually grows all year long. Brassavolas thrive in average temperatures.

nodosa pp. 134, 135
Lady of the Night. This species is from Mexico and Central America. The 2- to 3-in. (5.0- to 7.5-cm) flowers are very fragrant at night. Clusters of flowers appear on plants from 10 to 15 in. (25 to 38 cm) high from winter into spring, but some clones bloom almost continually if grown well.

Brassia
Orchid family
Orchidaceae

Brass´ee-uh. These are the fantastic plants known as spider orchids, much appreciated for their arching sprays of honey-scented yellow flowers that are beautifully spotted with brown. In some species, flowers are 12 in. (30 cm) tall, measured from the tip of the top petal to the bottom of the flower. With an average of 10 to 15 flowers per spike, brassias are sure to create a sensation during their fall-to-winter flowering season. Most popular *Brassia* species come from Central America. In addition to the pure species, several hybrids between the most spectacular species are available.

How to Grow
Although these are epiphytes, they have thinner roots than cattleyas and similar orchids. A standard epiphyte potting mix is suitable, but add some chopped sphagnum moss or a fine grade of tree fern to retain enough moisture to keep the pseudobulbs plump. Brassias have thin leaves that grow from both sides of flat pseudobulbs. The flower spikes grow from between the leaves and pseudobulbs. To avoid rot, keep water away from the new growth.
Moderate temperatures are fine. When plants are growing actively, making new pseudobulbs and foliage, fertilize with every other watering. If the brassias continue to grow and light is bright, keep adding fertilizer to every other watering. Should the plants stop producing new growth, which may happen after flowering, cut back on watering and eliminate fertilizer. Sometimes brassias grow plantlets on top of the older pseudobulbs. These can be removed once a few roots form—an easy form of propagation.

gireoudiana pp. 134, 135
This species has 10- to 12-in. (25- to 30-cm), spidery, fragrant flowers, usually yellow to olive-yellow, and usually spotted with dark brown. They bloom from spring to summer.

Broughtonia
Orchid family
Orchidaceae

Brow-toe'nee-ah. Most taxonomists agree that this genus has but a single species, *B. sanguinea*, a dwarf epiphyte from the sunny island of Jamaica. It has variable flower size and color, from light pink or even white to a dark rich red.
Some taxonomists separate a larger-flowered form as *B. negrilensis*.

Broughtonias are ideal for cramped quarters. The hybrids produced with related genera are suitable for growing in bright windows or under broad-spectrum fluorescent lamps. Since *B. sanguinea* has compact growth and flowers with very brilliant colors, orchid breeders have used the species to create dwarf, red-flowered hybrids. In recent years broughtonia hybrids have received awards from orchid societies around the world. Some of the best known and most suitable hybrids for flower form, color, and vigor are: *Hawkinsara*, a blend of *Broughtonia, Cattleya, Laelia,* and *Sophronitis;* and *Cattleytonia,* a combination of *Broughtonia* with *Cattleya.*

How to Grow
Broughtonias thrive when mounted on slabs of dense tree fern or cork bark. Species hybridized with other genera grow slightly better if potted in relatively small, well-drained pots in a mixture of hardwood charcoal, bark, or tree fern. Moderate temperatures are ideal. For maximum bloom and for healthy plants, provide bright light. Broughtonias are more susceptible to fungus attacks under poor conditions than most hard-leaved orchids. Chemical sprays such as insecticides can damage *Broughtonia* foliage more easily than that of other orchids.

negrilensis* × *sanguinea *pp. 146, 147*
This 6- to 8-in. (15- to 20-cm) plant is a hybrid between 2 forms within the genus. It is more vigorous than either parent. Similar hybrids sometimes occur naturally in the wild, resulting in populations of plants that confuse botanists.

Browallia
Nightshade family
Solanaceae

Brow-wall'ee-a. This genus of tropical American plants includes a species that makes a good temporary indoor plant, *B. speciosa*.

How to Grow
Browallias are annuals and should be discarded after blooming. To keep them in flower as long as possible, give them 4 hours of sun each day in a cool room. Let the soil

dry out slightly between waterings. Fertilize every 2 weeks. Propagate from seeds in spring.

speciosa p. 174
Bush Violet; Amethyst Violet. This purple-flowered plant grows to a height of 12 in. (30 cm). There are several named cultivars, including some with white flowers.

Bulbophyllum
Orchid family
Orchidaceae

Bulb-oh-fill'um. The popular *Bulbophyllum* species for contemporary collections are dwarf creeping epiphytes from India and Southeast Asia. These charming miniature orchids are well suited to light gardens, large terrariums, and humid situations where light is bright but diffuse. The flowers of a few species smell unpleasant (in order to attract flies, which pollinate the flowers), so they are seldom found in cultivation.

How to Grow
Use small clay pots filled with unmilled sphagnum moss or tree fern over hardwood charcoal. Clumps of mature bulbophyllums often thrive on slabs of tree fern or cork when humidity is kept above 60 percent. Average to warm temperatures are best. Fertilize with a water-soluble balanced formula every second or third watering as new pseudobulbs are being made. Withhold fertilizer and water after flowering since most species have a 6- to 8-week rest at that time, usually in mid-winter.

blumei pp. 126, 127
This species is native to Java and New Guinea. It grows 6 to 8 in. (15 to 20 cm) tall and produces 1 to 2 in. (2.5 to 5.0 cm) flowers.

Caladium
Arum family
Araceae

Ka-lay'di-um. With their large, colorful, mostly heart-shaped leaves, caladiums are among the most gorgeous of foliage plants. There are dozens of named horticultural varieties to choose from. As indoor plants, they have just one limitation—they need to spend 3 or 4 months completely dormant. During this time, they are nothing more than little dried-up brown tubers. It doesn't matter when they rest, however, so you can schedule a series of plants to come into leaf whenever you want them. Outdoor plants are usually started in late winter or early spring; for an indoor display, it might be better to let your caladiums rest in summer so you can enjoy their color during the winter months.

How to Grow
You can buy either plants already in leaf or tubers. If you choose tubers, be sure your choice is pictured in a catalog. Otherwise, you may not know what your plant will look like until it develops. During growing season, caladiums need warm temperatures, never below 65° F (18.5° C) during the day. Give them extra humidity by misting or setting the pot in a tray of pebbles. They like bright light but no direct sun, and drafts are a danger. Water freely while the plants are growing and fertilize them every 2 weeks.
When the leaves die down, let the soil dry out. Store the tubers in their pots or in dry peat moss in a cool place (55 to 60° F; 13.0 to 15.5° C) for at least 2 months. Repot the tuber in a 5-in. (12.5-cm) pot, using an all-purpose soil mix. Water the soil and place the pot in a warm, humid place. When shoots appear, gradually move the plant into bright light and water it frequently. Propagate by separating clumps of tubers and potting them up individually.

× *hortulanum* pp. 109, 112, 113
Fancy-leaved Caladium. Grows to a height of 2 ft. (60 cm). The hybrids 'Candidum', 'Rosalie', 'Crimson Glow', and many other named varieties come in a range of colors and color combinations.

Calathea
Arrowroot family
Marantaceae

Kal-a-thee'a. Calatheas are among the most exotic of the foliage houseplants. They are sometimes confused with plants in the genera *Maranta, Ctenanthe,* and *Stromanthe,* all members of the same family and all with beautifully marked leaves.

How to Grow
Calatheas prefer medium light and temperatures from 60 to 70° F (15.5 to 21.0° C). If your room is warmer, it is essential to provide extra humidity. A daily misting is helpful, too.
In spring and summer, water generously, making sure that the soil is always moist. In winter, let the soil dry out a bit between waterings. Calatheas are often potted in a soilless mix and consequently need fertilization every 2 weeks while they are actively growing. Don't feed them in winter. Repot in early spring using either a soilless mix or an all-purpose soil generously enriched with peat moss. Propagate by division in spring.

makoyana p. 99
Peacock Plant. This 2 ft. (60 cm) plant is the best known of the calatheas. Its common name refers to the pattern on its leaves, which resembles the markings on a peacock's feathers.

picturata p. 97
This calathea has round to oval, silvery leaves that are edged in green with purple undersides. It will reach a height of 2 ft. (60 cm).

roseopicta p. 104
This 8-in. (20-cm) plant has leaves that are green on top with a red midrib and a bright red patch near the margin that fades to pink in age. The undersides of the leaves are purple.

vittata p. 103
This 3-ft. (90-cm) plant can have 18-in. (45-cm) leaves that are light green striped with white and yellow-green underneath.

zebrina p. 100
Zebra Plant. The name of this plant refers to the dark green marks on the emerald-green leaves; their undersides are purple. It will grow to 15 in. (38 cm) high. Two other houseplants, *Aphelandra squarrosa* and *Cryptanthus zonata,* have the same common name.

Calceolaria
Figwort family
Scrophulariaceae

Kal-see-o-lay′ri-a. There are 500 species of
Calceolaria, but the ones sold as houseplants
are usually the hybrids called *C. herbeohybrida.*
They are grown as annuals from seed.

How to Grow
Calceolarias should give you a month of
flowers if you keep your plants in bright
light but not direct sun. They also like cool
temperatures. Water them plentifully, and
never let the soil dry out completely. Watch
out for aphids. When your plant has
finished blooming, throw it away.

herbeohybrida p. 162
Slipper Plant; Pocketbook Plant. These odd
little plants are from 6 to 12 in. (15 to
30 cm) tall and are covered with masses of
pouch-shaped flowers in shades of yellow,
bronze, pink, red, or reddish brown. The
flowers are mostly speckled.

Camellia
Tea family
Theaceae

Ka-mee′li-a. The species of camellia usually
grown indoors is *C. japonica,* from which
more than 2000 cultivars have been derived.

How to Grow
Camellias will not flower in the average
home. They need a cool porch, greenhouse,
or garden room where the daytime
temperature is no more than 65° F (18.5°)
and the night temperature ranges from 45 to
50° F (7 to 10° C). They also need high
humidity and don't like being moved around
when in bud. Give them bright, filtered
light and keep the soil evenly moist. Fertilize
them every 2 weeks in spring and summer
with an azalea-type acid fertilizer. Repot after
flowering, if needed, in a half-and-half
mixture of peat moss and all-purpose soil.
Propagate by tip cuttings.

japonica p. 192
If you can satisfy a camellia's fussy needs, it
will live for many years. Be careful not to
touch the flowers with your hands or they
will turn brown. The dark, glossy leaves

make this an attractive houseplant even
when it is not in bloom.

Capsicum
Nightshade family
Solanaceae

Kap'si-kum. The ornamental Christmas
Pepper, *C. annuum,* belongs to the same
species as the many edible peppers. It is
usually bought when the fruits have become
brightly colored and discarded after they
drop. The peppers are extremely hot and best
kept away from children and pets.

How to Grow
Keep your ornamental pepper plant in bright
light, in average room temperatures, and
water it freely. When it has finished fruiting,
throw it out. Peppers are annuals, raised
from seed in small pots and transplanted
later.

annuum p. 194
Christmas Pepper. These are cheery plants
for late fall or winter color. They rarely
grow more than 12 to 15 in. (30 to 38 cm)
high.

Carissa
Dogbane family
Apocynaceae

Ka-ris'sa. Dwarf cultivars of the Natal Plum,
C. grandiflora, make beautiful houseplants
and are often trained as indoor bonsai. They
have shiny green leaves and an occasional
scented white flower.

How to Grow
Natal Plums need at least a half day of
sunshine and temperatures that never drop
below 60° F (15.5° C). Keep the soil moist
at all times and feed the plants every 3 or 4
months. Repot only when the roots have
filled the pot, using an all-purpose soil mix.
Propagate at any time by taking stem
cuttings.

grandiflora p. 191
Natal Plum. The dwarf cultivars, growing
no taller than 2½ ft. (75 cm), include
'Minima', 'Nana', and 'Nana Compacta'.

Caryota
Palm family
Palmae

Carry-o'ta. Caryotas, or fishtail palms, are named for their ribbed, wedge-shaped leaves that look quite unlike those of a typical palm. These are among the easiest palms to grow indoors.

How to Grow
Since palms usually come from hot, dry climates, most are well suited to indoor life. Grow them in medium to bright light, but never in direct sun. These plants like average temperatures and humidity; never let the temperature dip below 55° F (13° C). In very hot rooms they may be subject to attack by spider mites. To prevent this, increase the humidity by placing the pot on a tray of moistened pebbles.

Water palms thoroughly in spring and summer and moderately in winter. Never let the soil dry out completely, but don't let the pot stand in water, either. Fertilize once every 2 weeks in spring and summer. Palms don't have a well-defined resting period, but growth may slow in winter.

Palms are long-lived, and most grow very slowly indoors. The Burmese Fishtail may grow only a few inches a year until it reaches its maximum indoor height of 8 ft. (2.4 m). Fronds will die off occasionally; just cut them back. However, never prune the tip of a palm or cut off the newest frond since that will stop all growth.

If you move your palm outside for the summer, be very careful to keep it out of the sun and protected from wind. Bring it back inside before the temperature starts to fall. These plants need repotting only every 2 to 3 years; they actually do best in rather tight-fitting pots. Use an all-purpose potting soil and be sure to put plenty of pebbles or broken clay shards in the bottom for drainage. Propagate from suckers or offsets.

mitis p. 229
Burmese Fishtail Palm. Grows to a height of 8 ft. (2.4 m). The main stem of this palm has as many as 8 fronds, and there are many shorter fronds clustered at the base of the stem, giving this species a full, leafy appearance. *C. urens,* with fewer leaflets, is a more open plant. Because of their easy care

and long life, both of these palms are often used as decoration in commercial buildings.

Cattleya
Orchid family
Orchidaceae

Cat'lee-ya. Cattleyas have become world famous because they are so often included in corsages. The original species come from Latin America, where they grow as epiphytes on trees or sometimes on mossy rocks. During the past 50 years, hybridizers have created hundreds of new hybrids, often breeding cattleyas with related genera such as *Brassavola, Laelia,* and *Sophronitis. Cattleya* species are more demanding in cultivation than many of the available hybrids. Modern techniques of propagation permit commercial growers to offer the very best cattleyas and related hybrids at a relatively low price.

How to Grow
Pot cattleyas in an epiphyte mix of cork, bark chips, or tree fern and give them excellent drainage. A few dwarf species, such as *C. aclandiae,* will grow on slabs of bark or tree fern provided humidity and light are ideal; the larger plants do best in pots. Cattleyas have thick, water-storing pseudobulbs and flat, leathery leaves; they aren't especially attractive except when graced with flowers. Moderate temperatures and bright light are ideal for these plants. Some that have been crossed with miniature *Sophronitis* or the Mexican *Laelia* species will succeed with nights in the low 50s (10 to 12° C).
With so many hybrids available, you can easily select cattleya-type orchids to fit your taste in color, flower form, and flowering season. Hybridizers have recently created an array of charming dwarf-growing hybrids that have 2- to 4-in. (5- to 10-cm) flowers on plants less than 12 in. (30 cm) high, sometimes only 4 to 6 in. (10 to 15 cm) in total height. Fertilize growing plants with water soluble formulas: Use a 30-10-10 balance for plants grown in pure bark mixtures, and a 20-20-20 type ratio for other potting mixes. Repot plants every 2 to 3 years just as new growth is starting.

Laeliocattleya **Park Ridge** *pp. 142, 143*
This hybrid of *Lc.* Spring Comet with

C. mossiae blooms in the spring and is 12 to 15 in. (30.0 to 37.5 cm) tall. The species *C. mossiae* is known as the Easter orchid since its fragrant flowers are popular for corsages during Easter.

Sophrolaeliocattleya Jewel Box *p. 122, 123*

This compact-growing hybrid of *C. aurantiaca* and *Slc.* Anzac is popular because it is easy to grow and blooms in winter and spring. The clone 'Scheherazade' has won an Award of Merit from the American Orchid Society and is offered by many commercial firms.

violacea pp. 148, 149

This South American species has a compact growth habit with red-flushed pseudobulbs, each topped with 2 stiff leaves 4 to 6 in. (10 to 15 cm) long. The 4- to 5-in. (10.0- to 12.5-cm) flowers appear on a short spike, usually from spring to summer. They have an unusually flat shape, intense violet color, and heavy perfume.

walkerana pp. 148, 149

This dwarf-growing Brazilian species is usually 6 to 8 in. (15 to 20 cm) high and has flat, fragrant 3- to 4-in. (7.5- to 10.0-cm) flowers, usually blooming from late winter into spring. As a pure species this is difficult to grow, although some succeed with plants grown on hardwood logs or on slabs of dense tree fern. Hybrids of *C. walkerana* are easier to grow, yet often inherit the species' dwarf growth and flower fragrance.

Cephalocereus
Cactus family
Cactaceae

Sef-fal-lo-seer-e'us. This genus of desert cacti contains one species, *C. senilis,* that is commonly grown as a houseplant. In the wild, it can reach a height of 50 ft. (15 m), but indoors it is more likely to grow to just 12 in. (30 cm).

How to Grow
To encourage the growth of the long white hairs that make this so distinctive, grow it in full sun that lasts all day. Be careful if you stroke those hairs; they cover sharp spines. Average temperatures are fine, with a maximum of 65° F (18.5° C) in winter.

Keep the soil evenly moist when the weather is warm, but let it dry out quite a bit in winter. Fertilize once a year in spring. Repot only when the roots have completely filled the pot, using a cactus soil mix. Propagate from seeds.

Ironically, with old age the white hairs of an Old-man Cactus can turn brown. More often, however, the brown color means the hairs are dirty. You can give your cactus a shampoo by covering the soil with wax paper or foil and then brushing the hair with a mixture of detergent and warm water. Be sure to rinse it out.

senilis p. 261
Old-man Cactus. When very young, these plants may not yet be covered with white hairs. At this stage, keep them out of direct sun at midday.

Ceropegia
Milkweed family
Asclepiadaceae

Seer-ro-pee′ji-a. *Ceropegia* is a genus of vines and subshrubs, including several plants that are popularly grown indoors, often in hanging baskets.

How to Grow
Several hours of sunlight, average room temperature, and moderate watering during the growing season are virtually all it takes to make this intriguing little vine flourish. Let the soil dry out considerably between waterings and keep it almost constantly dry in winter. Young plants don't need fertilizer; feed older plants with half-strength fertilizer every 2 weeks in spring and summer. Repot when the plant has outgrown its pot, using a cactus soil mix. Propagate by planting the little tubers that appear on the vines.

woodii p. 87
Hearts-on-a-string; String-of-hearts; Rosary Vine. This is a good plant for a small hanging pot. The delicate stems grow out of a tuber, which sits on the soil.

Chamaecereus
Cactus family
Cactaceae

Kam-ee-seer′e-us. Chamaecereus is a small cactus from Argentina. There is only one species in the genus, *C. sylvestri,* which is related to the lobivia.

How to Grow
Follow the instructions for *Lobivia* in caring for the Peanut Cactus. Plenty of sun is essential.

sylvestri p. 266
Peanut Cactus. This is a fast-growing cactus with many stems, each 6 in. (15 cm) long. The 3-in. (7.5-cm) flowers appear in spring.

Chamaedorea
Palm family
Palmae

Kam-ee-dor′ee-a. There are more than a hundred species in this genus of slender, tropical-rainforest palms. One of them, *C. elegans,* is the most popular indoor palm.

How to Grow
Chamaedoreas thrive in medium to bright light and in average room temperatures. Unlike most other palms, however, they need additional humidity. Stand the pot on a tray of moistened pebbles. Water lavishly from spring to fall, then moderately during the cooler months. Feed once a month in spring and summer, using half-strength fertilizer. Repot only when the plant has clearly outgrown its pot, and be careful not to hurt the rather brittle roots. Use all-purpose potting soil mixed with an equal amount of peat moss. It is not easy to propagate this palm in the home. For more on how to grow palms, see *Caryota.*

elegans pp. 230, 231
Parlor Palm. Growing outdoors, this palm can reach a height of 6 ft. (1.8 m), but it is rarely more than 3 ft. (90 cm) tall indoors. Formerly it was called *Neanthe bella.* 'Bella', a popular cultivar, is more compact.

Chamaerops
Palm family
Palmae

Kam'ee-rops. The single species in this genus
is the sturdy *C. humilis,* the only native
European palm.

How to Grow
Unlike the tropical palms, which cannot
stand temperatures below 55° F (13° C),
C. humilis can survive 50° F (10° C)
temperatures and actually benefits from
being placed in a cool room in winter.
However, it will also do well in average to
warm room temperatures. This palm needs
bright light, preferably with a few hours of
direct sun. In all other respects, its culture is
the same as for *Caryota.*

humilis *p. 233*
European Fan Palm. The sharply cut and
angled leaves make this a dramatic palm.
New leaves are covered with fine gray hairs
that eventually fall off. There are a number
of named cultivars available, all of them
quite similar to the parent species, which
grows to a height of about 4 ft. (120 cm).
'Elegans', with silvery leaves, is somewhat
smaller.

Chlorophytum
Lily family
Liliaceae

Clow-ro-fy'tum. Legend has it that Goethe,
fascinated by the way this plant produces
miniature plantlets at the end of its strawlike
stolons, was the first person to bring it into
the house. True or not, the Spider Plant is a
perennial favorite among indoor gardeners. It
is an ideal hanging basket plant and one that
tolerates dry rooms.

How to Grow
Ideally, give the Spider Plant average room
temperatures and bright light with some
winter sun. Note, however, that it can adapt
to medium light. Water it thoroughly and
let the soil dry out slightly between
waterings—overwatering can lead to rotted
roots. Fertilize every 2 weeks in spring and
summer.
Spider Plants produce their offspring most
liberally when potbound. When repotting,

be sure to leave at least an inch of space between the top of the soil and the rim of the pot. The fat succulent roots of the plant will push up the soil, and if you haven't allowed for this, you'll have no place to water. Use all-purpose soil when you repot. Propagate by snipping off a plantlet that has started to form roots and putting it in water. When the roots are an inch or so long, pot the plantlet in soil. Use several plants in a basket to get the full look you want.

comosum p. 85
Spider Plant. This plant has narrow green leaves 8 to 12 in. (20 to 30 cm) long, with a central stripe of creamy white. Stems grow to 5 ft. (1.5 m) long. There are many cultivars, with leaves of various lengths and colorings. 'Vittatum' is probably the most familiar.

Chrysalidocarpus
Palm family
Palmae

Kris-sal´i-do-kar-pus. The only species of this genus that is grown as a houseplant is *C. lutescens*. It is commonly called the Areca Palm.

How to Grow
The Areca Palm is slightly more demanding than most palms. It needs a warm room, ideally 65 to 75° F (18.5 to 24.0° C) year round, with a good deal of additional humidity to keep the beautiful fronds in good condition. Water it thoroughly and keep the soil moist, but never let the pot stand in water. Filtered sunlight is also necessary. Feed the palm once a month in spring and summer and watch closely for spider mites. In all other respects, culture is the same as for *Caryota*.

lutescens p. 232
Areca Palm; Yellow Palm; Butterfly Palm. This slow-growing palm can reach 10 ft. (3 m), but a height of 5 ft. (1.5 m) is more likely. The long, graceful fronds grow from a cluster of thin, bamboolike canes.

Cissus
Grape family
Vitaceae

Sis'sus. Two of the easiest, most tolerant, and most beautiful hanging basket plants belong to this genus, including the popular grape ivy, *C. rhombifolia*. A fourth, *C. discolor,* is even prettier, but is only for those who can supply its greenhouse demands.

How to Grow
Except for *C. discolor,* these vines will flourish under almost any conditions. They do need good drainage, however, so put a layer of pebbles in the bottoms of their pots. Average, slightly cool temperatures are ideal. They need bright light or some indirect sun, but can tolerate medium, or even low light. Water freely in spring and summer, but never let the soil become soggy. Fertilize every 2 weeks or once a month in spring and summer, depending on how fast you want your plant to grow. Keep in mind that plants grown in low light should not be given much fertilizer. Pinch back the growing tips regularly to keep the plants bushy. Repot when necessary, using an all-purpose potting soil. Propagate by stem cuttings.

antarctica *p. 76*
Kangaroo Vine. This plant comes from Australia, not Antarctica, as the species name suggests. It presumably got its common name because it grows in leaps and bounds. The most rampant of the species, the Kangaroo Vine can easily grow to 10 ft. (3 m) in length. Keep it tamed and bushy by constantly pinching the ends.

discolor *p. 81*
Trailing Begonia Vine. This beautiful greenhouse vine has no relation to the true begonias. It has simple oval leaves, each 4 to 6 in. (10 to 15 cm) long, that are finely toothed and highly colored: silver and green on top; purple blotched with white, pink, reddish purple, or all three colors beneath. This vine is difficult to grow.

rhombifolia *p. 207*
Grape Ivy. This is the easiest cissus vine to grow and one of the best in all respects. The 3-part, somewhat heart-shaped leaves have a metallic sheen when young; later, they turn a rich green with rusty hairs on the veins

below. 'Ellen Danica' has larger, rounder leaves.

Citrus
Rue family
Rutaceae

Sit'rus. Several edible citrus bushes make excellent indoor plants. They bear beautifully scented flowers and, in the case of the orange, fruit that can be made into an excellent marmalade.

How to Grow
To ensure fruit and flowers, grow your plant in average temperatures, give it at least 4 hours of sun a day, and let it summer out of doors. Let the soil dry out a bit between waterings, and fertilize with an acid fertilizer every 2 weeks while the plant is actively growing. Pinch the growing tips frequently to keep the plant bushy. Repot in spring, using an all-purpose potting mix with some peat moss added. Propagate by taking tip cuttings. Watch out for spider mites and scale insects.

× *citrofortunella mitis* *p. 218*
Calamondin Orange. This hybrid is almost always sold as *C. mitis*. It often bears flowers and fruit at the same time. In the house, it rarely grows more than 4 ft. (120 cm) tall.

limon 'Meyer' *p. 218*
Meyer Lemon. This 4-ft. (120-cm) dwarf tree is the hardiest of the lemons. It produces 3-in. (7.5-cm) fruit.

Cleistocactus
Cactus family
Cactaceae

Kly-sto-cac'tus. These tall, slender desert cacti rarely bloom before they are 3 ft. (90 cm) tall. They are grown primarily for their interesting shape.

How to Grow
These cacti need sunshine all year, average temperatures from spring to fall, with cool (50 to 55° F; 10 to 13° C) temperatures in winter. Let the soil become almost dry between waterings and fertilize monthly in

spring and summer. Repot when necessary, using a cactus soil mix. Propagate from seeds.

strausii p. 263
Silver Torch. A mature plant can reach 5 to 6 ft. (1.5 to 1.8 m). The flowers, when they bloom, barely open—*Cleistocactus* means "closed cactus."

Clerodendrum
Vervain family
Verbenaceae

Kler-ro-den'drum. There are 450 species of clerodendrums, or glory bowers, but only one, *C. thomsoniae,* is commonly grown indoors. It makes an attractive hanging plant.

How to Grow
Clerodendrums will flower in spring and summer if they are given half sun and half bright, indirect light, temperatures that never go below 60° F (15.5° C), and extra humidity. Under ideal circumstances, they may even flower all year. While they are actively growing, keep the soil constantly moist and feed them every 2 weeks. Watch for white flies, which can be a problem. Once flowers fade in fall, reduce the water and don't feed them in winter. Prune back the stems after they finish flowering to keep the plant bushy and under control. These plants flower best when potbound. When repotting is necessary, use an all-purpose soil mix. Propagate from stem cuttings.

thomsoniae p. 193
Bleeding Glory-bower; Bleeding-heart Vine. The crimson flower protruding from the large, white calyx accounts for the plant's popular name. The plant will grow to 10 ft. (3 m) high but is best kept lower by pruning.

Clivia
Amaryllis family
Amaryllidaceae

Kly'vi-a. *Clivia* is a small genus of plants with handsome, strap-shaped leaves and spectacular orange flowers.

How to Grow

Clivias need bright light and average room temperatures. They are relatively easy to grow, provided you can give them 6 to 8 weeks of rest in the winter. During this rest period, they should be kept at 50 to 55° F (10 to 13° C) and quite dry to ensure flowering. In spring and summer, when the plants are in active growth, keep the soil uniformly moist. In winter, move your plant to a cool room and let the soil become almost dry; when a flower stalk emerges, increase the amount of water. Fertilize every 2 weeks in spring and summer.

These plants flower best when they are potbound, so repot only when you see roots on the surface, usually in about 3 years. Use all-purpose potting soil and move to a pot just one size larger. Because these are heavy plants, use clay pots instead of lighter plastic ones, which might tip over. Propagate by offsets.

miniata p. 155

Kaffir Lily. To 2 ft. (60 cm) high and 3 ft. (90 cm) wide. If cared for properly, this plant can bear 12 to 20 orange, trumpet-shaped flowers atop 18-in. (45-cm) stalks in spring. The leaves are 18 in. (45 cm) long, thick and glossy.

Codiaeum
Spurge family
Euphorbiaceae

Ko-di-ee′um. Crotons are tropical shrubs that make handsome houseplants if you can provide the full sun they need to develop their brilliantly colored leaves.

How to Grow

Crotons prefer a warm room with a good deal of humidity, but they will thrive in average indoor conditions as long as they get full sun for part of the day. Water sparingly in winter; otherwise, keep the soil evenly moist. Fertilize every 2 weeks from spring to fall. Repot in spring, using an all-purpose soil mix. Propagate by taking cuttings from side shoots.

variegatum pictum pp. 204, 223, 224

Croton. This 3-ft. (90-cm) species is the parent of almost all of the cultivars available today. 'Fascination' has leaves marked haphazardly with red, orange, and shades of green. The leaves of 'Punctatum Aureum' are thinner and green with yellow spots.

Coffea
Madder family
Rubiaceae

Kof'fee-a. Shrubs in the genus *Coffea* are the source of the world's coffee. Coffee beans are actually the seeds of the plant's pulpy fruit.

How to Grow
Coffee plants will thrive in average indoor conditions if they are given at least 4 hours a day of filtered sunlight. Keep the soil moist at all times, and fertilize the coffee plant every 2 weeks from spring to early fall. The beautifully–scented white flowers, followed by red berries, do not bloom until the plant is several years old. The leaves turn brown if they are brushed against, so keep your plant out of the way of traffic. Repot in spring, using an all-purpose soil mix. Propagate by taking tip cuttings before they have hardened. Take the cuttings from upright shoots; side shoots will produce unattractive, badly-shaped plants.

arabica p. 217
This species is the major source of the best-quality coffee and the only plant that is grown indoors, where it rarely becomes taller than 3 to 4 ft. (90 to 120 cm).

Coleus
Mint family
Labiatae

Ko'lee-us. Coleus are fast growing plants that are usually bought in spring and disposed of in fall. Most of the varieties for sale are hybrids.

How to Grow
Plants bought in spring should be grown in bright light with some sun and in average room temperatures; they like extra humidity. Water your plants copiously and fertilize them every 2 weeks. Watch closely for mealy bugs. Repot as soon as roots fill the pot; this is one plant that doesn't like being potbound. In the summer, take tip cuttings,

and throw out the old plants in fall. When
the cuttings have rooted, plant them in an
all-purpose soil mix. Pinch out the young
growing tips often to keep the plant bushy.
In spring, resume fertilizing schedule.

× *hybridus* *pp. 95, 96, 113, 114*
Painted Nettle. There are more than 200
named cultivars to choose from. Often they
are listed, incorrectly, as hybrids of the
species *C. blumei*. A few of the many
names on the market are 'Red Lace Leaf',
'Reasoner's Fancy Leaf', 'Lacey Leaf', and
'Wizard Mixture'. They grow to a height of
3 ft. (90 cm).

Columnea
Gesneriad family
Gesneriaceae

Ko-lum'ne-a. These Central American jungle
plants are spectacular in hanging baskets.
Their bright red, orange, or yellow flowers
look something like goldfish when they are
fully open. The flowers are long-lasting, and
a large plant can have a hundred flowers
blooming at one time.

How to Grow
Columneas need bright light but no direct
sun. Average home temperatures are fine, but
additional humidity is essential. Supply this
with a room humidifier, by daily misting, or
by putting small pots on a tray of moistened
pebbles. Water moderately and let the soil
dry out between waterings. Spring-blooming
species need a rest period in winter, with
slightly cooler temperatures and just enough
water to keep the roots from drying out
completely.
Don't fertilize a plant that is resting, but
otherwise, fertilize columneas each time you
water them with a one-quarter-strength
solution of liquid fertilizer. Since columneas
are epiphytes, you can plant them in
sphagnum moss, in an African violet soil
mix, or in a soilless potting mix. Repot
them at any time. If you don't want them to
outgrow their containers, slice off
one-quarter to one-third of the root ball and
put it back in the same box or container. To
propagate, take 4-in. (10-cm) stem cuttings
after flowering. Prune your plants after
flowering to keep them bushy.

'California Gold' *p. 185*
Hybrid Goldfish Plant. This hybrid
columnea really resembles its namesake: It
has yellow, fish-shaped flowers trimmed with
orange.

hirta p. 269
Goldfish Plant. The green leaves and reddish
stems of this columnea are densely hairy.
The vermilion flowers are also covered
with hairs.

Cordyline
Agave family
Agavaceae

Kor-di-ly′ne. A genus, related to *Draceana,*
of tropical plants grown for their
handsomely-colored foliage.

How to Grow
Average room temperatures and bright light,
but no direct sun, are fine for cordylines, but
extra humidity is a necessity. Stand the pot
on a tray of moist pebbles, mist the leaves
daily, or use a room humidifier. In spring
and summer, keep the soil evenly moist and
fertilize every 2 weeks. In winter, let the soil
dry out slightly between waterings. These
plants prefer to be potbound. Repot only
every 2 or 3 years, using a standard potting
mix or a soilless mix. When your plant
becomes leggy, you can easily propagate it by
taking 3-in. (7.5-cm) stem cuttings; root
them in sand. You can also propagate by tip
cuttings, air layering, or from purchased
seeds.

terminalis p. 116
Ti Plant. To 2 ft. (60 cm). The leaves of
these handsome foliage plants come in
variegated colors, with stripes of maroon,
red, purple, white, pink, and green. Most
often it has red leaves with darker red
markings. Among the many cultivars are
'Lord Robertson', with green leaves marked
in pink and cream; 'Prince Albert', with
green and red leaves; and 'Red Edge', with
green leaves edged with red and streaked
with red.

Crassula
Orpine family
Crassulaceae

Krass-you'la. The genus *Crassula* includes the enormously popular Jade Plant, which can grow as tall as 4 ft. (120 cm) indoors, as well as the tiny Toy Cypress, which rarely outgrows a 3-in. (7.5-cm) pot. All are easy to grow.

How to Grow
Bright light, preferably with some sun, and average-to-cool room temperatures suit these succulent plants. The only way to harm them is by overwatering. Water moderately during the spring and summer, letting the soil dry out between waterings, and only occasionally in winter. Fertilize every 2 weeks during the growing season. Repot every 2 years, or when the plant becomes root-bound, using a mixture of 2 parts all-purpose potting soil and 1 part perlite. Propagate by taking tip cuttings, which will root almost anywhere, including the pot in which the parent plant is growing.

argentea p. 287
Jade Plant. With its thick trunk and shiny, fleshy oval leaves, this is a long-lived indoor plant, one that can grow to 4 ft. (120 cm), tall enough and stout enough to fill a large tub. It can be kept smaller and more compact and shapely by regular pinching of the growing tips. There is a miniature variety, which is attractive in dish gardens. In a very cool room that gets winter sun, an old jade plant may even bloom.

falcata p. 283
Propeller Plant; Airplane Plant; Sickle Plant. Although the propeller plant has several 8-in. (20-cm) stems arising from the base, one usually takes off and grows as long as 12 in. (30 cm). The leaves growing out from the stem look like the propellers on an airplane. Clusters of red flowers appear in summer. In addition to rooting the tips, you can propagate this species by potting up offsets.

lycopodioides p. 265
Rattail; Toy Cypress. A small species, rarely more than 8 in. (20 cm) high, the Toy Cypress has slender stems covered with tiny, scaly leaves. Several grown in one pot make a better showing than a single plant.

rupestris p. 284
Buttons-on-a-string; Rosary Vine; Bead Vine.
The stems, or "strings," of this species pierce
the roundish leaves, or "beads," accounting
for the various popular names. It is small
and spreading and sometimes produces little
yellow flowers at the end of the stems.

Crossandra
Acanthus family
Acanthaceae

Kros-san'dra. The only species of
Crossandra grown as an indoor plant is
C. infundibuliformis, the Firecracker Flower.

How to Grow
Crossandras need warm temperatures and
plenty of humidity; in a hot, dry room they
are subject to spider mites. Give them
medium light in summer, when they usually
flower, and some sun in winter, when they
usually rest. With half a day of sun in
winter and continuous fertilizing, a plant
may flower all year long. Water actively-
growing plants moderately, letting them dry
out a bit between waterings, and feed them
every 2 weeks. If the plant rests in winter,
water only enough to keep the soil from
drying out completely and don't feed it.
Repot in the spring using all-purpose potting
soil. Propagate by taking tip cuttings, or
grow from seed.

infundibuliformis p. 188
Firecracker Flower. Grows to 2 ft. (60 cm)
high. Prized for its salmon-colored flowers
and glossy green leaves, this is a difficult
plant for the home but a good one for a
greenhouse. The cultivar 'Mona Wallhed'
is more compact, growing to about 18 in.
(45 cm).

Cryptanthus
Bromeliad family
Bromeliaceae

Krip-tan'thus. Plants in the genus
Cryptanthus are known as earth-stars because
of their flattened, star-shaped rosettes. They
are grown for their leaves, not their flowers,
and there are many species and cultivars
available. Most of them are quite small.

How to Grow
See *Aechmea* for the culture and propagation
of bromeliads. Cryptanthuses rarely need
fertilizing, although you might occasionally
want to spray a weak solution of plant food
on the leaves or put some in the plant's
central cup.

acaulis p. 276
Starfish Plant. This nearly stemless bromeliad
has 6-in. (15-cm) leaves that are green on
top and whitish beneath, with wavy, prickly
edges.

bivittatus p. 274
The arching, spiny, 3- to 4-in. (7.5- to
10.0-cm) leaves of this cryptanthus are
greenish-brown, each with two long, reddish
or pink stripes. 'Pink Starlight' looks more
rosy overall.

'Starlite' p. 275
This hybrid is probably related to
C. bivittatus. Its leaves are a bit longer, and
it is distinguished by the pink color in the
center of the rosette.

zonatus p. 275
Zebra Plant. The undulating, 9-in. (22.5-cm)
leaves are light green and crinkly with cross
bands of white, green, or brown.

Cuphea
Loosestrife family
Lythraceae

Kew'fee-a. The cuphea most commonly
grown indoors has thin, bright red flowers
that look like little firecrackers.

How to Grow
Cupheas need bright light, with some sun,
and, if possible, cool winter temperatures.
Let the soil dry out a bit between waterings
and fertilize every 2 weeks while the plants
are actively growing. Repot when necessary,
using an all-purpose soil mix. Propagate by
taking tip cuttings in fall.

ignea p. 182
Cigar Flower; Firecracker Plant. This plant
grows to 2 ft. (60 cm) and is usually
discarded after two years, when it tends to
lose its looks.

Cyanotis
Spiderwort family
Commelinaceae

Sy-an-o'tis. Cyanotis is a genus of trailing plants with fleshy leaves that are often covered with very fine hairs. They are related to the tradescantias.

How to Grow
These plants have certain contradictory needs that make them a little difficult to grow. They look best in hanging baskets but need extra humidity, which should not be supplied by misting since their hairy leaves tend to get water spotted. Average temperatures are fine, but they need bright light and some sun to keep their growth compact. Let the soil dry out a little between waterings. Fertilize once or twice a year. These plants rarely need repotting. Propagate in spring by taking tip cuttings, and pot up the new plants, when they have rooted, in cactus soil mix or a half-and-half mixture of all-purpose potting soil and cactus soil mix.

kewensis p. 110
Teddy-bear Plant. The name comes from the fine brown hairs that cover the stems and leaves. Another species, with white hairs, is *C. somaliensis,* sometimes called Pussy-ears.

Cycas
Cycas family
Cycadaceae

Sy'kas. Although the word *cycas* is from the Greek for palm tree, the most important member of this genus, *C. revoluta,* or Sago Palm, is not a palm at all, but the descendant of an ancient family of fernlike or palmlike plants that once covered the earth. Today it is more widely grown for funeral wreaths than any other plant in America.

How to Grow
Sago Palms must have bright light, with or without direct sun. Otherwise, they tolerate a wide range of home conditions, including low humidity. Water thoroughly and let the soil dry out slightly between waterings. If your plant is in lower-than-bright light in winter, reduce the amount of water. Fertilize once a month during the spring and

summer. Under ideal circumstances, the Sago
Palm is not likely to produce more than one
new leaf a year, so repotting won't be
necessary very often, if at all. When you do
repot, use an all-purpose potting mix and
add sand or perlite for additional drainage.
Cycases are commercially propagated by
suckers or seed, but neither method is
practical for the home grower.

revoluta p. 230
Sago Palm. This is a strikingly handsome
houseplant and a particularly good choice if
you want a plant that will never outgrow its
location. The young plant you buy, with
frondlike leaves up to 3 ft. (90 cm), is
probably about 10 years old and still too
young to have a trunk.

Cyclamen
Primrose family
Primulaceae

Sy′kla-men; also Sick′la-men. Although the
florist's cyclamen, *C. persicum,* has been
around for years, the newer, compact
cyclamen cultivars developed from this
species and the smaller *C. purpurascens* are
more satisfactory for the home. Some of
them have been given such operatic names as
Carmen, Tosca, and Boheme, and there
certainly ought to be a Madame Butterfly if
there isn't one.

How to Grow
Cyclamens are usually bought in flower.
They need cool temperatures; in a warm
room their blooming period will be short.
Placing them on a tray of moistened pebbles
can help prolong their flowering. Give
cyclamens bright light but no sun. Water
thoroughly, but never let them sit in water,
and feed them every 2 weeks while they are
in flower. Remove dead flowers and leaves
with scissors.
Cyclamens have the well-deserved reputation
of being difficult to bring into flower a
second year. If you want to try it, after the
plant finishes flowering, gradually reduce the
watering. When all the leaves have turned
yellow, let the soil dry out almost completely.
Store the plant in a cool place over the
summer. When growth begins in fall, repot
the tuber in all-purpose soil, bring the pot
into the light, and start watering. Until the

leaves are developed, keep the soil barely moist. Then increase watering and start fertilizing according to the directions given above.

persicum p. 168
The dwarf hybrids of this species and *C. purpurascens* rarely exceed 6 in. (15 cm) in height. The charming pink or white flowers are often referred to as butterflies. Other forms grow 10 to 12 in. (25 to 30 cm) high. 'Shell Pink' has lovely magenta flowers.

Cymbidium
Orchid family
Orchidaceae

Sim-bid'ee-um. Of all the orchids, cymbidiums are the easiest to grow. Modern hybridization has resulted in robust epiphytes and semi-terrestrial types that thrive in composts of bark, sphagnum moss, coarse perlite, gravel, and hardwood charcoal. In semi-tropical parts of California, many gardeners can even grow cymbidiums outdoors in beds alongside more common plants. Indoors, the best cymbidiums are crosses between dwarf species and standard hybrids that have recently appeared on the market. This mixture produces what are known as miniature cymbidium hybrids. Despite their name, some of these easy-to-grow plants can reach a height of 2 ft. (60 cm), bearing towering flower spikes of 3 ft. (90 cm); even so, they are smaller than standard hybrids.
A few rare dwarf species from Japan and China are sometimes grown for the glorious fragrance of their drab green or cream-colored flowers. Most orchid growers, however, prefer modern hybrids for their choice of flower color, blooming season, and size. The flowers come in all shades but blue and true red—the most popular are shades of green, white, and yellow.

How to Grow
Cymbidiums thrive in epiphyte mixtures enriched with unmilled sphagnum moss, oak leaf compost, and coarse peat moss to hold more moisture. These plants have very thick roots that grow from sturdy pseudobulbs. Strong light will encourage healthy growth and produce the most flowers. Cymbidiums are ideal for a greenhouse, sun room, or

spacious, sunny window. The bulbs are crowned with thin, straplike leaves that grow in a pleasant arch.

To prevent rot, keep water out of the new growth. Provide moderate temperatures when plants are actively growing. Standard-sized cymbidiums require a cool 6- to 8-week period, with night temperatures of 45 to 50° F (7 to 10° C), if they are to flower well. The modern miniature hybrids will bloom well with nights in the 60s (15.5 to 20.5° C). All types appreciate frequent fertilizing when new growth is forming. Repot or divide when new growth begins, usually in the spring.

Gainesville × Dan Carpenter *pp. 130, 131*
This recently-created hybrid was bred to produce standard-sized cymbidiums that bloom well with moderate temperatures. And it is a success—the plants flower well in Central Florida. Their flowers are 3½ to 4 in. (9 to 10 cm) wide.

Cyperus
Sedge family
Cyperaceae

Sy-peer′us. This large genus of sedges and grasses includes *C. papyrus,* the Bulrush of the Bible, also used to make writing paper in ancient Egypt. The species commonly grown indoors is *C. alternifolius,* an ideal plant for anyone given to overwatering, since almost its only absolute requirement is that its roots be kept soaking wet.

How to Grow
Umbrella Plants do well almost anywhere. Fertilize once a month throughout the year. If your plant begins to look tired and shabby, cut it back to the roots and let it start all over again. Repot when necessary, using 2 parts all-purpose potting soil, 1 part sand, and 1 part perlite. Propagate by division. You can also cut off leaf clusters, including a small portion of the stem, and root the clusters in sand.

alternifolius p. 233
Umbrella Plant. 2 to 4 ft. (60 to 120 cm) tall. This plant's need for constantly wet roots is best met by standing the pot in a good-sized saucer of water. From the roots grow a number of slender stems topped by

clusters of narrow, umbrella-shaped leaves.
C. a. gracilis, a smaller version of the same
plant, rarely exceeds 18 in. (45 cm) in
height.

Cyrtomium
Polypody family
Polypodiaceae

Sir-tō′mi-um. Only one member of this
small genus, *C. falcatum,* can be grown
indoors. It is relatively easy to cultivate.

How to Grow
Bright light and average to cool
temperatures are best for *C. falcatum.*
If your room gets warmer than 70° F (21° C),
give your plant extra humidity. Water it
thoroughly, letting the soil dry out between
waterings, and feed it every 2 weeks with
half-strength fertilizer. Don't fertilize your
plant in the winter if it is in a cool room.
When the roots have completely filled
the container, repot using a mixture of
all-purpose potting soil and peat moss.
Propagate by division.

falcatum p. 240
Holly Fern. A stiff, erect fern, 1 to 2 ft.
(30 to 60 cm) tall, with shaggy leafstalks,
shiny fronds, and deep green, glossy
segments that resemble holly leaves.

Davallia
Polypody family
Polypodiaceae

Da-val′li-a. The davallias are pretty, feathery
ferns, easy to grow indoors, and prized for
their long furry rhizomes, which give them
the common names Rabbit's-foot Fern,
Deer's-foot Fern, and Squirrel's-foot Fern. In
growth and appearance the species below are
similar, and the popular names are often
used indiscriminately.

How to Grow
Average home temperatures and medium
light suit these plants. Although they are
more tolerant than most ferns of low
humidity, they should be misted often if
your room is warm. Keep the soil barely
moist at all times. Davallias are not heavy

feeders; fertilize them only twice a year with half-strength fertilizer. Beware of overfertilization: Ferns can be damaged more easily by it than most plants. To propagate davallias, cut off 2 to 3 in. (5.0 to 7.5 cm) of the rhizome's growing tip and place it on a pot of moist sand. Fasten it down with 2 wire hoops so it is always in contact with the sand. Enclose the pot in a plastic bag until roots form and new growth begins.

fejeensis p. 250
Rabbit's-foot Fern. This is a large davallia, with fronds up to 2 ft. (60 cm) long. The light brown, furry rhizomes are ½ in. (13 mm) thick.

trichomanoides p. 247
Squirrel's-foot Fern. This fern's thick rhizomes are densely covered with whitish to tan fur. The fronds are 18 in. (45 cm) long.

Dendrobium
Orchid family
Orchidaceae

Den-dro′bee-um. Dendrobium blooms are sold around the world as cut flowers. The gracefully arching sprays of modern *D. phalaenopsis* and *D. gouldii* hybrids are long-lasting, travel well, and come in colors that range from white through yellow to bright purple. For home gardeners, the most suitable types are compact evergreen *D. phalaenopsis* hybrids, such as 'Muang Thai'.
Another group of *Dendrobium* orchids is made up of hybrids produced from the species *D. nobile*. A third group is based on tall-growing evergreen species from New Guinea, such as *D. gouldii*. These warm-growing hybrids are often called antelope dendrobiums because of the twisted petals of the colorful flowers. In addition to these 3 broad groups, the genus *Dendrobium* includes hundreds of other species, from creeping miniatures 1 to 2 in. (2.5 to 5.0 cm) high to towering 8-ft. (2.4-m) giants.

How to Grow
Since so many species are available from different areas in Asia, it is not practical to give precise directions for all dendrobiums. Culture for the most popular types is

similar in that all need to be potted as epiphytes, in mixtures of tree fern, bark, or cork, often with addition of hardwood charcoal. Use small clay pots for quick drying of the roots and to add weight to tall plants. All dendrobiums respond well to fertilizer when in active growth.

Provide bright light, at least 50 percent humidity, and moderate to warm temperatures. The *D. nobile* hybrids must have nights in the 50s (10 to 15° C) in the fall after growth is completed to form flower buds along the canes. If nights remain too warm, the plants form offsets rather than flowers. *D. phalaenopsis* hybrids usually have a rest period after flowering. During this time give no fertilizer and less water. The tall antelope types need water and fertilizer all year long plus bright light.

primulinum pp. 146, 147

This is a popular fragrant species from India and se. Asia. Plants have pendulous stems 10 to 12 in. (25 to 30 cm) long that lose their leaves at the end of each growing season. The 1- to 2-in. (2.5- to 5.0-cm) flowers appear along the stems each spring.

Tangerine × Mushroom Pink pp. 130, 131

These flowers are typical of the warm-growing evergreen antelope type dendrobiums. This hybrid is 10 to 12 in. (25 to 30 cm) high, much shorter than the 3- to 6-ft. (0.9- to 1.8-m) stems more common in the cut-flower types grown throughout Asia and in Hawaii.

Dieffenbachia
Arum family
Araceae

Dee-fen-bak'i-a. Some plants are so attractive, so well suited to the indoor environment, and so easy to take care of that they have become very common houseplants. It's difficult to see them with fresh eyes. Just because they are so often a part of shopping malls and other commercial landscapes, they shouldn't be any less desirable for the home. The dumb canes fall into this category.

How to Grow
Dumb canes tolerate most indoor conditions but prefer bright light. Water thoroughly

and let the soil dry out between waterings. Fertilize every 2 weeks during the warmer months. Repot using an all-purpose soil mix only when necessary; this plant likes to be potbound. If your plant becomes too leggy, you can cut it down to within a few inches of its base and new growth will sprout from the cut-off stump. Be careful when you cut into your plant. The sap of dieffenbachia contains calcium oxalate, which can cause painful swelling and even temporary dumbness if it gets on your tongue. Be sure to wear gloves when handling the plant and wash your hands afterwards. Propagate by taking tip cuttings, stem cuttings, or (carefully) by air layering.

amoena p. 97
The largest of the dumb canes, this plant grows 5 to 6 ft. (1.5 to 1.8 m) high on a single trunk. The leaves are 18 in. (45 cm) long and 12 in. (30 cm) wide. 'Tropic Snow' has dark green leaves with lighter centers than those of the species.

'Camille' p. 96
This handsome hybrid has bright green leaves whose light yellow centers spread almost to the edges. It will grow 3 to 4 ft. (90 to 120 cm) high.

maculata p. 203
Spotted Dumb Cane. This is the most popular of the dieffenbachias. It grows 4 to 5 ft. (1.2 to 1.5 m) high, and there are several cultivars with dramatic yellow or white markings.

Dizygotheca
Ginseng family
Araliaceae

Di-zee-go-thee'ka. A genus of about 15 species of shrubs or small trees, several of which make graceful indoor trees. These plants don't branch out; they eventually lose their lower leaves and can become scraggly. To avoid this, buy a pot filled with several small plants, preferably of different sizes. If you already own a lanky dizygotheca, buy a few new plants and pot them with the old one.

How to Grow
Grow your plant in a room where the

temperature never goes below 60° F (15.5° C), even in the winter. Stand the pot on a tray of moistened pebbles to ensure that the plant has adequate humidity. Provide bright light but no direct sun. Water sparingly at all times, allowing the soil to dry out slightly between waterings. Never overwater, and don't move the plant around, either; both can cause the leaves to drop. Fertilize every 2 weeks during the spring and summer. Repot only when the plant has outgrown its container, using all-purpose soil. Be very careful not to move the plant to a pot more than one size larger, since the extra soil might become waterlogged.

elegantissima p. 222
False Aralia. It would be hard to name a more elegant plant. Its slender, glossy leaflets are copper colored at first, then darken to almost blackish green. This plant grows to 6 ft. (1.8 m) high. *D. veitchii* is a similar plant; it has slightly wide, sturdier leaflets.

Dracaena
Agave family
Agavaceae

Dra-see′na. These handsome foliage plants come in a variety of shapes, sizes, and colors and grow in different ways. They are among the most reliable of indoor plants—no matter how dark or sunny your home, you could easily find the right place for each of them. They range in size from 18 in. (45 cm) to 6 ft. (1.8 m); the larger ones are particularly attractive when young.

How to Grow
Bright light but no direct sun is best to keep the leaves colorful, but dracaenas often do quite well in medium light, too. Like most foliage plants, they appreciate extra humidity. Water them freely from spring to fall, keeping the soil evenly moist; in winter, let it dry out somewhat between waterings. Fertilize your plants every two weeks during the growing season.
Repot using an all-purpose soil mix whenever it becomes necessary. *D. surculosa* usually needs repotting only every 2 to 3 years. To propagate an old dracaena with a long trunk, use air layering. Young plants can be propagated by taking tip or stem cuttings.

deremensis 'Warneckii' *p. 227*

Striped Dracaena. The leaves of this cultivar are similar to those of the Corn Plant, but shorter and thinner and in general more delicate. The plant can grow to 15 ft. (4.5 m) in the wild, but is most attractive when it is young, without a stalk. The leaves are bright green with 2 white stripes.

fragrans 'Massangeana' *p. 226*

Corn Plant. When the plant is young, the broadly spreading leaves grow in a rosette from the soil. The leaves have striking green borders and yellowish stripes. As a Corn Plant matures, it develops a thick trunk, and gradually loses its bottom leaves until it resembles a tall palm tree topped by a tuft of leaves. The plant can grow taller than 5 ft. (1.5 m) indoors. If you cut off the trunk when it is 3 to 4 ft. (90 to 120 cm) tall, 1 or 2 clumps of leaves will develop on the side of the blunt-cut top. But plants treated this way can look awkward. If your plant grows too tall for its setting, try one of two things: Either cut it down completely, to within a few inches of the base, and let the new plants develop at that level, or air layer the top. If you choose air layering, you can either throw the old plant away when the new one roots, or you can cut it down to the base, as above, and end up with 2 plants.

marginata *p. 236*

Dragon Tree. This is one of the easiest dracaenas to grow—it can even touch your ceiling if you want it to, albeit after quite a few years. The narrow green leaves have purple edges; they gradually drop off at the bottom, but the trunk is considerably more graceful than that of the Corn Plant. If you buy a pot that contains 3 Dragon Trees, each a different height, you won't face the problem of what, if anything, to do about a leggy tree for years. A very pretty cultivar is 'Tricolor'; it has stripes of green, pink, and cream and needs more light than the species.

sanderana *p. 224*

Belgian Evergreen. This dracaena has slender leaves of green and white stripes. It grows to 3 ft. (90 cm).

surculosa *p. 91*

Gold-dust Plant. This dracaena is quite different from the others, rarely growing more than 18 to 24 in. (45 to 60 cm) tall. Its many branches bear oval leaves that are pointed at both ends and heavily spotted with cream or white. Propagate by taking tip cuttings. You may find this sold under its former name, *D. godseffiana*.

Dyckia
Bromeliad family
Bromeliaceae

Dike′ee–a. Dyckias are tough, spiny-leaved bromeliads that can stand a reasonable amount of neglect. Small plants, they grow in clumps. Unlike most of their relatives, dyckias don't die after blooming.

How to Grow
Dyckias thrive in average room temperatures with dry air and bright sunlight. Water them moderately and let the soil dry out somewhat between waterings. Fertilize once a month from spring to fall. See *Aechmea* for more information on the care and propagation of bromeliads.

fosterana *p. 282*
The orange flowers grow on 12-in. (30-cm) spikes and bloom in summer. Handle this plant carefully; its spines are murderous.

Echeveria
Orpine family
Crassulaceae

Ech-e-veer′i-a. The genus *Echeveria* contains about 100 species of succulents generally known as hen-and-chickens. Most of those offered for sale are hybrids or cultivars.

How to Grow
Echeverias grow best with a half day of sun, but they can manage in very bright light. Average temperatures are fine. Water them thoroughly during the growing season and let the soil dry out almost completely between waterings. In winter, water only enough to keep the leaves from shriveling. Feed once a year in the spring with a half-strength fertilizer and repot whenever necessary using a cactus soil mix. Propagate from offsets.

'Black Prince' *p. 286*
This cultivar is named for the dark color of

its leaves, which form rosettes about 3 in. (7.5 cm) across.

elegans p. 268
Mexican Gem; Mexican Snowball; Pearl Elegans. The bluish-green leaves with reddish tips form a tight rosette 4 in. (10 cm) across. The rose-and-yellow flower grows from a 12-in. (30-cm) stem.

runyonii p. 285
The leaves of this species are flatter than those of *E. elegans,* but the rosettes are of similar size. The flowers are pink.

Echinocactus
Cactus family
Cactaceae

Ee-ky'no-kak-tus. Most of these plants are large, slow-growing cacti that can take a hundred years to reach 4 ft. by 4 ft. (120 cm by 120 cm) in the wild. Indoors, they are rarely more than a few inches in diameter. The only one that is likely to bloom has the unfriendly names of Eagle Claws or Mule-crippler Cactus.

How to Grow
These cacti need sunshine all year, average temperatures from spring to fall, and cool (50 to 55° F; 10 to 13° C) temperatures in winter. Let the soil become almost dry between waterings and fertilize monthly in spring and summer. Repot when necessary, using a cactus soil mix. Propagate from seeds.

grusonii p. 257
Barrel Cactus; Golden Ball Cactus. In 20 years, the Golden Ball will have a diameter of 10 to 12 in. (25 to 30 cm). Young plants look very similar to *Mammillaria* species.

horizonthalonius p. 257
Eagle Claws; Mule-crippler Cactus. This plant grows to a height of 12 in. (30 cm) and a width of 6 in. (15 cm), but it may bloom when it is only half that size.

Echinocereus
Cactus family
Cactaceae

Ee-ky-no-seer′ee-us. *Echinocereus,* or Hedgehog
Cactus, is a satisfying plant to grow indoors
because, given full sun all year, it will bloom
when very young.

How to Grow
These cacti need sunshine all year, average
temperatures from spring to fall, and cool
(50 to 55° F; 10 to 13° C) temperatures in
winter. Let the soil become almost dry
between waterings and fertilize monthly in
spring and summer. Repot when necessary,
using a cactus soil mix. Propagate from
seeds.

pectinatus *p. 262*
Rainbow Cactus. This slow-growing plant
takes years to reach its maximum height of
about 12 in. (30 cm).

Echinopsis
Cactus family
Cactaceaé

E-kin-op′sis. *Echinopsis* is a showy genus of
mostly night-blooming flowers. Some
Echinopsis plants have been crossed with
plants in the genus *Lobivia.*

How to Grow
See *Lobivia.* Unlike plants in the genus
Lobivia, however, echinopsises should be
fertilized only once a year, and many of these
hybrids bloom during the day.

multiplex *p. 256*
Barrel Cactus; Easter-lily Cactus. The
sweet-smelling flowers may be 8 in. (20 cm)
across—as wide as the cactus is tall.

Epidendrum
Orchid family
Orchidaceae

Ep-ee-den′drum. This is a genus of about
1000 species. Most of the popular, showy
epidendrums are from tropical areas of Latin
America, but the dwarf *E. conopseum* is
cold-hardy enough to be found wild in the

southeast U.S. Species vary from the sprawling, grasslike, reed-stem *E. radicans* to types with hard pseudobulbs and waxy strap-shaped leaves that resemble those of small *Cattleya* orchids. This second group is separated into the genus *Encyclia,* but many catalogues and all hybrid registrations retain the genus as *Epidendrum.*

Some *Epidendrum* flowers have a honey scent and a shape resembling cattleyas, although they are only a few inches across. Hybrids combining *Epidendrum* with *Cattleya, Laelia,* and related genera exist; these broaden blooming season, flower form, and color variations. As a group, epidendrums are adaptable spray-flowered orchids well-suited to the home horticulturalist.

How to Grow

Reed-stem species thrive outdoors in raised beds with direct sun. Indoors, these vinelike epidendrums do well trained on tree-fern poles. Usually many fine white roots hang free in the air. Add some unmilled sphagnum moss to compost, or use a standard cymbidium/paphiopedilum mix for these semi-terrestrial epidendrums. The species with pseudobulbs (the *Encyclia*) thrive when grown like cattleyas, under bright light, with 50 percent humidity and moderate temperatures.

A few thin-leaved species, such as *E. cochleatum,* 'Cockelshell' orchid, will bloom well in medium light or under broad spectrum fluorescent lamps. Some of the smaller species do well on chunks of cork or tree fern. Larger types do best in clay pots filled with epiphyte mixtures of bark, tree fern, coarse perlite, or cork, often with the addition of hardwood charcoal. Fertilize plants that are actively growing every 2 weeks with balanced, water-soluble fertilizer.

cordigera pp. 150, 151

Spice Orchid. This 8- to 15-in. (20- to 38-cm) epidendrum has been shifted by botanists to a new genus, *Encyclia.* For many years, this fragrant plant was grown as *E. atropurpureum.* Most clones have blooms of 1 to 2 ft. (30 to 60 cm) in the spring, with pink to rose–red lips with brown petals. Some white types are available. *E. cordigera* is popular in making *Epicattleya* hybrids.

radicans pp. 124, 125

This rambling, almost vinelike species is easy to grow in full sun. An established plant will have many thin stems 3 to 5 ft. (0.9 to 1.5 m) high, covered with short waxy leaves and sprouting many thin roots. These roots absorb moisture from the air and will grow into any compost they touch. In the wild, this species rambles through brush and over grassy banks. Most forms of *E. radicans* have clusters of 1- to 1½-in. (2.5- to 4.0-cm) flowers with bright yellow lips. Some taxonomists include *E. radicans* under *E. ibaguense*. With this inclusion, forms in white, yellow, and various shades of lavender are available. Hybrids of reed-stem epidendrums and some select forms of the pure species bloom off and on all year.

Epiphyllum
Cactus family
Cactaceae

Ep-i-fill'um. The "epiphyllums" sold today are almost always hybrids between the genus *Epiphyllum* and one of the other jungle cactus genera. Their spectacular flowers have given these plants their common name, orchid cacti. The drooping stems make them a good choice for a basket.

How to Grow
Epiphyllums need bright light. In spring and summer, they should be kept at temperatures of 70 to 85° F (21.0 to 29.5° C) during the day, 10 degrees lower at night. In winter, they are best grown at night temperatures of 50 to 55° F (10 to 13° C); in higher temperatures they produce leaves, not flowers. In early spring and summer, keep the soil evenly moist and fertilize your plants every 6 weeks with a low-nitrogen fertilizer such as 2-10-10. In fall and winter, water them less frequently and never apply fertilizer. Keep the stems under control by occasionally pinching back the tips when they aren't flowering. Repot when necessary, using an African violet potting mix. Propagate by taking stem cuttings in summer.

'Ackermannii' *p. 271*
Red Orchid Cactus. This is a free-flowering plant that will often bloom not only in the summer but into fall and winter. The flowers are 4 to 6 in. (10 to 15 cm) long and the stems up to 3 ft. (90 cm).

Epipremnum
Arum family
Araceae

Epi-prem'num. A small genus of climbing
vines similar to philodendrons.

How to Grow
The most popular plant in this genus,
E. aureum, is an excellent choice for any
less-than-ideal condition. In bright light, its
leaves will become more richly marked with
yellow or white. If you grow your plant in
low light, be careful not to overwater it. Let
the soil dry out slightly between waterings.
These plants are best in hanging baskets.
Periodically take the plant to the sink and
spray its leaves with water. Fertilize no more
than 2 or 3 times a year, and always when
the plant is actively growing. If your vines
become lanky, cut it back. Propagate by
taking tip cuttings.

aureum *pp. 92, 93*
Pothos; Devil's Ivy. This climbing or trailing
vine can grow "like the devil," but is usually
6 ft. (1.8 m) long indoors. Its heart-shaped
leaves are marked with white or yellow.
'Golden Queen' has leaves and stems that are
almost entirely yellow. 'Marble Queen' has
white and green variegated leaves and stems.

Episcia
Gesneriad family
Gesneriaceae

Ep-piss'i-a. Episcias have striking foliage,
colorful flowers, and trailing strawberry-like
stolons. Unfortunately, they are difficult to
grow outside a greenhouse since they need
constant high humidity.

How to Grow
Episcias require bright light but no direct
sun and relatively warm temperatures of 70
to 75° F (21 to 24° C) at night. Although
they want a lot of humidity, never spray
them, since water spots their velvety leaves.
Keep the soil uniformly moist, but not
soggy. Fertilize every 2 weeks from spring to
fall with half-strength liquid fertilizer. In a
greenhouse, fertilize every week all year with
a quarter-strength liquid fertilizer.
If you want to grow episcias in the house,

do so under lights on a tray of moistened pebbles. Pot them in shallow African violet pots using an African violet soil mix. Propagate by planting the runners.

cupreata p. 108
This plant has coppery leaves and lipstick-red flowers. A number of other species and hybrids have differently colored foliage and flowers. Most bloom in spring or summer, but 'Cygnet' can often be forced to bloom on and off all year if the stolons are pinched off as soon as they appear.

Euonymus
Staff-tree family
Celastraceae

You-on'i-mus. This genus of shrubs, vines, and trees contains about 170 species. Only 1 is usually grown inside, but there are many variegated types of *E. japonica,* or Spindle Tree, available.

How to Grow
Most euonymuses are outdoor shrubs, and even the Spindle Tree likes bright light and cool temperatures—never above 65° F (18.5° C). Give it about 4 hours of sun as well in winter, but keep it cool—preferably 50 to 55° F (10 to 13° C)—and relatively dry. In spring and summer, water more often, but let the top soil dry out a bit between waterings. Feed twice a month but not at all in winter. Repot as often as once a year, in spring, until the plant reaches the desired size—usually 4 ft. (120 cm) high. Propagation is by tip cuttings, but this is rather difficult. Watch for powdery mildew, which sometimes plagues these plants.

japonica 'Mediopicta' p. 215
Spindle Tree. This is one of the many variegated cultivars of the species. Its glossy green leaves have bright yellow centers.

Euphorbia
Spurge family
Euphorbiaceae

You-for'bi-a. The genus *Euphorbia* consists of more than 1600 species, including 2 very popular indoor plants—Poinsettia,

E. pulcherrima, and Crown-of-thorns, *E. milii.*
It is typical of the genus that these two
plants are very different in both appearance
and growth; the one thing they have in
common is the milky juice that flows when
they are cut or bruised.

How to Grow
Since the culture and care of these plants
differs for each, this information is discussed
under the specific species.

milii pp. 170, 197
Crown-of-thorns. This spiny, shrubby plant
grows to 3 ft. (90 cm) and has small, sparse
leaves on very prickly stems. There are dwarf
forms that grow about 12 in. (30 cm) high.
The flowers usually appear in summer; under
ideal conditions, the plant may blossom on
and off all year. The Crown-of-thorns grows
well in normal warm room temperatures, in
bright light with a lot of sun. When the
plant is in flower, water it thoroughly and
let the soil dry out somewhat between
waterings. In winter, water sparingly, but
don't let the soil get completely dry.
Fertilize every 2 weeks from spring to fall.
Repot only when necessary, using a mixture
of all-purpose potting soil and sand or perlite
for drainage. You can cut back a leggy plant
before repotting or at any time, preferably in
spring. To stanch the flow of the milky
latex, put cold water on the cut end.
Propagate by taking tip cuttings. Let the
cutting dry out for a day or so before
potting it up in sand or sand and peat
moss. Until it roots, keep it damp but not
soaking wet.

pulcherrima p. 199

Poinsettia. When it was discovered growing
wild in Mexico in the 19th century, the
Pointsettia was a rangy 6-ft. (1.8-m) bush.
Today's ubiquitous Christmas plant holds its
large red, cream, or pink flowers on sturdy
stems that may be as short as 8 to 10 in.
(20 to 25 cm) while the plant grows to a
height of 2 ft. (60 cm). The blooms are not
really petals but colorful bracts surrounding
an insignificant greenish flower. Poinsettias
are always bought in bloom and can be kept
blooming for 2 to 3 months under the right
conditions. They need relatively cool room
temperatures, preferably not above 70° F
(21° C) during the day or 55° F (13° C) at
night. Keep the plant in bright light and

out of drafts. Water it thoroughly but let the soil dry out somewhat between watering. Do not feed. If the soil is too wet or too dry, the leaves will drop.

Although it is possible to hold a Poinsettia over until the next winter or to take cuttings from your plant, it is difficult and really not worth the trouble because you will never get a plant as attractive as one you can buy. In addition to following a rigorous 8-week regimen of total uninterrupted darkness for 14 hours each night, commercial growers also treat their Poinsettias with growth-inhibiting hormones to create short-stemmed, stocky plants.

tirucalli p. 272
Milkbush; Pencil Tree. This succulent euphorbia can reach a height of 6 ft. (1.8 m) indoors and has the same cultural needs as *E. milii*. To propagate, take stem cuttings in spring. *E. tirucalli* has a great deal of milky juice; when you take cuttings, stanch their flow by dipping the cutting in cold water, then spray the wound on the parent plant with cold water. Let the cutting dry out for a few days before potting it up.

Exacum
Gentian family
Gentianaceae

Ecks'a-kum. The representatives of this genus grown indoors are *E. affine* and its cultivars.

How to Grow
This cheerful little plant has flowers that virtually cover its waxy leaves and is almost always bought in flower. To extend its blooming period, pick off the dead flowers. When the plant begins to look straggly, take tip cuttings and throw away the parent. After the cuttings have rooted, pot them in African violet soil, keep them moist at all times, and fertilize them every 2 weeks. They need bright light, average temperatures, and some extra humidity.

affine p. 175
Persian Violet; German Violet; Arabian Violet. This plant grows to a height of 2 ft. (60 cm). Choose a well-rounded plant, one covered with small flowers, which are lavender with yellow centers. 'Blithe Spirit'

has white flowers. 'Midget' is a smaller plant with bright blue flowers.

Fatshedera
Ginseng family
Araliaceae

Fats-hed'e-ra. This genus consists of a single species, a botanical wonder that is a cross between 2 distinct species belonging to 2 genera, *Fatsia* and *Hedera.* Although this is of more interest to botanists than to the average grower, the resultant plant, *Fatshedera lizei,* is a superlative foliage plant and very easy to grow.

How to Grow
Grow *Fatshedera* in any room temperature; in the winter, it prefers cool rooms. Give it medium or bright light and let the soil dry out a bit between waterings. Fertilize every 2 weeks while the plant is actively growing. Repot in spring using an all-purpose soil mix and insert supporting stakes into the new pot. Propagate by taking tip or stem cuttings. If an old plant gets too leggy, you can cut it back to the base. Watch out for aphids—they are attracted to *Fatshedera.*

lizei *p. 207*
Aralia Ivy; Tree Ivy; Botanical-wonder; Ivy Tree. This plant usually grows 3 to 4 ft. (90 to 120 cm) indoors, but it needs staking. When potting up your own cuttings, put several into a pot to make a shrubby-looking bush. 'Variegata' has white leaf markings; it needs bright light.

Fatsia
Ginseng family
Araliaceae

Fat'si-a. The only species in this genus is *F. japonica,* a fast-growing, large-leaved foliage plant.

How to Grow
Fatsias do best in quite cool temperatures, not above 65° F (18.5° C) and as low as 45° F (7° C) in winter. They can manage in more normal indoor temperatures if placed on a tray of moistened pebbles for extra humidity. Give them bright light. Water

plentifully during the active growth period and more moderately in winter, letting the soil dry out a little between waterings. Feed every 2 weeks during the period of active growth. To keep these fast-growing plants manageable, you can cut them back by half in spring. Repot in spring, using all-purpose potting soil. Propagate by taking stem cuttings from the shoots that appear at the base of the plant.

japonica p. 210

Japanese Fatsia; Formosa Rice Tree. This species has large, dramatic leaves. It can grow to a height of 5 ft. (1.5 m). 'Variegata' has green leaves with white margins. The cultivar 'Moseri' is more compact.

Ficus
Mulberry family
Moraceae

Fy'kus. This huge genus of more than 800 species of chiefly tropical trees, shrubs, and vines includes half a dozen of our most popular indoor foliage plants, as well as the edible fig, *F. carica,* which will not grow fruit indoors. The best plants for the house range in size from the tiny creeping *F. pumila* to the tree-sized *F. benjamina.*

How to Grow
In general, figs are adaptable, easy-going plants that do well in medium to bright light and normal household temperatures. However, sudden changes in temperatures or drafts will cause the leaves to drop (although they will usually come back). Plants with variegated leaves need bright light, preferably with some sun, to keep their color. Except for *F. pumila,* which should be kept uniformly moist, figs should be watered thoroughly and then allowed to dry out slightly.

Keep the large-leaved varieties clean by gently sponging the leaves with tepid water. To repot, use standard soil; add peat moss for *F. pumila.* Figs do best when they are cramped or potbound, so repot only every 3 or 4 years. If the plant has reached the maximum size for your room, root-prune it instead of moving it to a larger pot. You may also pinch off the growing tip, but if you do, be sure to dust the cut with powdered charcoal or ashes to stanch the flow of milky sap. Except for *F. pumila,* propagate by air layering. *F. pumila* roots easily from tip cuttings. Air layering is also a good treatment for plants that have become leggy. In hot, dry rooms, these plants are subject to spider mites. *F. benjamina* is prey to scale.

benjamina pp. 90, 216
Weeping Fig; Java Fig. A graceful, birchlike tree, from 2 to 18 ft. (0.6 to 5.5 m) high, with spreading and drooping branches. The leaves are 2 to 4 in. (5 to 10 cm) long, rather leathery, with a tapering tip. 'Variegata' has white-edged leaves. This is one of the most deservedly popular trees used for landscaping large indoor areas. The young plant is bushy and attractive in a smaller room.

deltoidea p. 219
Mistletoe Fig. A shrubby, miniature tree to 3 ft. (90 cm) high. The leaves are variable in shape—another, incorrect name for this plant is *F. diversifolia*—dark green above, lighter below. Even the small plants bear tiny, yellowish, inedible figs all year long.

elastica p. 205

Rubber Plant. This old workhorse of house-plants is one of the most popular ficuses, though not the most attractive one. Among newer varieties is 'Decora', with dark, oval leaves up to 15 in. (38 cm) long. The plant can easily reach 6 ft. (1.8 m) on a single trunk, but it can also be induced to branch by air-layering or cutting off the tip. 'Robusta' has even larger, rounder leaves. Variegated cultivars include 'Tricolor', with green leaves with cream and pink patches; 'Schrijvereana', with pale yellow-green patches; 'Doescheri', with a pink central rib and cream and gray patches; and 'Variegata', with yellow markings and a yellow border.

'Elegante' p. 219
This hybrid has short, glossy green leaves arranged on branching stems. It will grow 3 to 4 ft. (90 to 120 cm) high.

lyrata p. 205
Fiddle-leaf Fig. The common name comes from the large, fiddle-shaped leaves, which are often 15 in. (38 cm) long and have noticeable white veins. Although it may grow as tall as *F. elastica* on a single stem,

this plant will branch if you cut off the growing tip.

pumila p. 208
Creeping Fig; Climbing Fig. A popular vine that grows flat against walls in a greenhouse or outdoors in the South. Inside, this fast-growing vine makes a good plant for a hanging basket or a shelf. It can stand a somewhat dimmer light than the other figs but must be kept moist.

Fittonia
Acanthus family
Acanthaceae

Fit-toe′ni-a. There are only 2 species of fittonias, one of which is a good choice for a terrarium or in a shady part of a greenhouse.

How to Grow
These creeping plants need steady warmth, humidity, and medium or bright light—conditions that are best supplied in a terrarium. In a dry room, they require constant attention. Keep the soil moist but not wet, and feed every 2 weeks with half-strength fertilizer. Pinch the ends frequently and, instead of repotting, take tip cuttings and start the new plants. Pot them in a soillesss mix.

verschaffeltii argyroneura p. 107
Mosaic Plant; Nerve Plant. This is a pretty little plant with bright green leaves and white veins. It is sometimes called Silver-nerve Fittonia. The typical *F. verschaffeltii* has dark green leaves with rosy red veins.

Fuchsia
Evening Primrose family
Onagraceae

Few-sha; but properly Fuke′zi-a. There are more than 100 species of fuchsias, but the ones that are grown as basket plants, indoors or out, are all hybrids.

How to Grow
Although many people try to bring their outdoor fuchsias indoors after the summer, this is the least satisfactory way to grow

these plants. Instead, start with newly
purchased or propagated plants. Fuchsias
require cool temperatures and several hours
of sun every day. Water them liberally while
they are actively growing and feed them
every 1 or 2 weeks. After they stop
blooming, take tip cuttings to make new
plants or winter them over and take cuttings
in spring. Some fuchsias can be cut back to
6 to 8 in. (15 to 20 cm) in fall and will
grow again from the old plant. Whatever
method you use, the plants need to be kept
in a very cool place (40 to 50° F; 4.5 to
10.0° C) over the winter and watered only
enough to keep the soil from drying out
completely. Use all-purpose potting soil
when planting. Fuchsias are susceptible to
aphids and white flies.

× **hybrida** *pp. 176, 177*
Lady's Ear-drop. The graceful, drooping
flowers of the many fuchsia hybrids available
are usually 2-toned in combinations of red,
purple, magenta, and white.

Gardenia
Madder family
Rubiaceae

Gar-den'i-a; also Gar-din'i-a. The only
gardenia usually grown indoors is
G. jasminoides. Unfortunately, as anyone
knows who has brought home a plant
covered with buds, only to watch them drop
off one by one, it is a highly temperamental
houseplant.

How to Grow
Temperature and sunlight are crucial in
making gardenias flower. They need at least
4 hours of sun a day. Although they are not
fussy about daytime temperatures, in order
to set blossoms, they need nighttime
temperatures no warmer than 62° F
(16.5° C)—even 1 warm night can prevent
bud formation. When the buds do form,
pinch them off until late September, for
midwinter bloom. Gardenias also need
constant moisture, in both the air and the
soil. Feed them once a month with an acid,
or azalea-type, fertilizer. If you live in an area
where the water is alkaline, feed your plants
with a solution of iron chelate every 2 or 3
months.
Bud drop can be caused by dry air, drafts,

too much or too little water, or too many
dark winter days. To help a new plant adjust
to your home, put it on a dish of wet
pebbles and mist it several times a day for a
few weeks. Repot only when the roots have
filled the pot, using an equal mix of peat
moss and all-purpose potting soil, or a
special mix for acid-loving plants. Propagate
by taking 5-in. (12.5-cm) stem cuttings.

jasminoides p. 189
Gardenia; Cape Jasmine. The delicious scent
of the waxy white flowers is enough to make
gardeners willing to endure a great deal of
trouble to make these plants blossom. This
plant can reach a height of 2 ft. (60 cm).

Gasteria
Lily family
Liliaceae

Gas-steer′ri-a. *Gasteria* is a genus of stemless
succulents with interesting markings on their
leaves. They are very easy to grow.

How to Grow
Normal room temperatures, medium or
bright light, and moderate amounts of water
make the care of these plants simple. They
never need to be fed. When the plant has
outgrown its container, repot into a wide,
shallow pot using a cactus soil mix.
Propagate by potting up the offsets.

liliputana p. 278
Dutch-wings. This is one of the smallest
gasterias but a particularly appealing one. It
rarely grows more than 2 to 4 in. (5 to 10
cm) tall.

Gesneria
Gesneriad family
Gesneriaceae

Jez-near′ee-a. Gesnerias are native to the
West Indies and South America. The only
species commonly grown indoors is
G. cuneifolia.

How to Grow
Gesnerias need warmth, high humidity, and
bright light. They are really suitable only to
terrariums, where they may bloom all year

long. Water thoroughly, but be sure that the soil is only moist, never wet. Fertilize when you water, using one-eighth-strength fertilizer. When planting, use an African violet soil mix with a tablespoon of dolomite lime to each cup of soil. Propagate by dividing the underground stolons.

cuneifolia p. 182
This slow-growing species, rarely more than 6 in. (15 cm) tall, has red flowers. There are cultivars with orange and yellow flowers.

Grevillea
Protea family
Proteaceae

Gre-vil'lee-a. The only *Grevillea* species grown indoors is *G. robusta,* an Australian timber tree that in its native habitat can reach a height of 150 ft. (45 m).

How to Grow
Grevilleas need bright light. It is helpful to give them some sun in winter. They prefer cool temperatures (between 60 and 65° F; 15.5 and 18.5° C) but will do well in a warmer room if you give them additional humidity. Water thoroughly, but let the soil go almost dry between waterings. When the plant is growing actively, fertilize every 2 weeks. Repot whenever necessary, using an all-purpose soil mix. Prune heavily in spring to keep this vigorous grower under control. Propagate from seeds.

robusta p. 222
Silk Oak. Although this plant can grow to 6 ft. (1.8 m) within a few years, it is also attractive as a seedling.

Guzmania
Bromeliad family
Bromeliaceae

Guz-man'i-a. Most of the guzmanias grown indoors are varieties of the species *G. lingulata.* They bear small white flowers that bloom in winter; the showy red bracts that follow last for weeks or even months.

How to Grow
See *Aechmea* for directions on how to grow
and propagate bromeliads. Place your plant
near a window to encourage flowering.

'Cherry' *p. 156*
New *Guzmania* cultivars continue to be
derived. This one has a red flower head, 18 in.
(45 cm) tall, that is quite striking.

lingulata *p. 156*
The red bracts of this species surround inner
bracts of orange tipped with yellow or white.
The plant is about 12 in. (30 cm) high.

Gymnocalycium
Cactus family
Cactaceae

Jim-no-cal-iss'ee-um. There are about 40
species and numerous varieties of chin cacti,
all from South America. The common name
comes from the cleft under the spines in
some species.

How to Grow
See *Lobivia* for general advice on growing
cacti. Consider grouping several of these
plants together.

mihanovichii *p. 256*
This cactus only grows to 3 in. (7.5 cm)
high, but its lovely pink or yellow flowers
will bloom when it is quite young.

Gynura
Sunflower family
Compositae

Jy-noor'a. The plants in this genus are
grown for their lustrous, velvety, purple
foliage. If your gynura produces flowers, snip
the buds off before they bloom—the flowers
aren't particularly attractive, and they have
an unpleasant odor.

How to Grow
These plants do best in warm, sunny rooms,
and they need both warmth and sun to keep
their foliage colorful. Given only low light,
they'll soon become dullish green. Water
them moderately, keeping the soil barely
moist at all times. Feed once a month with

half-strength fertilizer. Be sure to keep your gynura pinched back; pinching will keep it compact and shapely, and it will ensure new growth, which is much more attractive than the old. When your plant outgrows its container, repot using an all-purpose soil mixture; don't try to keep a gynura, though, for more than 2 years, as old gynuras are unattractive. Instead, start new plants by taking tip cuttings. Watch out for aphids.

aurantiaca p. 117
Purple Velvet Plant. The cultivar 'Purple Passion' is particularly attractive and sturdy. This species is also sold as *G. sarmentosa*.

Hatiora
Cactus family
Cactaceae

Ha-ti-or′ra. The cacti in this genus are spineless epiphytes, found in the tropics rather than the desert. *H. salicornioides* is the only species usually cultivated.

How to Grow
These plants are closely related to *Rhipsalis* and should be grown the same way.

salicornioides p. 246
Drunkard's Dream. The common name is said to refer to the bottle-shaped branchlets of this many-branched species. Small salmon-colored flowers may appear in late winter. The branches can grow to 6 ft. (1.8 m) long.

Haworthia
Lily family
Liliaceae

Ha-wor′thi-a. Haworthias are succulents that are very easy to grow, and there are many species to choose from. The 2 most popular are *H. fasciata* and *H. margaritifera*.

How to Grow
Normal household temperatures and bright to medium light suit these easygoing plants. Water them moderately, but let the soil dry out a bit between waterings. Water less often in winter, but never let a plant become completely dry, and never fertilize. Repot in

spring using cactus soil and a shallow pot.
Propagate by taking offsets with their
attached roots.

fasciata p. 279
Zebra Haworthia. The handsomely striped
leaves account for this plant's common
name. Many cultivars are available.

margaritifera p. 279
Pearl Plant. This plant has dark green leaves
heavily spotted with white. Like *H. fasciata,*
many cultivars are available.

Hedera
Ginseng family
Araliaceae

Hed'er-ra. There are 5 species in the genus
Hedera, but the one most frequently used as
a houseplant is *H. helix,* English Ivy. This
species has more than 200 cultivars and
natural mutations—enough to keep a
national ivy society busy trying to keep
everything straight.

How to Grow
Although ivies will grow in a warm room,
they prefer temperatures ranging from 65° F
(18.5° C) during the day to 45° F (7° C) at
night. In hot rooms, ivies tend to get spider
mites. One way to avoid these pests is to
shower your plants in the sink regularly.
Bright light and normal room humidity are
satisfactory. Water thoroughly, but let the
soil dry out somewhat between waterings.
Pinch back new tips to encourage bushiness
and fertilize in spring and again in summer.
Repot whenever necessary, using an
all-purpose potting soil. Propagate from
tip cuttings.

helix pp. 77, 78, 79
English Ivy. The leaves of this species are
typical of ivy plants—5-lobed, dark green,
and about 2 in. (5 cm) long. The leaves of
varieties may be oval, pointed, heart-shaped,
or erect; crinkled, crested, ruffled, or waved;
and mottled or variegated. 'Ripples' has
irregularly lobed leaves with curled or crested
margins; 'Sagittaefolia' has purplish stems
and gray-green leaves with a whitish midrib;
and 'Harald' has shallow-lobed leaves with
cream-colored edges.

Heptapleurum
Aralia family
Araliaceae

Hep-ta-plur'um. The single species in this genus resembles plants in the genus *Brassaia,* which explains why it is sometimes called Dwarf Schefflera.

How to Grow
Treat this large foliage plant as you would *Brassaia.* Be sure to pinch tips out from time to time to discourage legginess.

arboricola p. 211
Dwarf Schefflera; Hawaiian Elf. The 7 to 8 leaflets of this 4- to 6-ft. (1.2- to 1.8-m) plant radiate from the stems on long stalks, giving it an airy look. Staking may become necessary as the plant reaches its full height.

Hibiscus
Mallow family
Malvaceae

Hy-bis'kus. There are 250 hibiscus species, 2 of which are grown indoors. By far the more popular is *H. rosa-sinensis.*

How to Grow
Under the right circumstances, hibiscus plants will flower all year long, every year, for many years. They require direct sunlight for several hours every day, temperatures in the high 70s (about 25° C) during the day and not below 60° F (15.5° C) at night, constantly moist soil, and monthly feedings. Prune your plant to a height of about 3 ft. (90 cm); if it gets too leggy, cut it back a bit in spring. Repot in spring using an all-purpose soil mix. Propagate by taking stem cuttings.

rosa-sinensis p. 188
Chinese Hibiscus; Rose-of-China. The red or yellow flowers are about 5 in. (12.5 cm) across. The fully open flower lasts for 1 day, but the attractive buds take several days to bloom. There are varieties with white, pink, or orange flowers and one—'Cooperi'—with variegated leaves.

Howea
Palm family
Palmae

How'ee-a. The 2 species in the genus *Howea* can be grown indoors. Known today as sentry palms, they are often called kentia palms, their former name.

How to Grow
Except for propagation, which is not possible for an amateur grower, these palms have the same cultural requirements as plants in the genus *Caryota.*

belmoreana *p. 232*
Sentry Palm; Kentia Palm; Curly Palm. Graceful dark green fronds and the ability to survive fairly harsh indoor conditions make this palm a favorite. It can reach a height of 8 ft. (2.4 m) with a 6-ft. (1.8-m) spread. A much wider spreading species is *H. forsterana*; it is also somewhat faster growing.

Hoya
Milkweed family
Asclepiadaceae

Hoy'ya. Hoyas are vines that twine and climb. *H. carnosa* is an old-fashioned houseplant with flowers that smell intensely sweet. One cultivar of *H. carnosa* is grown for its oddly contorted leaves, not its flowers.

How to Grow
Hoyas never flower until they are mature plants, or until their vines are about 3 ft. (90 cm) long. If you prune them back, you'll never get a blossom, since the flowers grow on the leafless spurs that extend out of the main stems. One popular solution to the problem of long trailing vines is to insert a hoop of wire into the pot and then train the vines around and around the wire. Hoyas do well in average room temperatures. If possible, give them bright light and sun. During the winter, or when the plants are too young to flower, water only enough to keep the soil from drying out completely. Feed once a month in spring and summer. Remove faded flowers very carefully; don't cut off the spur, since that's where future flowers will grow. Repot once every 2 or 3 years when necessary. Propagate by taking tip cuttings in spring.

carnosa *p. 80*
Wax Plant. Several cultivars are available,
most with pink or white flowers with a
red center. A smaller species, *H. bella,* or
Miniature Wax Plant, has white flowers with
a purple center.

carnosa **'Krinkle Kurl'** *p. 267*
Hindu-rope; Green Curls. The oddly folded
and contorted leaves make this an interesting
choice for a hanging basket.

Hypoestes
Acanthus family
Acanthaceae

Hy-poe-est′ees. Shrubs in the genus *Hypoestes*
have spotted leaves. The only species grown
as a houseplant is *H. phyllostachya.*

How to Grow
Filtered sunlight or very bright light is
necessary to keep the dotted leaves colorful.
Average room temperatures are fine. Let the
soil dry out a bit between waterings and
fertilize every 2 weeks during the spring and
summer. Repot when the roots have filled
the present container, using an all-purpose
potting soil. Since these plants tend to get
leggy as they age, it is best to replace them
every few years with new plants made by
taking tip cuttings. *Hypoestes* plants can also
be started from seeds.

phyllostachya *p. 214*
Polka-dot Plant; Measles Plant; Freckle-face.
Although this plant can grow to 3 ft.
(90 cm), it is most attractive when kept
pruned to 12 to 18 in. (30 to 45 cm). It is
sometimes sold as *H. sanguinolenta.*

Impatiens
Balsam (or Touch-me-not) family
Balsaminaceae

Im-pay′shens. Several garden flowers and
native American wildflowers are found in
this genus. The plants we call impatiens are
hybrids of *I. wallerana.*

How to Grow
Most impatiens are grown as annuals and
thrown away after they have finished

blooming. They will flower in bright light in average temperatures. The New Guinea hybrids need full sun to produce their colorful leaves and unusually large blossoms. Let the soil dry out somewhat between waterings and feed them every 2 weeks while they are actively growing. Instead of repotting, take tip cuttings in summer and root them in water. Pot them up in an all-purpose soil mix. If the air is dry, watch out for spider mites, aphids, and white flies.

New Guinea hybrids *p. 198*

These plants were recently developed from *I. wallerana.* They have long, variegated yellow and green or pink and green leaves and bright orange, pink, or red flowers that are much larger than those of the species. They are bushy plants 10 to 16 in. (25 to 40 cm) high.

wallerana *pp. 170, 171*
Busy Lizzy; Patient Lucy. The original plants of this species tended to be tall and lanky. The newer hybrids are stockier and sturdier, and their flowers and white, red, salmon, and purple, as well as pink. They grow 12 to 15 in. (30 to 38 cm) high and look nice in a hanging basket. The cultivar 'Twinkles' has red flowers with white stripes. 'Super Elfin Blush' has light pink flowers, and 'Liegnitzia' and 'Nana' are low and compact.

Iresine
Amaranth family
Amaranthaceae

Eye-re-sy'ne. *Iresine* is a genus of ornamental foliage plants including one species, *I. herbstii,* that is grown for its bright red leaves.

How to Grow
These plants need bright light with some sun to keep their color. They thrive in normal room temperatures. Water freely when actively growing, more sparingly in winter, and feed every 2 weeks during spring and summer. To keep your plant bushy, occasionally pinch back its tips. These are fast-growing plants; you may need to repot more often than once a year. Do so when roots appear on the surface and use a standard potting soil.

herbstii p. 117
Beef Plant; Beefsteak Plant. This 2-ft. (60-cm) plant has red stems and red leaves with paler red veins.

Ixora
Madder family
Rubiaceae

Icks-ō′ra. These handsome plants bear bright flowers. They cannot tolerate changes in temperature or humidity.

How to Grow
Ixoras need at least half a day of sun, temperatures that never fall below 60° F (15.5° C), and extra humidity. Let the soil dry out a little between waterings and feed every 2 weeks during the spring and summer. In winter, keep the soil somewhat dry. Repot in spring, using a mixture of all-purpose potting soil, peat moss, and sand. Propagate by taking cuttings.

coccinea p. 187
Flame-of-the-woods; Jungle Geranium. Grown indoors, these shrubs can reach 4 ft. (120 cm). 'Fraseri', with brilliant salmon-red flowers, is one of the most popular cultivars.

Jasminum
Olive family
Oleaceae

Jas′mi-num. These beautifully scented flowers bloom in the winter, making them highly desirable indoor plants.

How to Grow
To bloom, jasmines need bright light and several hours of sun a day. *J. nitidum* and *J. sambac* 'Maid of Orleans' need 60° F (15.5° C) nights and 80° F (26.5° C) days. The other species here prefers cool temperatures, about 60° F (15.5° C). Water plentifully in spring and summer and feed every 2 weeks. Let the soil dry out a bit between waterings in fall and winter and don't fertilize then. Prune the stems back in spring and then repot, using an all-purpose soil mix. Propagate by taking tip cuttings in summer or fall.

nitidum p. 190
Angel-wing Jasmine; Star Jasmine. This jasmine bears sweet-smelling white flowers. With half a day of sun, it may bloom all year long, not just in winter. It is sometimes sold as *J. ilicifolium.*

polyanthum p. 192
Winter Jasmine. This winter-blooming species has beautifully fragrant white flowers that open from pink buds when the plant is less than a year old. It is a vigorous climber, but should be kept under control with pruning.

sambac 'Maid of Orleans' p. 190
Arabian Jasmine. *J. sambac* is one of the oldest jasmine species in cultivation, and this new cultivar, with its intensely fragrant flowers, is one of the best.

Justicia
Acanthus family
Acanthaceae

Jus-tiss′i-a. The species in this genus most commonly grown indoors is *J. brandegeana,* which is almost always sold under its old name, *Beloperone guttata.*

How to Grow
Average to slightly cool temperatures with bright light and some sun suit these plants. Keep soil constantly moist, except in winter, when it should be allowed to dry out a bit between waterings. Fertilize every 2 weeks in spring and summer. To keep the plant shapely, prune it back to half its size in spring and pinch out the growing tips once to encourage bushiness. Repot in spring, using a mixture of 2 parts all-purpose potting soil and 1 part peat moss. Propagate by taking tip cuttings in spring, as you cut the plant back.

brandegeana p. 184
Shrimp Plant. This plant can reach a height of 2 ft. (60 cm). Its popular name comes from the pinkish-tan, shrimplike bracts that often remain for most of the year. Keep your plant pruned to about 12 in. (30 cm) for a bushy effect.

Kalanchoe
Orpine family
Crassulaceae

Kal-an-ko'ee. Kalanchoes are succulents
grown for their foliage or for their beautiful
flowers that bloom in winter.

How to Grow
K. blossfeldiana is usually bought in bloom
and discarded after it finishes flowering. For
care of the other kalanchoes, see *Crassula*.

blossfeldiana *p. 187*
New cultivars of this species range in height
from 6 to 12 in. (15 to 30 cm) and bloom
in brilliant reds, oranges, and yellows. They
will bloom for 2 to 3 months.

pumila *p. 283*
With its silvery leaves and pink flowers, this
makes a striking plant for a hanging basket.

tomentosa *p. 282*
Pussy Ears; Panda Plant. The plushy leaves
of this 10-in. (25-cm) plant are covered with
silvery hairs. The edges have rusty brown
hairs.

Kohleria
Gesneriad family
Gesneriaceae

Ko-lee'ree-a. Kohlerias, known as tree
gloxinias, grow from scaly rhizomes. The
plants sold today are usually hybrids.

How to Grow
Kohleria hybrids flower at different times of
the year. They need bright light with several
hours of sun during the blooming period.
These plants will grow in average room
temperatures, but they need a great deal of
additional humidity, which may be difficult
to provide since their drooping habit makes
them best suited for hanging baskets. Keep
the soil moist when the plant is in flower,
but the rest of the time let it dry out
between waterings. While the plant is in
active growth, use one-quarter-strength
fertilizer each time you water. Repot after
flowering, using African violet soil mix.

'Dark Velvet' *p. 181*
Tree Gloxinia. The dark green leaves with

red undersides and bright orange tubular flowers make this a striking hybrid kohleria. It is about 12 in. (30 cm) high.

Laelia
Orchid family
Orchidaceae

Lay'lee-a. Laelias are native to Mexico and to Central and South America. Mexican and Central American species, such as *L. anceps,* will thrive in cool to moderate temperatures. South American species that bear larger flowers, such as *L. purpurata,* do best with moderate temperatures. *Laelia* species are often bred with *Cattleya* species to create *Laeliocattleya* hybrids. Many laeliocattleyas have deeply colored lips. Recently, some dwarf Brazilian species, such as *L. pumila* and *L. milleri,* have been crossed with species in the genera *Cattleya* and *Sophronitis* to create a new race of compact-growing orchids that have relatively large flowers in colors ranging from pink to orange, yellow, and dark red.

How to Grow
Laelias are epiphytes that thrive in the orchid-potting mixtures of bark, cork, tree fern, and charcoal. A few dwarf species, such as *L. anceps* and *L. rupestris,* will grow on slabs of cork or tree fern, provided they are given adequate humidity. These orchids need bright diffuse light; in winter months, when the sun is cooler, even full sun is safe for species with hard leaves.
A few dwarf Brazilian species grow wild on mossy rocks under sun so strong it turns the plants a deep maroon. Laelias from high altitudes and semi-tropical Mexico tolerate cool temperatures. Most popular hybrids and the majority of *Laelia* species will thrive in moderate temperatures. Feed actively-growing plants every 2 weeks with a water-soluble fertilizer. When plants stop producing new growth, water less frequently and stop fertilizing.

anceps pp. 150, 151
This compact-growing, winter-blooming orchid is native to Mexico and Honduras. It adapts well when grown on a slab of cork or tree fern. The 2- to 4-ft. (60- to 120-cm) upright to slightly arching flower stem has blossoms 2 to 4 in. (5 to 10 cm) wide

growing mainly at the top. Many forms within the species are fragrant. The common type has rose-pink flowers with dark purple lips. Some rare clones have white flowers.

Lantana
Verbena family
Verbenaceae

Lan-ta′na. Only one species in this genus of low-growing shrubs, *L. camara,* or Yellow Sage, grows well indoors. It has lovely, fragrant clusters of small flowers that bloom in early spring.

How to Grow
Yellow Sage is usually sold in bloom in spring and often discarded after the flowers drop in autumn, but it can be carried over into another season relatively easily. Provide bright light, with some direct sun to encourage flowering. Normal temperatures are fine; lower temperatures, around 55°F (13°C) during the winter rest are desirable but not essential. Extra humidity helps in higher temperatures. Keep the soil moist during the growth season and slightly dry in winter. Feed twice a month and repot whenever necessary using an all-purpose potting mixture. Propagate by cuttings of non-flowering stems in summer. Watch for whiteflies, which frequently plague these plants.

camara pp. 185, 189
Yellow Sage. Keep this plant about 12 in. (30 cm) high by pinching it back, which will also improve its shape. The flower clusters are 1 to 2 in. (2.5 to 5.0 cm) wide and yellow at first, turning to orange or red; all 3 colors may appear at once in a single cluster. There are many hybrids of this species, which can also have white or pink flowers.

Lithops
Carpetweed family
Arizoaceae

Lith′ops. These South African desert plants are a curiosity; children particularly find them entertaining. The "stones" they bear are actually a pair of fleshy leaves, barely an inch high, that resemble the stones among which they grow in nature. In late summer or early fall, a yellow or white daisylike flower sprouts from the crevice between the leaves. After the plant finishes blooming, its leaves shrivel up slowly and a new pair replaces them.

How to Grow
Average to cool room temperatures and low humidity suit these succulents, but several hours of sunlight each day are essential. Water sparingly from spring until fall. From the time the flower dies until the following spring, do not water lithops at all. This is undoubtedly the hardest thing for owners to accept and almost all disasters with lithops come from failure to heed this warning. If you overwater this plant, it will turn to mush. Never fertilize. Although the plant is barely an inch tall, it has a long taproot and requires a standard flower pot. These are slow-growing plants and may not need to be repotted for several years. When repotting is necessary, use a cactus soil mix. Propagate by division, separating overcrowded clumps in spring or summer.

lesliei p. 284
Living Stones. The color of the leaves of this species can range from rosy gray to dark greenish gray with rust brown spots on top. The bright yellow flowers with pink undersides are about 1 in. (2.5 cm) wide.

Livistona
Palm family
Palmae

Liv-i-stow′na. Palms in the genus *Livistona* are tall trees native to Asia, Australia, and the Pacific islands. Several species are grown indoors, notable *L. chinensis,* the Chinese Fan Palm.

How to Grow
Culture for *Livistona* is the same as for *Caryota.* These palms, however, cannot be propagated by the amateur grower.

chinensis p. 234
Chinese Fan Palm; Chinese Fountain Palm. This is a large plant, growing in nature to a height of 10 ft. (3 m), with fanlike leaves

as much as 2 ft. (60 cm) across. Indoors, however, the Chinese Fan Palm will be smaller, 5 to 6 ft. (1.5 to 1.8 m) high.

Lobivia
Cactus family
Cactaceae

Loe-biv′ee-a. Lobivias are very easy to grow, but if you want them to flower they need winter temperatures below 50° F (10° C). Their name is an anagram for Bolivia, where they grow in high, cold country. They are commonly called Cob Cacti.

How to Grow
Plenty of sun all year, normal temperatures except in winter, and moderate watering during the periods of active growth is the correct regimen for these cacti. In winter, give them only enough water to keep the soil from drying out completely. Feed every 2 weeks in spring and summer with a high-phosphorous fertilizer. Repot when the roots fill the pot, using a cactus soil mix. Propagate by potting up the offsets that appear at the base or by sowing seed.

arachnacantha p. 262
Cob Cactus. This 3-in. (7.5-cm) cactus produces gold flowers that contrast nicely with its dark stems.

leucomalla p. 258
Cob Cactus. Singly, or in clusters, the stems grow only 1 to 2 in. (2.5 to 5.0 cm) high. They bear white spines and beautiful yellow flowers.

Lycaste
Orchid family
Orchidaceae

Lie-kass′tee. Lycastes come from tropical areas in Mexico and Central and South America, where they grow as epiphytes or semi-terrestrials. Flowers range in color from the pristine white of *L. skinneri* (national flower of Guatemala) to pinks and orange. Lycastes are relatively large plants; in many species, the palm-like foliage spreads out from each pseudobulb for 15 to 24 in. (38 to 60 cm). Many species lose their leaves during each 12-month cycle. The deciduous sorts need less light and water when they are resting. *Lycaste* hybrids have longer blooming seasons and more color choices. The 4- to 6-in. (10- to 15-cm) flowers range from green with yellow lips to purples, lavender pinks, and yellows. Most lycaste flowers are pleasantly fragrant.

How to Grow
These orchids thrive in cool to moderate temperatures. When plants are producing new growth, bright diffuse light will increase flower production and reduce foliage fungus problems. Pot lycastes in mixtures of unmilled sphagnum moss with tree fern, cork, or bark chips.
Pseudobulbs store moisture, so lycastes should dry out slightly at the roots between soakings. When plants are first sprouting new leaves, the foliage forms a funnel that easily catches water; avoid letting water remain in this leaf cluster, especially at night. Wet lycaste foliage often suffers from rot or fungal problems. Fertilizer should be applied to growing plants every 2 weeks at regular strength, or more frequently if diluted to one-quarter-strength. Repot lycastes when new growth starts to send out roots.

cruenta pp. 128, 129

This fragrant species comes from Mexico and Central America, where it lives under cool to moderate conditions. In the spring, waxy 3- to 4-in. (7.5- to 10.0-cm) flowers appear on stalks 5 to 8 in. (12.5 to 20.0 cm) long that grow from the base of each pseudobulb.
L. cruenta is deciduous—the broad leaves fall off at the end of each growing season.

Malpighia
Malpighia family
Malpighiaceae

Mal-pig'i-a. This genus of evergreen shrubs and trees includes a species that grows no taller than 3 ft. (90 cm) outdoors; indoors, it rarely exceeds 12 in. (30 cm).

How to Grow
These plants are easy to grow if you can give them several hours of sunlight each day. Otherwise, they won't flower.

Average temperature and humidity are fine.
Let the soil dry out between waterings and
fertilize monthly from spring to fall. To keep
your plant compact and shapely, prune it
after it flowers. Repot only when the roots
have filled the pot. Propagate by taking tip
cuttings.

coccigera p. 253
Miniature Holly; Singapore Holly; Dwarf
Holly. This plant is not a holly, but its
glossy leaves have hollylike spines and its
pink flowers are followed by red berries.

Mammillaria
Cactus family
Cactaceae

Mam-mill-a′ri-a. This large New World
genus contains 150 species of cacti, many of
which have the same common name. Those
listed below are just a sampling of the
mammillarias available today.

How to Grow
Mammillarias need sun all year long and do
especially well if you can put them outdoors
in spring and summer. See *Lobivia* for more
information.

bocasana pp. 260, 261
Snowball Cactus; Powder-puff Cactus. One
of the most popular of the mammillarias,
this plant reaches a height of 4 to 6 in. (10
to 15 cm). It forms clusters of individual
heads.

camptotricha p. 258
Bird's-nest Cactus. Like most mammillarias,
this is a decorative plant, even if it never
blooms it will reach a height of 4 in.
(10 cm). Its flowers are small, but they
have a pleasant smell, like limes.

guelzowiana p. 259
Strawberry Cactus. The 2-in.- (5-cm-) long
purplish flowers of this species bloom from
spring to fall. Its stems grow 2½ in. (6 cm)
high.

hahniana p. 260
Old-woman Cactus; Old-lady Cactus. This
plant is rounded and has long spines and red
flowers. It grows to a height of 8 to 10 in.
(20 to 25 cm). It might be a nice

companion to the Old-man Cactus,
Cephalocereus senilis.

Maranta
Arrowroot family
Marantaceae

Ma-ran'ta. Marantas are colorful foliage
plants. Although only one species,
M. leuconeura, is generally grown indoors,
there are many cultivars available, with
different markings.

How to Grow
Marantas are closely related to calatheas and
grown the same way. Be sure to keep them
away from bright sun to protect leaf color.

leuconeura p. 101
Prayer Plant. The popular name comes from
the way the beautifully colored leaves of this
12-in. (30-cm-) high plant fold up in the
evening like a pair of praying hands.

leuconeura kerchoviana p. 101
Prayer Plant. In this 12-in. (30-cm) variety,
the leaf's upper surface is light green, with a
row of dark brown or dark green markings
on both sides of the vein.

Masdevallia
Orchid family
Orchidaceae

Maz-de-vah'lee-a. Orchids in the genus
Masdevallia are native to mountain slopes in
Central and South America. Many of the
most popular types are from the Andes
Mountains; there they thrive under
cloud-forest conditions. In captivity, these
orchids demand cool, airy but humid
conditions. Botanists have recently
segregated a group of large-flowered
masdevallias into the new genus *Dracula.*
Hybrids between these two genera are placed
in the genus *Dracuvallia.* The original
Masdevallia species and some hybrids are well
worth growing for their compact form and
oddly shaped, sometimes brightly colored
flowers.

How to Grow
The growth requirements of each species are

based on their native habitats. For most gardeners, the best choices come from moderate elevations, under 5,000 feet; these plants will thrive in cool to moderate night temperatures. Cloud-forest species are difficult to grow outside a well-managed greenhouse. Pot masdevallias in well-drained pots of unmilled sphagnum moss or tree fern. Some species have waxy succulent leaves; these require still more moisture and humidity levels of 50 to 60 percent. Moving air will help keep foliage clear of fungal problems. Keep a small fan going constantly so air will circulate around the plants. Masdevallias and the related draculas grow continually. Fertilize them with one-quarter-strength water-soluble fertilizer every other watering.

Marguerite 'Selby' *pp. 126, 127*

This modern hybrid was produced at the Marie Selby Botanical Gardens in Florida. The parents are the cool- to intermediate-growing *M. infracta* from Brazil and *M. veitchiana,* a cool-growing species from Peru. Blending these two species creates offspring more tolerant of warm conditions than most masdevallias. In the spring, *M. Marguerite* produces one or two 3½- to 4-in. (9- to 10-cm) long flowers.

Miltonia
Orchid family
Orchidaceae

Mil-tone'ee-a. Miltonias are called pansy orchids because many of them have flat flowers marked with contrasting colors, much like the garden pansy. Recently, taxonomists divided the genus into 2 separate genera. The large-flowered species, mainly from South American Andean habitats, are called *Miltoniopsis.* The warm-growing Brazilian species are retained in the genus *Miltonia.* In horticultural circles, both groups are commonly called miltonias. Andean types have large, flat flowers that last several weeks but soon wilt if picked, quite unlike most orchids, which make long-lasting cut flowers. Brazilian miltonias make good cut flowers.

How to Grow
Miltonias are epiphytes with fine roots, pseudobulbs, and thin leaves. They do best

in pots that permit only enough space for 2 years' growth. Pot in a mixture of unmilled sphagnum moss and tree fern. Brazilian *Miltonia* species and their hybrids thrive on logs of tree fern. Andean types do best in pots. Provide moderate temperatures for Andean (*Miltoniopsis*) types and intermediate to warm night temperatures for the Brazilian miltonias. Keep the compost evenly moist when plants are producing new growth. Fertilize active plants every 2 weeks or sprinkle slow-release orchid fertilizer around the plants. Let the compost dry out slightly between soakings when plants are not in active growth.

Miltonias thrive under broad-spectrum fluorescent lights and are compact enough to be suitable for light gardens. Miltonia foliage will stay free from fungal attacks if plants are given good circulation and bright diffuse light. Be sure the foliage is dry by nightfall. Recent hybrids between Andean and Brazilian types have extended the range of colors, patterns, and flowering seasons available.

flavescens pp. 136, 137

This Brazilian species has 3-in. (7.5-cm), fragrant flowers borne on arching stems, usually in summer months. It requires moderate to warm temperatures. In most forms, the white lips are decorated with purple lines.

Monstera
Arum family
Aracee

Mon-steer'ra. *Monstera* is a genus of South American climbing plants noted for their perforated leaves. *M. deliciosa* is especially dramatic indoors. *M. obliqua* is an attractive, smaller species.

How to Grow
These plants grow best in warm room temperatures and in bright to medium light. In light that is less than bright, the leaves will show fewer of their characteristic cuts and incisions. During the warmer months, water thoroughly and let the soil dry out a little between waterings; water less frequently in winter. Keep the leaves clean by sponging them gently with plain tepid water.

Like philodendrons, with which it is often confused, *Monstera* has aerial roots. To keep the plant from sprawling widely, stake it to a piece of bark and spray the bark with water until the roots take hold. Feed monthly from spring to fall. Repot in spring using an all-purpose potting soil. When the plant has reached the largest container that is manageable, leave it in the pot and replace the top inch or two of soil with fresh all-purpose potting soil. Propagate by air layering or by taking tip cuttings.

deliciosa p. 211
Swiss-cheese Plant; Hurricane Plant; Split-leaf Philodendron. This plant is a good choice for a large empty corner. It can grow to 6 ft. by 6 ft. (1.8 m by 1.8 m) without much effort on your part. The young leaves are heart-shaped and undivided. In bright light, the older leaves can be 18 in. (45 cm) wide, deeply incised, often with holes like those in Swiss cheese. The name Hurricane Plant apparently derives from the idea that these holes and incisions keep the leaves from tearing in a high wind.

obliqua p. 92
The leaves of this smaller species are heart-shaped and perforated, but not as deeply as those of *M. deliciosa.* They grow to 8 in. (20 cm) long and 2½ in. (6 cm) wide.

Nematanthus
Gesneriad family
Gesneriadeae

Nee-ma-tan'this. There are over 30 species in this genus of epiphytic gesneriads. The hybrids described below make colorful houseplants, with their glossy leaves and pouchlike flowers.

How to Grow
Nematanthus resemble columneas and should be grown in the same way. Be sure to provide extra humidity and protection from direct sun.

'Castanet' p. 184
This hybrid is a bushy, compact plant with shiny, dark green leaves and a profusion of dangling, orange-red, bell-shaped flowers. It grows 10 to 12 in. (25 to 30 cm) high.

'Tropicana' *p. 183*
The yellow flowers of this 10- to 12-in. (25- to 30-cm) plant are decorated with maroon stripes and surrounded by salmon-colored bracts.

Neoregelia
Bromeliad family
Bromeliaceae

Nee-o-ray-jeel'ee-a. These bromeliads are grown for their extraordinary colorful rosettes of leaves. The flowers, which bloom at any time of the year, are not particularly interesting, but they are accompanied by a flush of color in the leaves that lasts for months.

How to Grow
Like most bromeliads, these plants need bright light with some sun. See *Aechmea* for details.

carolinae 'Meyendorffii Flandria' *p. 161*
Blushing Bromeliad. This cultivar grows to 8 in. (20 cm) high by 18 in. (45 cm) wide. It has green leaves tinged with copper that blush a dark red just before the plant puts out its purple flowers.

carolinae 'Tricolor' *p. 161*
Blushing Bromeliad. The variegated leaves blush red or purple when the plant is about to flower; the shorter leaves in the center turn fiery red.

Nephrolepis
Polypody family
Polypodiaceae

Nee-froll'e-pis or Neph-ro-lee'pis. Ferns in the genus *Nephrolepis* are commonly known as sword ferns because of their long, narrow, pointed fronds. Only a few of the 35 species are good indoor plants; one of them is the parent of the Boston Fern, the most deservedly popular house fern in this country.

How to Grow
These tough ferns can thrive in normal home conditions. They need medium or bright light, with no direct sun. Normal

room temperatures on the warm side are fine; additional humidity is always helpful. Water freely and keep the soil moist. A good way to water an overgrown fern is to immerse it in a pail of water. Feed once in early spring and again in summer; if you don't want these fast-growing plants to outgrow their containers, occasionally withhold plant food. Repot when necessary, using an all-purpose potting mixture. If your fern is becoming too large, cut the fronds down to their base and cut the plant in 3 or 4 sections, planting each section in a pot the same size as that of the parent plant. This is one of the few times you should use a pot that seems too large. Propagate by division, as above, or by pinning the fern's runners onto pots of moist soil. When they have rooted, cut them away from the parent plant.

cordifolia p. 244

Sword Fern; Erect Sword Fern. The fronds are 2 ft. (60 cm) tall, stiff and erect; the plant grows from runners that take root in the pot. There are several cultivars available, including some with variegated fronds.

exaltata 'Bostoniensis' *p. 248*

Boston Fern. The Boston Fern originated by chance in the 1890s when a shipment of *N. exaltata* was sent from Philadelphia to Boston. One plant in the shipment had more gracefully drooping, somewhat broader 3-ft. (90-cm) fronds, and it grew faster than the others. This "sport," or natural mutation, was given the varietal name *bostoniensis.* Since that day, millions of Boston Ferns have been sold and dozens of cultivars have been named. None, however, exceeds the toughness and usefulness of the original Boston Fern. Among the best cultivars are 'Compacta', with 18-in. (45-cm) fronds; 'Fluffy Ruffles', a more erect fern with double-edged 12-in. (30-cm) fronds; 'Verona', a lacy plant with triple, filmy 12-in. (30-cm) fronds; and 'Dallas', a miniature.

Nerium
Dogbane family
Apocynaceae

Neer'i-um. The only *Nerium* species that is cultivated is *N. oleander,* all parts of which are very poisonous if eaten. If you have small children or pets, choose another plant.

How to Grow
Oleanders need sunlight all year long in order to flower. They will grow well in normal room temperatures, but they prefer slightly cooler temperatures in winter. Water them thoroughly and let the soil dry out a little between waterings. Feed every 2 weeks while the plant is actively growing and repot when necessary, using an all-purpose soil mix. Propagate by rooting tip cuttings in water. Watch out for scale insects.

oleander p. 196
Common Oleander; Rosebay. This slender 6-ft. (1.8-m) shrub is sometimes sold as *N. indicum* or *N. odorum,* especially if it is one of the scented varieties. Its flowers are rose-colored, but some varieties have red, yellow, orange, or purple blossoms. There are also dwarf forms that grow only 3 to 4 ft. (90 to 120 cm) high.

Nidularium
Bromeliad family
Bromeliaceae

Nid-you-lay′ri-um. Plants in the genus *Nidularium* are grown for their beautiful foliage and the brightly-colored bracts surrounding their inconspicuous flowers. When the plant is about to flower, the base of the leaves near the center of the rosette turns color, usually rosy red.

How to Grow
These bromeliads can grow in medium as well as bright light. Otherwise, their culture and propagation are the same as that of *Aechmea.*

billbergioides p. 157
The long, straplike leaves of this species have pale green centers. The bracts that grow on a 9-in. (22.5-cm) stem are yellow to pink.

'Ra Ru' × 'Sao Paulo' p. 157
This hybrid nidularium has broader leaves than *N. billbergioides* and its bracts are red. It grows 12 to 18 in. (30 to 35 cm) high.

Odontoglossum
Orchid family
Orchidaceae

Oh-dont-oh-gloss′um. Odontoglossums are native to Latin America, from Mexico into the Andes. They are epiphytes but may sometimes be seen as semi-terrestrials growing on well-drained slopes with thick moss around the roots.
Odontoglossum flowers are well displayed on arching sprays 1¼ to 3 ft. (38 to 90 cm) long. Many modern hybrids are available, some made with related genera to extend flowering season, increase heat tolerance, and broaden the flower color range. All of the odontoglossums and related hybrids thrive in cool to moderate conditions.

How to Grow
Odontoglossums and hybrids with other Andean species do well in cool nights, bright diffuse light, good air circulation, and small pots. Odontoglossums from warmer habitats, such as *O. bictoniense* and hybrids with *Oncidium* or *Miltonia,* thrive in average temperatures. All types grow well in small pots filled with unmilled sphagnum moss over pea gravel. Hardwood charcoal and ground tree fern is another good potting mix. Odontoglossums have pseudobulbs to store water, but their roots are fine so the mix should never dry fully. Use small, well-drained pots and water frequently.
The most popular odontoglossum hybrids have flowers 3 to 4 in. (7.5 to 10.0 cm) wide on 2- to 3-ft. (60- to 90-cm) arching stems. These are crosses of *Odontoglossum crispum* and its hybrids, often with a genetic sprinkling from the genus *Cochlioda,* whose flowers are much smaller but bright red. Crossing the two creates the man-made genus called *Odontioda.*

bilobum *pp. 140, 141*
This spring-blooming species comes from Bolivia. Its flowers are 1½ to 2 in. (4 to 5 cm) wide.

Odontioda Memoria Len Page *pp. 142, 143*
This orchid is a cross of *Odontioda* Dalmar with *Odontoglossum* Connero. The 3½-in. (9-cm) flowers appear on long spikes in late spring.

Oncidium
Orchid family
Orchidaceae

On-sid'ee-um. This genus is made up of about 700 species, all from tropical areas of Latin America. Many oncidiums are called dancing dolls because their small yellow flowers are beautifully displayed on arching sprays. Another type of oncidium has succulent leaves 4 to 8 in. (10 to 20 cm) tall and shorter spikes of multi-colored flowers. The succulent sorts, called equitant oncidiums, are from the Caribbean islands, where they live in bright, dry conditions. Most of the popular species adapt to moderate conditions, making them good choices for the home grower. Hybrids between *Oncidium* and related genera, such as *Ondontoglossum* (*Odontocidium*) and *Miltonia* (*Miltassia*), are usually more adaptable than pure species. With so many types to choose from, you can easily find several to suit your desires. The equitant sorts are so small that 50 or more grown on chunks of cork or tree fern can be displayed in a sunny window. Other types, such as *O. sphacelatum* with its 3-ft. (90-cm) flower spike, can fill a 12-in. pot in just two seasons.

How to Grow
Oncidiums are epiphytes, but not all have pseudobulbs. The succulent equitant types have clusters of waxy leaves. Other species have leaves 1 to 2 ft. (30 to 60 cm) tall that resemble mules' ears. To grow and flower well, the succulent sorts need very bright light. Thin-leaved oncidiums thrive with diffuse sun. Small species thrive on slabs of tree fern or cork bark. Larger types are best grown in pots filled with an epiphyte mixture. Fertilize growing plants every 2 weeks. Some of the mules'-ear species rest for a month or two at which time they need no fertilizer and less water. Propagate by division as new growth sends out roots. Hybrids between species and related genera are easier to grow than pure species.

Equitant hybrids *pp. 120, 121*
O. William Thurston 'Orchidglade' and *O.* Golden Sunset × *O.* Orglade's Rose Claret are typical miniature equitant, or succulent-leaved, oncidiums bred from the species *O. triquetrum* and *O. desetorum*. Such tiny plants, 1 to 6 in. (2.5 to 15.0 cm) high, produce spikes 12 to 15 in. (30 to 38 cm)

high with clusters of 1-in. (2.5-cm) flowers
from spring into summer.

maculatum pp. 132, 133
This species is native to Mexico and Central
America. It produces long arching clusters of
1- to 2-in. (2.5- to 5.0-cm) flowers that vary
in color and color pattern. Most have white
lips and petals with brown blotches.

viperinum pp. 128, 129
This species comes from Brazil. Its flowers
are 1 to 2 in. (2.5 to 5.0 cm) wide; the plant
itself grows 8 to 12 in. (20 to 30 cm) high.

Oplismenus
Grass family
Gramineae

O-plis'me-nus. The variegated form of
O. hirtellus, or Basket Grass, is appropriately
named since it is an attractive, hanging
foliage plant. The other 20 or so species in
this tropical genus are not usually cultivated.

How to Grow
Basket Grass needs bright light and about 3
hours of sun a day to keep its leaves colorful.
It is not particular as to temperature, but the
soil should be kept moist except in winter,
when you should let it dry out slightly
between waterings. Feed monthly during
active growth. Discard the plant when it
begins to lose its leaves, after about a year,
replacing it with a new plants made from tip
cuttings, which root easily.

hirtellus 'Variegatus' p. 252
Basket Grass. The branching stems grow to
12 in. (30 cm) long and carry 4-in. (10-cm)
leaves striped with white. Very bright light
can make the white turn pinkish.

Opuntia
Cactus family
Cactaceae

O-pun'ti-a. This genus of cacti includes
almost 300 species. The best known for
indoor gardens are *O. microdasys* and its
cultivars.

How to Grow
Like most desert cacti, opuntias like lots of
sun. See *Lobivia* for details on their care.
Propagate from cuttings or seeds.

microdasys p. 263
Rabbit-ears; Bunny-ears. The common name
is derived from the flat, oval segments that
distinguish this cactus and give it its appeal.
It can grow to a height of 3 ft. (90 cm) and
may need to be staked.

subulata p. 265
Eve's-pin Cactus. This fast-growing plant can
reach a height of 6 ft. (1.8 m) indoors in
just a few years. To keep it under control
and to encourage branching, cut off the top
of the stem.

Osmanthus
Olive family
Oleaceae

Oz-man'thus. The sweet olive, *O. fragrans,*
has tiny, unimpressive flowers that have a
heavenly fragrance. They start blooming
when the plant is only a few inches tall.
O. heterophyllus is a dead ringer for a holly
bush.

How to Grow
Sweet olives like cool temperatures and will
do well in bright light, preferably with some
direct sun. Keep the soil evenly moist at all
times and feed them once a month. Repot
only when the roots have filled their
present pot, using a mixture of equal parts
of all-purpose potting soil and peat moss.
Propagate at any time by taking stem
cuttings.

fragrans p. 90
Sweet Olive; Fragrant Olive. In about a
hundred years, this plant can grow into
a small tree, even indoors. More often,
however, it grows to a height of 1 to 2 ft.
(30 to 60 cm).

heterophyllus 'Variegatus' p. 215
False Holly; Holly Olive. There are many
cultivars of *O. heterophyllus,* and most of
them have variegated leaves. Indoors, this
plant grows to a height of about 3 ft.
(90 cm).

Pachyphytum
Orpine family
Crassulaceae

Pack-i-fy'tum. These succulents are closely related to the echeverias, and there are many hybrids between the two genera.

How to Grow
Pachyphytums thrive in normal room temperatures with at least 4 hours of direct sun a day. From spring to fall, let the soil dry out moderately between waterings; in winter, water only enough to keep the leaves from shriveling. Never fertilize. In spring, repot using a cactus soil mix and propagate by taking stem cuttings.

oviferum p. 268
Moonstones. This plant rarely grows taller than 3 in. (7.5 cm). The glaucous leaves are sometimes tinged with lavender.

Pandanus
Screw pine family
Pandanaceae

Pan-day'nus. Screw pines are not actually pines. They are graceful foliage plants native to Malaysia.

How to Grow
Ideally, these plants need greenhouse conditions. If you grow them in your house, provide bright light, warmth, and extra humidity. Keep the soil constantly moist from spring to fall; in winter, water only enough to keep it from drying out completely. Fertilize every 2 weeks during the growing season and repot in spring, using an all-purpose potting mixture. Old screw pines develop trunks with offsets at the base, which may be potted up.

veitchii p. 237
Screw Pine. This plant has handsome, striped green-and-cream leaves that twist out of the soil in a spiral. The strap-shaped leaves have prickly edges and are 2 to 3 ft. (60 to 90 cm) long and 2 to 2½ in. (5 to 6 cm) wide. A smaller cultivar named 'Compacta' has shorter, stiffer leaves and less of a spread.

Paphiopedilum
Orchid family
Orchidaceae

Paf-ee-oh-ped′i-lum. The paphiopedilums are aptly called lady slipper orchids. *Paphiopedilum* species and the numerous hybrids provide long-lasting waxy flowers in most colors except blue and true red. Hybridizers have worked with this genus for more than a hundred years. Currently 2 major types are popular. There are large-flowered hybrids created for their full, round form and hybrids made by crossing 2 pure species. These have more refined, delicate-looking flowers and are more compact. All paphiopedilums have long-lived flowers—some look beautiful for a month or more.

How to Grow
These are terrestrial orchids that lack pseudobulbs. Foliage is leathery but not very thick. Compared to other orchids, these plants have fewer roots and are easily damaged by overwatering. Pot paphiopedilums in commercial mixes made for terrestrial orchids, or mix your own by blending unmilled sphagnum moss, medium-to-fine-ground bark, granulated hardwood charcoal, coarse peat, and perlite. Species from limestone areas, such as *P. niveum,* do better with a dusting of granulated dolomite limestone added to the mix. Keep the potting mix evenly moist and never let it become soggy.
Diffuse sunlight or broad-spectrum fluorescent light are ideal for all types of paphiopedilums. The best temperature range depends upon the origin of each species. These are tropical Asian orchids that range in nature from sea level to chilly mountain slopes. In general, species with plain green foliage thrive in cool to low-moderate temperatures. Types with patterned or mottled leaves do best in moderate temperatures. Modern hybrids adapt to moderate conditions as well.

Maudiae *pp. 138, 139*
This popular hybrid of *P. callosum* with *P. lawrenceanum* has silver-mottled foliage and blooms as each growth matures. Established clumps are 6 to 8 in. (15 to 20 cm) high and may bloom in summer, winter, and spring. Clone 'Magnificum' has white and green flowers on 10- to 15-in. (25- to 38-cm)

stems. Some other clones have purple
flowers.

Passiflora
Passionflower family
Passifloraceae

Pass-i-flow′ra. Passionflowers are vigorous
climbing vines that have showy red, white,
or purple flowers.

How to Grow
Passionflowers are perfect for a greenhouse or
a sun room. They need warm temperatures
and at least 4 hours of direct sun all year
long. Keep the soil very moist while they are
actively growing and flowering; at other
times, let it dry out somewhat between
waterings. Fertilize every 2 weeks during the
period of active growth. After the plant has
finished flowering, cut it back to within 6 in.
(15 cm) of the soil. When the plant fills a
6-in. (15-cm) pot, it is better to top-dress it
with fresh all-purpose soil mix than to repot
it. Propagate at any time by taking stem
cuttings.

caerulea p. 209
Blue Passionflower. This plant has white
petals and sepals; the 4 central rings of
filaments are purple, white, and blue. It can
grow to a height of 20 ft. (6 m). Cultivars
include 'Grandiflora' and 'Constance Elliott'.

coccinea p. 209
Red Passionflower; Red Granadilla. The
blossoms of this passionflower have deep
orange to scarlet petals and a 3-ring corona
of filaments that are pale pink at the base
shading to deep purple.

Pelargonium
Geranium family
Geraniaceae

Pee-lar-go′ni-um. The plants we call
geraniums belong to the genus *Pelargonium*.
Those grown indoors are usually hybrids.

How to Grow
Except for geraniums with scented leaves,
which are grown for their aroma and not for
their insignificant flowers, geraniums need

full sun for at least half a day. Scented geraniums need only bright light.
Water actively growing geraniums moderately and let the soil dry out between waterings. Don't mist these plants or give them additional humidity; they are susceptible to stem rot, which is caused by too much moisture in the soil or the air. Fertilize every 2 weeks from February until October.
Keep your geraniums in a relatively small pot. When you do repot them, move them up just one size and use an all-purpose potting soil. Rather than letting a plant grow large and leggy, cut it back drastically or take tip cuttings and start new plants.

Cascade hybrids *pp. 172, 173*
These recently introduced types combine *P. peltatum* and *P. hortorum* to produce a hanging geranium more tolerant of heat than most other *P. peltatum* hybrids.

***hortorum* hybrids** *pp. 94, 199*
Zonal Geranium; Bedding Geranium. These are the geraniums that everyone knows, and many excellent hybrids are available. They grow to a height of 3 to 4 ft. (90 to 120 cm). The name zonal refers to the dark ring on the leaves. 'Mrs. Parker' has variegated leaves. *P. domesticum* hybrids, or Martha Washington Geraniums, have a shorter blooming season than *P. hortorum* hybrids, but they can also be grown indoors. They need a rest in winter like most geraniums. Martha Washingtons grow to 1½ to 2 ft. (45 to 60 cm) high.

***peltatum* hybrids** *pp. 172, 173*
Ivy Geranium; Hanging Geranium. These low, spreading plants are excellent for hanging baskets.

tomentosum *p. 180*
Peppermint Geranium. This geranium has mint-scented leaves and white to pink flowers. It reaches a height of 3 ft. (90 cm). Other scented-leaf species and cultivars include *P. quercifolium* (Oak-leaved Geranium) and a lemon-scented cultivar 'Lady Mary'. There are many others.

Pellaea
Polypody family
Polypodiaceae

Pell-ee′a. In nature, pellaeas, or cliff-brake ferns, mostly grow on rocks. Of the few species grown indoors, by far the most popular is *P. rotundifolia,* the Button Fern.

How to Grow
Medium light, additional humidity, and temperatures on the cool side will keep your *pellaea* healthy. Keep the soil constantly moist in summer; let it dry out slightly between waterings in winter. If your fern is growing in a soilless mix, feed it with half-strength fertilizer every 2 weeks from spring to fall. Feed it once a month, again with half-strength fertilizer, if it is potted in soil. Pellaeas don't develop large root balls and probably can go for several years before they need a bigger container. Use a shallow pot and either a soilless mix or a mixture of all-purpose potting soil and peat moss. Propagate by division. Be sure that each section you divide has both roots and fronds.

rotundifolia p. 252

Button Fern. This pretty little plant hardly resembles a fern. It has small, leathery, round leaves on either side of its arching 12-in. (30-cm) stems. The leathery leaves may lead you to believe that it will do well in a dry room, but in fact, like most ferns, this one needs extra humidity.

Pellionia
Nettle family
Urticaceae

Pell-i-o′ni-a. Pellionias are flat, creeping plants that do well in dish gardens or in hanging baskets.

How to Grow
Pellionias need bright light, but no direct sun, and they flourish in normal room temperatures. Keep the soil uniformly moist while the plants are actively growing and fertilize them every 2 weeks. In winter, let the soil dry out between waterings and don't fertilize. Repot when the roots fill the present pot, using a mixture of all-purpose potting soil and peat moss. Propagate by taking tip cuttings in spring.

daveauana p. 82

Trailing Watermelon Begonia. The pinkish stems of this species may grow to a length of 2 ft. (60 cm). The leaves are pinkish on the bottom and bronzy green with purple edges on the top.

Peperomia
Pepper family
Piperaceae

Pep-er-o′mi-a. This genus of low-growing foliage plants contains several species that do very well indoors.

How to Grow
Normal room temperature and bright or medium light suit peperomias. Put them on a tray of moist pebbles if your room is hot and dry. Be extremely careful not to overwater or overfeed these plants, either of which can kill them. When repotting, use a very porous soil or a soilless mix and let it dry out between waterings. Never let peperomias stand in water—not even for a short time. Feed with half-strength fertilizer once a month from spring to fall. When repotting, supply extra drainage by putting a layer of clay shards in the bottom of the pot. Propagate by taking tip or leaf cuttings.

argyreia p. 105

Watermelon Peperomia. This species has watermelonlike markings, red leafstalks, and a white flower spike that may or may not bloom. It grows 6 to 12 in. (15 to 30 cm) high.

caperata p. 107

Emerald Ripple Peperomia. Its deeply wrinkled leaves, small size, and compact shape make 'Emerald Ripple' one of the best of all peperomias. It reaches a height of 6 in. (15 cm).

obtusifolia p. 93

Baby Rubber Plant; American Rubber Plant; Pepper Face. This 6- to 8-in. (15- to 20-cm) plant has a number of cultivars. The new growth on 'Alba' is white-yellow marked with bright red.

scandens 'Variegata' p. 95

Philodendron Peperomia. This trailing vine has heart-shaped leaves that are almost completely yellow at first. Their centers turn green later, leaving the edges whitish yellow.

Phalaenopsis
Orchid family
Orchidaceae

Fal-ae-nop′siss. If you make a careful selection of species and modern hybrids, you can have a phalaenopsis plant in bloom every day of the year. Known as moth orchids, these are Asian epiphytes with broad flat leaves, many white roots, and no pseudobulbs. In the jungle, phalaenopsis live where light is diffuse and humidity high. They are ideal for growing in a greenhouse, light garden, or humid sun room.

A few species are small growing, but the most popular types reach 12 to 15 in. (30 to 38 cm) across, with arching sprays of 2- to 4-in. (5- to 10-cm) flowers. The flat flower shape of the classic white phalaenopsis, bred from the species *P. amabilis,* inspired the common name. A few species, such as *P. violacea,* have very fragrant flowers. Modern hybrids offer an array of round, flat flowers in many colors including white with pink or red stripes, yellow, yellow with red spots, deep pink, small waxy reds, and variations on the classic white in shades of light pink or with contrasting lip colors. Phalaenopsis flowers often last 3 to 4 weeks. Sprays will usually sprout a second time if the old mature spike is cut back to the second or third lowest bud.

How to Grow
Pot in a mixture suitable for epiphytes but with enough medium- to fine-grind material to assure constant moisture. Unmilled sphagnum moss and hardwood charcoal are good additions to phalaenopsis mixes. Keep the potting mix evenly moist with just slight drying between soakings. Maintain humidity at 50 percent or more, keep night temperatures above 65°F (18.5°C) for seedlings, down to 55°F (13°C) for fully mature plants. An average to warm range is best for continued growth.

Mature plants that fail to bloom can often be encouraged to do so if given 2 months with 50°F (10°C) nights in the fall. Fertilize with water-soluble orchid formulas every other watering during maximum growth. If no new leaves are being produced, stop fertilizing. Phalaenopsis may grow plantlets on the flower spike. These may be potted on their own once several roots have formed. Repot every 2 to 3 years as new roots begin.

Carnival Queen × Zauberot *pp. 144, 145*
This cross between a large, pink-flowered hybrid and a smaller, waxy-flowered yellow (bred from species *P. amboinensis* and *P. lueddemanniana*) has produced an adaptable hybrid with a slight sheen to the blooms.

stuartiana pp. 138, 139
Moth Orchid. This species from the Philippines usually blooms in the spring, but some clones bloom into the summer months. Leaves have attractive silver markings. The 2-in. (5-cm) flowers are white with a pink blush and many fine reddish to brown spots.

Philodendron
Arum family
Araceae

Fill-o-den'dron. Philodendrons are the best-known indoor foliage plants. They come in a variety of sizes, shapes, and growth habits that should suit every need. All are easy to grow.

How to Grow
Give philodendrons medium or bright light with little or no sun, average temperatures and humidity, and let the soil dry out a bit between waterings. Fertilize them every 2 weeks during spring and summer. Repot the plants when their roots have completely filled the pot, using an all-purpose soil mix with extra peat moss. The climbing or vining philodendrons are easily propagated by taking tip cuttings. The self-heading types such as *P. selloum* are best propagated from seed.

bipennifolium p. 206
Panda Plant; Fiddle-leaf Plant. A fast-growing climber that needs to be grown against a bark support. It can reach a height of 6 ft. (1.8 m). When small, the leaves are heart-shaped, but they achieve their distinctive violin shape as they age.

erubescens p. 206
Red-leaf Philodendron; Blushing
Philodendron. The leaves of this vigorous
climber are shiny dark green on top and
coppery underneath. Because it can reach
6 ft. (1.8 m), it needs to be staked.

pinnatilobum 'Fernleaf' p. 246
Fernleaf Philodendron. The climber is named
for its finely-cut leaves.

'Pluto' p. 243
The wavy edges of its leaves distinguish this
2-ft. (60-cm) cultivar.

scandens p. 76

Heart-leaf Philodendron. Although it has
aerial roots and can be trained against a bark
stake, this small-leaved vine is usually grown
as a trailing or hanging plant. It is
sometimes sold as *P. cordatum* or
P. oxycardium.

selloum p. 210
This philodendron reaches a height of 6 ft.
(1.8 m), and has several interesting cultivars,
including 'Miniate Selloum' and 'Golden
Selloum'.

Phoenix
Palm family
Palmae

Fee'nix. Although several species in this
genus are cultivated indoors, by far the most
elegant as well as the most manageable is
P. roebelenii, the Pygmy Date Palm.

How to Grow
The date palm needs bright light, with some
direct sun if possible, and average room
temperatures. If you can offer a winter rest
period in a room 55 to 60°F (13.0 to
15.5°C), so much the better. Water freely
in the warm months, but never let the palm
stand in water. In winter, keep the soil
barely moist. Fertilize every 2 weeks when
the plants are actively growing. Repot with
an all-purpose potting soil only when the
fine roots appear on the surface. Be careful
not to damage the roots when you tamp the
new soil around them. Phoenix palms
occasionally produce suckers, which can be
detached for propagation. More often they

are propagated by seed, a slow and difficult procedure for the amateur. For more information on growing palms, see *Caryota*.

roebelenii p. 231
Miniature Date Palm; Pygmy Date Palm. The graceful, delicate, arching fronds of this small date palm make it one of the most desirable of indoor plants. Eventually it can grow to 4 ft. (120 cm), with an even wider spread. If more than one stem develops, remove it to maintain the palm's symmetrical shape.

Phyllitis
Polypody family
Polypodiaceae

Fill-eye'tis. In this small genus of ferns, only one species is used as an indoor plant. There are several different cultivars, however, each with slightly different decorative fronds.

How to Grow
Put your fern where it will get medium light and no direct sun in any room that has average or cool temperatures. If the temperature goes above 65 to 70°F (18.5 to 21.0°C), set the pot on a tray of moistened pebbles for extra humidity. Water freely, but let the soil dry out a bit between waterings. Feed with half-strength fertilizer once a month throughout the year.
Repot only when the roots fill the pot, using a mixture of equal parts of all-purpose potting soil and peat moss. Propagate by division. Break off a 2- to 3-in. (5.0- to 7.5-cm) piece of the rhizome, making sure that it has some fronds attached, then partially bury it in a small pot filled with potting soil and peat moss.

scolopendrium 'Crispum' p. 242
Hart's-tongue Fern. The 12- to 18-in. (30- to 45-cm) fronds of this cultivar have beautiful frilled edges. Other cultivars have variously ruffled or crested edges.

Pilea
Nettle family
Urticaceae

Py'lee-a. These small plants have attractively marked and quilted leaves, making them good foliage plants for a terrarium or a dish garden.

How to Grow
Pileas need warmth and humidity, medium or bright light, but no direct sun. Although they want extra humidity, they cannot tolerate wet soil. Water your plant just enough to moisten the soil, then let it dry out between waterings. Feed every 2 weeks in spring and summer. Pileas don't age well; instead of moving them to larger pots, it is better to start over again by taking tip cuttings or dividing the roots in spring. When the plants are rooted, pot them in a mixture of peat moss and all-purpose soil mix.

cadierei *p. 99*
Aluminum Plant; Watermelon Pilea. This is the most popular pilea. It grows to a height of about 12 in. (30 cm), then begins to get leggy. A dwarf variety, *P. cadierei* 'Minima', is about 6 in. (15 cm) tall.

involucrata *p. 102*
Panamiga; Friendship Plant. This plant's leaves are bronzy green on top and purplish below. They show their color best in bright light, but keep them out of direct sun. It reaches a height of 6 to 8 in. (15 to 20 cm).

microphylla *p. 253*
Artillery Plant. The common name of this 12-in. (30-cm) species describes the forceful way the flowers eject the pollen.

nummulariifolia *p. 86*
Creeping Charlie. This flat little creeper is fast growing. It can be planted in a hanging basket or in a dish garden as a groundcover.

spruceana 'Norfolk' *p. 108*
Angelwings. The leaves of this 6- to 8-in. (15- to 20-cm) plant are striped with silver. They will become dark bronze in bright light.

402

Pittosporum
Pittosporum family
Pittosporaceae

Pit-toss'por-um. One of these evergreen trees
and shrubs makes a long-lived indoor plant
for a cool, sunny room.

How to Grow
Although for most of the year pittosporums
can thrive in normal room temperatures,
they need to be kept cool—down to 50° F
(10° C)—in winter. They also need several
hours of direct sun every day. Keep the soil
thoroughly moist while the plant is actively
growing, but in winter, water only enough
to keep it from becoming dry. Fertilize every
2 weeks from spring to fall and repot in
spring using an all-purpose soil mix.
Propagate in spring by taking tip cuttings.
To maintain its shapeliness, keep your bush
pruned and trimmed.

tobira p. 212
Japanese Pittosporum; Australian Laurel;
Mock Orange. Although these plants are
prized for their glossy leaves, they also have
fragrant white or lemon-yellow flowers. They
grow 3 to 4 ft. (90 to 120 cm) high.
'Variegata' has leaves marked with white.

Platycerium
Polypody family
Polypodiaceae

Plat-i-seer'i-um. Platycerium is a genus of
7 large ferns that grow on the branches or
trunks of trees. The large sterile frond is
round and platelike, enclosing the roots and
clasping the support on which the fern
grows. The fertile fronds are branched and
forked like a pair of antlers. The species most
often grown indoors is *P. bifurcatum,* the
Staghorn Fern.

How to Grow
Bright light with no direct sun, normal
room temperatures with good air circulation,
and a great deal of added humidity are
necessary to keep a Staghorn Fern healthy.
From spring to fall, water thoroughly but let
the soil dry out between waterings. In
winter, keep your plant barely moist. Since
these epiphytes are best grown on a piece of
bark—only very small ones can be grown in

a pot—the best way to water them is to soak them, bark and all, in a pail of water. Never fertilize. To attach a Staghorn Fern to a piece of bark, remove it from its pot and wrap the root ball in dampened sphagnum moss. Tie the ball to the bark and keep it damp until the round supporting frond attaches itself firmly. When these fronds have covered the bark completely, move the fern to a bigger support. The easiest way to do this is simply to nail the smaller bark onto a larger piece of bark. *Platycerium* is propagated by spores, a technique impractical in the home.

bifurcatum p. 240

Staghorn Fern. With forked fronds that can extend to a width of 3 ft. (90 cm), a well-grown staghorn fern closely resembles the antlers of its namesake. Unfortunately, it is difficult to grow to that size under normal home conditions.

Plectranthus
Mint family
Labiatae

Pleck-tran′thus. The botanical and common names of the most popular vine (Swedish Ivy) in this genus pose an intriguing question: How did an Australian plant in the mint family that isn't an ivy come to be called Swedish Ivy? Most likely its name stems from its great popularity in Sweden.

How to Grow
Swedish Ivy requires bright light and average home temperatures. Keep the soil uniformly moist and feed the plant every 2 weeks while it is in active growth. To keep the plant lush and bushy, pinch it back regularly. To propagate, root the tips you pinch in an all-purpose potting soil. Swedish Ivy doesn't age well. Instead of repotting an old specimen, root new ones and start over again.

australis p. 176
Swedish Ivy. This plant has round green leaves with scalloped edges. Its small, pale purple flowers appear only occasionally.

australis 'Purple Majesty' p. 81
This handsome cultivar has sturdy leaves that are green on the top and purple underneath.

coleoides 'Marginatus' *p. 94*
The leaves of this cultivar are wavy and edged with yellowish white. The species itself is seldom sold.

Pleomele
Agave family
Agavaceae

Plee-om'uh-lee. Correctly, pleomeles belong to the genus *Dracaena,* but since they are always sold under the name pleomele, they are described here separately. Similarly, the species *P. reflexa* is sometimes labeled *P. recurva.*

How to Grow
Pleomeles are easy-to-grow foliage plants for the house. For their culture, see *Dracaena.*

reflexa p. 225, 228
This plant has plain green leaves. It is usually kept to a height of 4 ft. (120 cm). The leaves of a handsome cultivar 'Variegata', called Song of India, have light yellow markings around the edges.

Plumbago
Plumbago (or Leadwort) family
Plumbaginaceae

Plum-bay'go. The species of leadwort usually grown indoors is *P. auriculata,* which was formerly called *P. capensis.* It is a spreading evergreen with blue-to-white flowers.

How to Grow
Direct sun and average temperatures suit the Cape Leadwort except in winter, when temperatures should be lower—about 50°F (10°C). Water generously during the spring and summer growth period and sparingly during the winter rest. Feed twice a month except in winter, and repot growing plants each spring until they mature. If you pinch out old flowering shoots in early spring, the plant will bloom all summer. The plant can be cut back quite severely in winter for best shape. Propagate by cuttings about 3 in. (7.5 cm) long, taken in spring and rooted in a mixture of sand or perlite and peat moss.

auriculata p. 195
Cape Leadwort. This 4-ft. (120-cm) plant has
attractive blue flowers. The var. *alba,* with
white flowers, is also available.

Podocarpus
Podocarpus family
Podocarpaceae

Po-do-kar′pus. In this genus of evergreen
conifers, only one plant, *P. macrophyllus,* or
Southern Yew, is grown indoors.

How to Grow
Podocarpus is best grown in bright light in
cool to average temperatures. Let the soil dry
out a bit between waterings and fertilize
every 2 weeks in spring and summer. Repot
only when the roots have filled the present
pot, using an all-purpose soil mix. Propagate
by taking cuttings from newly mature
shoots, ones that are neither too soft nor too
woody.

macrophyllus p. 223
Southern Yew; Japanese Yew; Buddhist
Pine. This plant grows 6 to 10 ft. (1.8 to
3.0 m) high. The dark green leaves are
actually flat needles. Crowded on the twigs,
they give the plant a full, lush look. Several
varieties are available.

Polypodium
Polypody family
Polypodiaceae

Pol-i-po′di-um. Of the 1,000 species in this
genus, the only one you are likely to find
indoors is *P. aureum,* the Rabbit's-foot Fern.

How to Grow
Normal room temperatures and medium
light are suitable for these ferns. If your
room is warmer than 70°F (21°C), give
them additional humidity. Keep the soil
moist at all times and feed every 2 weeks
with half-strength fertilizer. Repot when the
rhizomes have covered the surface of the soil.
Use a wide, shallow pot or a hanging basket
that will give the rhizomes plenty of room
to spread. Use a mixture of 1 part all-purpose
potting soil and 1 part peat moss. Propagate

in spring, following the directions given for
Davallia.

aureum *p. 241*
Rabbit's-foot Fern; Hare's-foot Fern. Unlike
the feathery *Davallia* that also goes by the
name Rabbit's-foot Fern, the *Polypodium* has
2-ft. (60-cm) fronds with deeply cut wavy
edges. The cultivar 'Mandaianum', or Blue
Fern, has beautiful blue-green fronds with
ruffled edges.

Polyscias
Aralia family
Araliaceae

Pol-lis′i-as. Several of the species in this
genus make decorative foliage plants for
warm rooms.

How to Grow
Aralias need warm temperatures, no lower
than 65° F (18.5° C), and extra humidity,
best supplied by putting the pot on a tray of
moistened pebbles. Grow your plant in
bright light and water it thoroughly, letting
the soil dry out a bit between waterings.
Feed every 2 weeks from spring to fall.
Repot when the roots start coming through
the drainage hole, using an all-purpose soil
mix. Propagate by taking tip cuttings in
early spring.

balfouriana *pp. 202, 203*
Balfour Aralia. The stems of this plant are
green with gray speckles. It grows to a
height of 3 to 4 ft. (90 to 120 cm). The
leaves are composed of round leaflets. In the
cultivar 'Marginata', the leaflets have white
edges. 'Pennockii' has larger leaflets and light
yellow-green markings.

fruticosa *p. 220*
Ming Aralia. The frilly, lacy foliage makes
this an elegant shrub. It reaches a height of
3 to 4 ft. (90 to 120 cm). 'Deleauna' is a
dwarf variety.

paniculata '**Variegata**' *p. 217*
This species has longer, more pointed leaflets
than *P. balfouriana.* They are dark green
with lighter green and cream markings. The
plant will grow to 3 to 4 ft. (90 to 120 cm).

Portulacaria
Purslane family
Portulacaceae

Por-tew-lak-cay′ri-a. There is only one species in this South African genus, *P. afra*, or Elephant Bush. It is a succulent shrub with small, rounded leaves.

How to Grow
This plant resembles the Jade Plant, *Crassula argentea*, and should be grown in the same manner.

afra p. 287
Elephant Bush. In the wild this plant grows to 12 ft. (3.5 m); indoors it will be 3 to 4 ft. (90 to 120 cm). It is sometimes called Baby Jade. A form with variegated white-and-pink leaves is also available.

Pteris
Polypody family
Polypodiaceae

Teer′is. Commonly called table ferns, dish ferns, or brakes, the varieties of *Pteris* most often found today are cultivars of 2 species, *P. cretica* and *P. ensiformis*.

How to Grow
These plants do well in average temperatures, but if your room is warmer than 65° F (18.5° C), be sure to place your fern on a tray of moistened pebbles. Bright light but no direct sun is best for variegated cultivars. Keep the soil moist throughout the year, but never let the plant stand in water. Fertilize every 2 weeks if you are using a soilless mix; otherwise fertilize once a month in spring and summer, using half-strength fertilizer. Repot in spring, using a soilless mix or a mixture of 1 part potting soil, 1 part peat moss, and 1 part sand. Propagate by division in spring.

cretica 'Alexandrae' p. 241
Cretan Brake; Ribbon Brake. There are many cultivars of *P. cretica*, some with crested tips, like 'Alexandrae', which has light green leaves. It grows to 18 in. (45 cm) high. 'Albolineata' has a white stripe running the length of each pinna, or leaflet.

ensiformis 'Victoriae' *p. 249*
Victoria Brake. The fertile fronds of the
Victoria Brake stand erect, to 20 in. (50 cm);
the sterile fronds are wider and only half as
tall. This cultivar has white-banded pinnae,
or leaflets.

Punica
Pomegranate family
Punicaceae

Pew'ni-ka. The edible pomegranate, one of
the 2 species in this genus, has many
cultivars. The best one for indoors is the
dwarf cultivar *P. granatum* 'Nana'.

How to Grow
During the spring and summer when it is in
flower, grow the plant in bright light with
some direct sun in average room temperatures.
Water it liberally and feed it every 2 weeks.
In autumn, after the leaves fall, move the
pomegranate into a cool room and water it
only enough to keep the soil from drying out.
Repot when the roots are very crowded,
using an all-purpose potting soil. Propagate
by taking stem cuttings in summer.

granatum 'Nana' *p. 220*
Dwarf Pomegranate. Outdoors this shrub
may reach 6 ft. (1.8 m). In the house it
infrequently grows taller than 3 ft. (90 cm)
but needs occasional pinching and pruning
to keep it shapely. It has bright red flowers
and fruits about 2 in. (5 cm) wide.

Rebutia
Cactus family
Cactaceae

Ree-boo'tee-a. These bristly little crown cacti
have abundant flowers and are popular with
cactus fanciers.

How to Grow
See *Cleistocactus*. Fertilize rebutias once a year
in spring, and propagate by seed or by
potting up offsets.

kupperana *p. 259*
Scarlet Crown Cactus. This little 3-in.
(7.5-cm) cactus has bright red flowers in
early summer.

Rhapis
Palm family
Palmae

Ray'pis. In this genus of reedlike palms, 2 species are grown indoors. The most popular is *R. excelsa.*

How to Grow
Grow these plants as you would those in the genus *Caryota.* They can stand temperatures down to 45° F (7° C).

excelsa p. 229

Bamboo Palm; Slender Lady Palm. This palm has multiple thin, reedy stems. The leaves are made up of wide, somewhat puckered leaflets. It grows to a height of 5 ft. (1.5 m) indoors. *R. humilis* is taller, with thinner stems and wider leaves.

Rhipsalidopsis
Cactus family
Cactaceae

Rip-sal'id-op-sis. Like the Christmas Cactus, *Schlumbergera,* the Easter Cactus is an epiphyte, a plant that grows on trees in the tropical forest.

How to Grow
These cacti require the same care as those in the genus *Schlumbergera.* Although their blooming schedule is somewhat different—or should be—the plants are treated the same way before and after flowering.

gaertneri p. 270

Easter Cactus. The pointed red flowers of this plant bloom at Easter time and sometimes in the fall. There are a number of hybrids available, with flowers ranging in color from pink to red.

Rhipsalis
Cactus family
Cactaceae

Rip'sa-lis. Rhipsalis is a genus of jungle cacti, most of which have trailing stems. Although they are well suited for hanging baskets, they demand a great deal of humidity, making them difficult to grow successfully outside of a greenhouse.

How to Grow
Average temperatures, bright light, and extra humidity are the proper conditions for growing these plants. Keep the soil uniformly moist from spring to fall; let it dry out just a little between waterings in winter. Feed once a month throughout the year. Repot in spring, using a cactus soil or mixture of 3 parts soilless mix plus 1 part sand. Propagate by cutting off a segment or a piece of the stem.

baccifera p. 272
Mistletoe Cactus. This is sometimes sold as *R. cassutha.* Its long, thin branches hang in strands. The cream-colored flowers precede a white, mistletoe-like fruit.

crispata p. 271
Wickerware Cactus. The flat stems of this species can reach 16 in. (40.5 cm) long. They are yellow-green and jointed. Flowers are pale yellow, and the fruit is white.

rhombea p. 269
The flat branches of this cactus are 2 ft. (60 cm) long with leaflike joints. The flowers are yellowish-white dotted with red.

Rhoeo
Spiderwort family
Commelinaceae

Ree'o. The genus *Rhoeo* consists of just one species, *R. spathacea,* yet that species has at least 10 common names, most of them variations on Moses-in-a-cradle.

How to Grow
Give *Rhoeo* bright light or direct sun, average room temperatures with additional humidity, and plenty of water during the warm months when it is actively growing. In winter, let the soil dry out between waterings. Fertilize every 2 weeks in spring and summer only. This plant likes to be somewhat crowded, so repot only when necessary, using an all-purpose potting soil mix. Propagate by offsets or division.

spathacea p. 227
Moses-in-the-cradle; Moses-in-a-boat;
Moses-in-the-bulrushes; Boat Lily; Oyster
Plant. The many names of this plant come
from the little white flowers that appear in
the boat-shaped purple bracts at its base.
Nevertheless, *Rhoeo* is grown mostly for its
handsome dark green and purple foliage,
which becomes more colorful in direct sun.
It grows to about 12 in. (30 cm). A
variegated form, 'Variegata' or 'Vitatta',
has leaves striped with pale yellow.

Rumohra
Polypody family
Polypodiaceae

Roo-moh'ruh. The one species commonly
grown is *R. adiantiformis,* sometimes
considered a species of *Polystichum.* By either
name, it is the Leather Fern often used by
florists.

How to Grow
Medium to bright light and temperatures no
lower than 55°F (14°C) at any time are
best for these plants. When the temperature
is warmer than 65 to 70°F (18.5 to
21.0°C), give the fern additional humidity.
Keep the soil moist at all times. Feed with
half-strength fertilizer once a month if the
plants are growing in soil, more often if they
are growing in a soilless mix or a mixture of
potting soil and peat moss. Propagate in
spring by division. To divide a plant, cut
through a rhizome with a sharp knife,
making sure that each piece of rhizome has
both roots and fronds, then repot.

adiantiformis p. 248
Leather Fern. Under ideal conditions the
leathery much-divided fronds can reach 3 ft.
(90 cm) high. They are dark green and grow
from a stout rhizome covered with brown,
papery scales.

Saintpaulia
Gesneriad family
Gesneriaceae

Saint-paul'i-a. African violets are the most
popular of all flowering houseplants and for
the most part they are easy to grow. There

are literally thousands of new cultivars, and
most of them flower throughout the year.

How to Grow
African violets need quite warm room
temperatures—at least 70° F (21° C) during
the day and 64 to 66° F (18 to 19° C) at
night. Supply extra humidity by placing the
pot on a tray of moistened pebbles. Keep the
soil uniformly damp but never soaking wet
and always use tepid water—if you do so,
you needn't worry about getting the leaves
wet. If you prefer to water from the bottom
of the pot, please read the information on
watering in the front of this book.
You can either fertilize once a month or use
one-quarter-strength fertilizer every time you
water. Keep these violets in bright light, but
out of direct sun. They do very well under
fluorescent lights. Repot only when roots
have completely filled the pot. Use African
violet soil mix and shallow pots. To
propagate, choose a medium-sized leaf and
snap it off, with its stem. Cut off all but 1
in. (2.5 cm) of stem and insert the stem
with the leaf attached into damp sand. Pot
up the little plantlets after they root.

'Jelly Bean' *p. 168*
Miniature violets are often displayed in
teacups. They are also pretty planted in a
dish garden. This one is 3 in. (7.5 cm) tall.

Optimara hybrids *pp. 166, 167*
These new hybrids are named for the states.
They grow 6 to 12 in. (15 to 30 cm) high.
Other excellent standard African violet
cultivars are the Ballet and Rhapsodie series.

'Pendula' *p. 174*
Violets grown in hanging baskets are
somewhat difficult to take care of because it
isn't easy to give them extra humidity.
Don't mist fuzzy-leaved plants, but do take
them to the sink from time to time to spray
the leaves with room-temperature water.

Sansevieria
Agave family
Agavaceae

San-se-ver′i-a. Sansevierias are native to
warm, dry climates. Most of the modern
houseplant cultivars derive from *S. trifasciata*.

How to Grow

Because these plants tolerate almost any level of neglect, they often look shabby and forlorn. With just a little attention, though, they can be quite handsome. They do very well in average room temperatures and in direct sun to medium or even low light. The only thing they cannot stand is overwatering. The lower the light, the less water they need, and the soil should always be allowed to dry out between waterings. From spring to fall, feed with half-strength fertilizer once a month. Sansevierias don't need to be repotted often. You may want to move the tall varieties to larger pots to balance the height and weight of the leaves. Use a cactus soil mix and propagate by taking offsets.

trifasciata 'Hahnii' *pp. 276, 277*

Bird's-nest Sansevieria. This rosette-shaped dwarf species grows to a height of about 6 in. (15 cm). 'Golden Hahnii' has broad yellow edges on its leaves and gray bands across the darker green centers.

trifasciata 'Laurentii' *p. 277*

Snake Plant; Mother-in-law's Tongue. This cultivar has lemon-yellow bands along the edges of the leaves. It grows to a height of 18 in. (45 cm). It is the most popular of the snake plants.

Saxifraga
Saxifrage family
Saxifragaceae

Sak'sif-ra-ga. In the large genus *Saxifraga*, one species, *S. stolonifera*, is commonly grown indoors. It has been given many common names, the most appropriate of which is Mother-of-thousands, because of its trailing shoots that carry little plants.

How to Grow

Temperatures between 50 and 60° F (10.0 and 15.5° C) are ideal, though this plant can tolerate warmer temperatures when it is actively growing from spring to late fall. Water freely during the growing season and fertilize no more than once a month. In winter, water only enough to keep the soil from drying out and don't fertilize. To propagate, detach one or more little plants from their stems and pot them in a mixture of peat moss and sand. When they are rooted, replant them in a standard potting mix.

stolonifera p. 106

Mother-of-thousands; Strawberry Geranium; Strawberry Begonia. This plant grows to a height of about 9 in. Although it is not a strawberry, a begonia, or a geranium, its round, silver-veined leaves make it easy to understand why it bears its common names. The long, trailing stems make Mother-of-thousands ideal for a hanging basket. If your plant becomes scraggly after a few years, replace it with young rooted plantlets. Formerly known as *S. sarmentosa.*

Schefflera
Ginseng family
Araliaceae

Sheff-leer'a. The plant that is popularly called schefflera is actually *Brassaia actinophylla.* The only houseplant in the genus *Schefflera* is *S. arboricola.* It is sometimes erroneously called *S. digitata* and *Heptapleurum arboricola.*

How to Grow
Follow the directions for growing *Brassaia actinophylla.* To keep your plant bushy, pinch out the growing tips from time to time. If the stems seem weak, stake them.

arboricola p. 213

Australian Umbrella Tree. To 6 ft. (1.8 m). Although it looks more delicate than the plant known as schefflera, this plant is easier to grow. In warm rooms it is less troubled by spider mites, although it, too, benefits from extra humidity.

Schlumbergera
Cactus family
Cactaceae

Shlum-ber-ger'a. Plants in this genus are native to moist tropical forests, where they grow on trees, and do best in conditions that mimic their original home. They are prized for their winter-blooming, brilliant, red, pink, yellow, or white flowers. These long-lived plants are often handed down from generation to generation. Commercial growers are skilled at forcing these plants to bloom exactly at Christmastime. Home gardeners should be delighted to approximate a Christmas blooming.

How to Grow
Normal room temperatures, medium to bright light without direct sun, and a rich, porous soil suit these jungle plants. Keep them well watered from spring until they finish blooming. In winter, let them dry out slightly between waterings. If you want the plant to set buds, keep it outdoors during the short days of September and October. Bring it indoors whenever frost threatens. Indoors again, keep it in a room that is dark in the evening, or move it to a closet whenever the sun goes down. Repot in spring, using an African violet soil mix. Propagate by taking stem cuttings in the spring.

bridgesii p. 270

Christmas Cactus. The branches grow to 12 in. (30 cm) long. A close relative, *S. truncata,* is known as the Thanksgiving Cactus and typically blooms several weeks before the Christmas Cactus. The Easter Cactus belongs to the genus *Rhipsalidopsis.*

Sedum
Orpine family
Crassulaceae

See'dum. Sedums are succulents with plump leaves and are often grown outdoors in rock gardens or in sandy soil. The best indoor sedum is *S. morganianum,* the Burro's Tail.

How to Grow
Average temperature and very bright light with some direct sun suit these plants. Water moderately from spring to fall and only enough in winter to keep the leaves from shriveling. Feed once a month during the warm months. Repotting, which is rarely necessary, is difficult because the fat little leaves break off easily when touched. Propagate by rooting the leaves in sand.

morganianum p. 267
Burro's Tail; Donkey's Tail. The blue-green leaves of this trailing plant have a whitish "bloom," much like that seen on blueberries.

Selaginella
Selaginella family
Selaginellaceae

See-laj-i-nell′a. Selaginellas are moss- or fernlike plants that reproduce via spores, not seeds.

How to Grow
These plants need warmth and high humidity and are really only suited to a greenhouse or a terrarium. Give them medium to low light. Keep the soil constantly moist and feed them once or twice a year. Repot whenever necessary using a shallow container and a soilless mix. Propagate by taking tip cuttings.

willdenovii *p. 249*
Peacock Fern. There is a slight bluish tint to the branching green leaves of this tropical, mosslike plant. It grows erect to about 12 in. (30 cm) high before it becomes a climbing plant.

Senecio
Composite family
Compositae

Sen-ee′si-o. There are between 2000 and 3000 species in this large genus, which includes succulents, ivylike vines, and *Cineraria,* a colorful, flowering annual that is often brought indoors during its blooming period.

How to Grow
The plants described here each have somewhat different cultural requirements. To find out how to grow them, see the plant descriptions below.

macroglossus 'Variegatum' *p. 79*
Variegated Waxvine. A handsome creeper that has ivylike leaves marked with yellowish-white, it does well under the same conditions as the String-of-beads. Repot it in a mixture of 2 parts all-purpose potting soil and 1 part perlite or sand. Propagate by taking tip cuttings. To keep your plant bushy, pinch its growing tips often. Watch out for aphids.

rowleyanus *p. 87*
String-of-beads. This succulent vine likes average temperatures and bright light,

preferably with some direct sun. Water moderately, and let the soil dry out a little between waterings. In winter, water just enough to keep the soil from drying out completely. Feed once a month from spring to fall. Repot using a cactus soil mix only when the plant has outgrown its present pot. Propagate by cutting off a "bead" and poking the end that was attached to the vine into sand.

Setcreasea
Spiderwort family
Commelinaceae

Set-cre′a-sea. Only one species of *Setcreasea* is grown indoors, and usually in one form. *S. pallida* 'Purple Heart' is sometimes sold as *S. purpurea*.

How to Grow
These trailing plants are grown for their purple stems and leaves, which need some direct sunlight each day in order to keep their intense color. Average temperatures and humidity are fine. Water thoroughly, but let the soil dry out a little between waterings. Feed monthly all year long, since the plants grow actively even in winter. Repot, whenever necessary, using an all-purpose soil mixture. Propagate by taking tip cuttings at any time. Setcreaseas do not age gracefully; after a year or two, replace your old plant with new ones made from cuttings.

pallida '**Purple Heart**' *p. 83*
Purple-heart. This trailing plant has small violet-purple flowers, usually produced in summer.

Sinningia
Gesneriad family
Gesneriaceae

Sin-nin′jee-a. This genus is somewhat confusing. It includes what is commonly known as the Florist Gloxinia but is not a true gloxinia, a group of plants that until recently were considered members of the genus *Rechsteineria,* and some miniature plants.

How to Grow

Grow these plants in a warm room and in bright light without direct sun. For their general care, follow the instructions given for African violets, with the following exceptions. Plants in the *Rechsteineria* group (including *S. leucotricha* and *S. cardinalis*) and hybrids of the Florist Gloxinia, *S. speciosa,* grow from tubers and have periods of dormancy. After they finish blooming, stop fertilizing and gradually reduce the watering. After the leaves die back, let the soil dry out until new growth starts. Repot *S. speciosa* tubers in fresh African violet soil. Plants in the *Rechsteineria* group can remain in the same pot for several years.

concinna p. 163

The stems, stalks, and veins of this 6-in. (15-cm) plant are red, and its woolly round leaves have crimped edges. Its trumpet-shaped flowers are lilac on top and paler underneath with purple spots inside the tube.

Miniature hybrids *p. 181*

These gloxinias grow to only 3 in. (7.5 cm) high and flower continuously. *S. pusilla* and its many hybrids are very popular miniatures. They have names like 'Doll Baby', 'Pink Petite', and 'Little Imp' and resemble *S. concinna.* Other miniatures, like the one shown, have been derived from *S. aggregata.*

speciosa p. 163

Florist Gloxinia; Velvet Slipper Plant. There are innumerable hybrids of *S. speciosa* and, where they once flowered only in summer, it is now possible to buy a gloxinia in flower at almost any time of the year. They grow to 12 in. (30 cm) high.

Sophronitis
Orchid family
Orchidaceae

Sof-roe-nye'tiss. *Sophronitis* orchids are dwarf epiphytes from Brazil. The best modern red *Cattleya* type hybrids have *Sophronitis* in the background, as the parent to contribute an intensely red flower color. Pure sophronitis species are a challenge to grow but worth extra care because of their showy 1- to 3-in. (2.5- to 7.5-cm) red, orange, or pink flowers produced on compact plants 3 to 8 in. (7.5 to

20.0 cm) high. In the Brazilian wild, some species, such as *S. coccinea,* live in treetops where sun is bright and the air filled with mist and breezes to keep the plants cool. Others, like *S. cernua,* come from lower elevations and tolerate warmer, less humid conditions.

Some primary hybrids of *Sophronitis* with related genera *Laelia* (called *Sophrolaelia*) and *Cattleya* (called *Sophrocattleya*) retain the dwarf habit and bright flower color of the *Sophronitis* parent but are easier to grow.

How to Grow
These orchids thrive in small clay pots filled with unmilled sphagnum moss over hardwood charcoal or grown mounted on slabs of tree fern. Sixty to seventy percent humidity and constant air movement are vital. As with most orchids, it is helpful to use a small fan to keep air moving around the plants constantly. Keep the potting mix evenly moist but never let it become soggy. When new growth is being produced, fertilize every week with water-soluble, balanced orchid fertilizer at half-strength. Provide cool temperatures for pure species native to high altitudes, and moderate temperatures for hybrids with related genera.

cernua *pp. 124, 125*
This species is popular because it will succeed in warmer temperatures than other *Sophronitis* orchids. The 1-in. (2.5-cm) flowers vary from orange to brilliant red-orange. Most clones flower from fall to winter.

Spathiphyllum
Arum family
Araceae

Spath-i-fill'um. Easy to care for, with beautiful glossy green leaves and the unusual ability to blossom in medium light, these are first-class indoor plants. The pure white flower that they bear changes to pale green after 10 days and then remains lovely for at least another month.

How to Grow
Spathe flowers tolerate medium light and average room temperatures. Water freely and

provide extra humidity—never let them
become dry. Fertilize the plants every 2
weeks throughout the year, but if
temperatures dip below 60° F (15.5° C) in
winter, let them rest. Repot in spring, using
a standard potting mixture, until your plant
reaches the largest pot size you can
accommodate. Then divide it or keep it in
the same pot and top-dress it with fresh soil.
Propagate by division. In direct sun, or if the
leaves touch a freezing window, ugly brown
spots may appear. Cut off the blighted leaves;
new ones will take their place.

'Mauna Loa' *p. 154*

The flower stalk of this 2-ft. (60-cm) hybrid
is 15 to 20 in. (38 to 50 cm) long. Its
spathe is slightly scented.

wallisii p. 154

This species grows to only 12 in. (30 cm)
high. Its flowers bloom in spring and
sometimes repeat in late summer. A similar
but larger spathiphyllum is *S.* 'Clevelandii'.

Stapelia
Milkweed family
Asclepiadaceae

Sta-pee′li-a. Stapelias are interesting South
African desert plants. Their flowers are large
and handsome—but unfortunately smell like
a full garbage can. They are commonly
known as carrion flowers.

How to Grow
To keep your stapelia from flowering, grow
it in bright light without direct sun—then
cross your fingers. If it does bloom, move it
outside. Average room temperatures are fine.
Water carefully; these plants will rot if the
soil is too soggy. In winter, water only
enough to keep them from shriveling. Repot
when necessary, using cactus potting soil,
and propagate by division.

hirsuta p. 264

Hairy Toad Plant. The flowers, which appear
near the base of the 8-in. (20-cm) stems, are
dark purplish-brown with cross-lines of cream
or yellowish-white.

leendertziae p. 280

The branching stems of this species are 4 in.
(10 cm) long and have small teeth, making

them look like cacti. The drooping flower is
purplish-red.

variegata p. 264

Toad Plant; Starfish Plant. This small stapelia
has 4-sided stems that grow to a height of
about 6 in. (15 cm). The flowers are a
modest 2 to 3 in. (5.0 to 7.5 cm) across but
can have a stronger odor than the Giant
Stapelia, which will bear flowers up to 18 in.
(45 cm) across, even though the plant is
rarely taller than 12 in. (30 cm).

Streptocarpus
Gesneriad family
Gesneriaceae

Strep-to-kar′pus. Plants in this genus are
relatives of African violets and have long,
primroselike leaves and trumpet-shaped
flowers. Some varieties have one large leaf
with several smaller ones growing from its
base. The more popular hybrids have a
rosette of leaves that are all about the same
size—usually 12 in. long and 2 to 3 in. wide.
Cape primrose is their common name.

How to Grow
Plants in the genus *Streptocarpus* need bright
light but no direct sun, and do well in
average room temperatures, preferably with
additional humidity. They appreciate a drop
of 5° F at night. Like African violets, these
are excellent plants for fluorescent light
set-ups. Water them freely and keep the soil
evenly moist while the plant is actively
growing; never let the soil become soggy.
While the plant is resting, let the soil dry
out between waterings. During active
growth, fertilize every 2 weeks with an
African violet fertilizer. Repot, using an
African violet soil mixture, when the roots
fill the pot. Use shallow pots. In deeper pots,
these plants stay wet too long and eventually
rot. To propagate, take leaf cuttings in the
spring.

'Constant Nymph' p. 165

The flowers of this popular hybrid are blue
with light yellow throats. They appear from
spring to fall on 6-in. (15-cm) stalks from
the center of the leaf rosette.

'Good Hope' p. 175

This relatively new cultivar technically

belongs in a subsection of the genus *Streptocarpus* called *Streptocarpella*. It is smaller and bushier than the typical plant and has become quite popular.

'John Innes' hybrids *pp. 164, 165*
These streptocarpuses have 8-in. (20-cm) flower stalks and resemble S. 'Constant Nymph' in leaf and flower shape. The flowers can be light pink, blue, or purple, and they bloom all year.

'Wiesmoor' hybrids *p. 164*
These types have light green leaves and the largest color range, including shades of white, pink, blue, and maroon. The ruffled petals are often marked with a darker color. They bloom from spring to fall.

Syngonium
Arum family
Araceae

Sin-go'nee-um. Syngoniums are climbing vines related to the philodendrons. The species most often grown indoors is *S. podophyllum*.

How to Grow
These plants have the same growing requirements as the philodendrons. As they age, the leaves of this plant become lobed rather than arrow-shaped. Prune the climbing stems if you prefer to see young leaves.

podophyllum *p. 103*
Arrowhead Vine; Nephthytis. This vine is a good choice for a hanging basket, or it can be trained against a bark stake.

Thunbergia
Acanthus family
Acanthaceae

Thune-ber'ji-a. The thunbergia most often grown indoors is *T. alata,* the Black-eyed Susan Vine. It is treated as an annual and discarded after it finishes flowering. *T. erecta* is an evergreen shrub that can be attractive in a large container.

How to Grow
Thunbergias do well in average or cool room

temperatures, with several hours of direct
sun. When small, water them moderately;
when they are in flower, keep the soil
continually moist. Fertilize every 2 weeks
and remove the dead flowers to extend the
blooming season. Start new *T. alata* plants
from seed in the spring. Propagate *T. erecta*
by cuttings.

alata *p. 194*
Black-eyed Susan Vine. The cheerful yellow
flowers have a dark center eye. Popular
cultivars include 'Aurantiaca', with orange
flowers, 'Alba', with white flowers, and
'Lutea', with yellow flowers.

erecta *p. 195*
King's Mantle. This shrub can grow to 6 ft.
(1.8 m) high. It bears 3-in. (7.5-cm) blue or
white flowers in summer.

Tillandsia
Bromeliad family
Bromeliaceae

Till-and'zi-a. *Tillandsia* is a large genus of
epiphytic bromeliads that includes the
Spanish Moss, *T. usneoides,* which hangs
from trees in the wild.

How to Grow
Tillandsias have very small root systems, so it
is important not to put them in an overly
large pot or to overwater them. Give your
plant extra humidity and keep the central
cup filled with water. For more on the care
and propagation of bromeliads, see the
information on genus *Aechmea.*

caput-medusae *p. 273*
This interesting plant has a bulblike base and
thin, curling, grayish leaves that suggest the
head of Medusa—hence its name. Its flowers
are purple, and it grows about 10 in.
(25 cm) high.

cyanea *p. 160*
Beautiful rose-colored bracts that last for
months surround the short-lived purple
flowers of this 10-in. (25-cm) plant.

didisticha *p. 160*
The thick gray leaves of this species grow to
12 in. (30 cm) long. The reddish bracts
surround small white flowers.

Tolmiea
Saxifrage family
Saxifragaceae

Tol'mee-a. Only one species, *T. menziesii,*
belongs to this genus. It is a hardy,
easy-to-grow plant, one that is attractive in
a hanging basket. Its fresh green leaves are
heart-shaped and hairy; new leaves appear to
ride on the backs of the old ones. Actually,
they are produced just at the juncture of the
stalk and the mature leaf.

How to Grow
These plants can tolerate average room
temperatures, but they do better in a cool
room. Water frequently and keep the soil
moist from spring to fall. In winter, let the
soil dry out slightly between waterings.
Fertilize every 2 weeks during spring and
summer. Although the leaves are hairy, they
can be showered off with room-temperature
water occasionally. In warm rooms, watch
out for mealybugs. Repot in an all-purpose
soil in spring. If your plant begins to look
old and scraggly, pot up some of the young
plantlets. Take leaf cuttings, taking care to
include a baby plantlet in each cutting
you make. Insert the stems in potting
medium; the little plantlets must touch
the soil.

menziesii p. 77
Piggyback Plant. This plant grows to about
12 in. (30 cm) high and just as wide. Its
small greenish flowers rarely appear indoors.

Trachelospermum
Dogbane family
Apocynaceae

Tra-kell-o-sper'mum. This genus of fragrant,
shrubby vines includes *T. jasminoides,* the
Star Jasmine, which starts flowering indoors
when it is a mere 6 in. (15 cm) tall.

How to Grow
Star Jasmines aren't actually jasmines. They
need bright indirect light with at least 4
hours of direct sun in winter. Average
temperatures are fine. Let the soil dry out
somewhat between waterings and feed them
every 2 or 3 months. Although these plants
are vines, they grow slowly and can be kept
as small shrubs if you continually pinch

them back. Unlike many other flowering
plants, these do not like to be potbound.
Repot them in winter or spring using an
all-purpose soil mix. Propagate from cuttings
taken in the fall.

jasminoides p. 191
Star Jasmine. This sweet-smelling plant
displays its star-shaped white flowers in
spring. If possible, move it outside in the
summer. It can grow to 8 ft. (2.4 m) but
will need support.

Tradescantia
Spiderwort family
Commelinaceae

Tray-des-kan'ti-a. Tradescantias are closely
related to plants in the genus *Zebrina* and
share with them the common name
Wandering Jew. Choose from several species
and many cultivars. They differ primarily in
the color of their flowers, which are small
and don't always appear indoors. The
markings on the leaves vary considerably;
they are the real attraction.

How to Grow
See *Zebrina*. It is a good idea to keep this
plant pruned to avoid weakness and
ranginess.

fluminensis pp. 82, 85
Wandering Jew. This easy-to-grow trailing
plant has leaves that are green on top and
purple underneath. Its flowers are white.
Aptly named, the cultivar 'Quicksilver'
grows rapidly; it has green leaves with white
stripes. 'Variegata' has yellow stripes.

Vanda
Orchid family
Orchidaceae

Van'dah. Vandas are Asian epiphytes with
flowers in all colors except black. Best
known are the pink- and white-flowered
hybrids grown for making leis in Hawaii.
The original *Vanda* species come from Asia,
but they have adapted to conditions in
Hawaii. Most popular in collections are the

strap-leaved types or hybrids between these and the tough, pencil-leaved vandas. All vandas require very bright light to reach their full potential. The strap-leaved hybrids are best for growing outside the tropics. Even more suitable for the average grower are hybrids with *Ascocentrum*. Although even compact vandas reach heights of 3 ft. (90 cm) after a few years, hybrids with *Ascocentrum* (called *Ascocenda*) stay compact while producing many vanda-type flowers in a wide range of colors.

How to Grow

Vandas have no pseudobulbs but do have abundant, thick white roots and thick foliage that conserves moisture. Pot vandas in slat baskets made of teak or cedar, or in very well drained pots using coarse mixtures of hardwood charcoal, tree fern, cork, or bark. Hanging the pots or baskets from a greenhouse rafter or hook is the best way to give vandas bright light and room for their roots to hang freely.

Give young vandas warm temperatures for best growth; moderate nights are suitable for mature plants. Keep humidity at 50 to 70 percent. In warm, sunny weather, mist the plants each morning. Vandas respond well to regular fertilizer. Feed growing plants with half-strength formula every week as new leaves are forming. In winter in cold climates where light is dim, stop giving fertilizer until late March. When light is inadequate, too much fertilizer will encourage weak growth.

Repot when potting mixes begin to break down, usually every 2 years. Spring is a good time to repot.

sanderana pp. 144, 145

This Philippine species is famous as a parent of many modern strap-leaved hybrids. Some taxonomists put this into a separate genus as *Euanthe sanderana,* but horticulturally it is still considered a vanda. It is a lovely, warm-growing, fall-blooming species that needs very bright light to produce abundant flowers. It will grow 2 to 4 ft. (60 to 120 cm) high. Crossed with *V. coerulea,* it makes the popular blue-flowered *V. Rothschildiana,* a hybrid that does well with slightly less light and cooler temperatures.

Vriesea
Bromeliad family
Bromeliaceae

Vreez'zi-a. There are many superb
houseplants in this genus of bromeliads.
V. splendens, or one of its cultivars, is an
especially good choice.

How to Grow
For detailed information on the culture and
propagation of bromeliads, see facts about
the genus *Aechmea.*

ensiformis p. 159
This species of *Vriesea* has shiny green leaves
and a flower spike that may be as high as
3 ft. (90 cm).

splendens p. 158
Flaming Sword. This plant has stiff green
leaves that are cross-banded in brown; the
bright red 2-ft. (60-cm) high "sword" lasts
for months.

Washingtonia
Palm family
Palmae

Wash-ing-toe'ni-a. There are only 2 species
in this genus, both of which make good
houseplants.

How to Grow
Washingtonias, popularly known as fan
palms, are easy-going plants that do well in
average temperatures and bright light. If you
can give them some sun, all the better. Keep
the soil thoroughly moist while they are
actively growing and let it dry out just a
little bit between waterings in winter.
Fertilize every 2 weeks during the period of
active growth. Repot every few years when
the roots appear on the surface of the soil.
Use a 2 to 1 mixture of all-purpose potting
soil and peat moss. Propagation is not easy
for the average gardener.

filifera p. 234
Desert Fan; Petticoat Palm. The 2-ft.
(60-cm) leaves on 18-in. (45-cm) stems
make this a handsome plant for a rather
large space. The fine hairs are a distinctive
feature of washingtonias.

Xanthosoma
Arum family
Araceae

Zan-tho-so'ma. There are 40 species in this tropical American genus, one of which is being grown more and more as a houseplant.

How to Grow
Treat these foliage plants the same way you would philodendrons. They resemble a green and white caladium but grow all year.

lindenii p. 105
Indian Kale; Spoon Flower. The white-veined leaves are arrow-shaped, and the plant grows 12 to 18 in. (30 to 45 cm) high.

Yucca
Agave family
Agavaceae

Yuck'a. Yuccas are native to the warm regions of North America. The species most often grown indoors is Y. aloifolia.

How to Grow
Never put these spiny-leaved plants where they might be brushed against. They are well suited for the dry air of the average home and will tolerate temperatures down to 50° F (10° C). Although bright light with some direct sun is best, these plants will also accept medium light. Water thoroughly, but let the soil dry out between waterings; in winter, water less frequently. Repot when necessary, using an all-purpose soil mix. Fertilize every 2 weeks during the warm months. Propagate by taking cane cuttings, if your plant is large enough to have a cane.

aloifolia p. 235
Spanish-Bayonet; Dagger Plant. Buy this as a small, stemless plant, with leaves up to 2 ft. (60 cm), or you can buy a 3- to 4-ft. (90- to 120-cm) plant made from a cane cutting.

elephantipes p. 235
Spineless Yucca. The rough, thick trunk of this species grows to 6 ft. (1.8 m). The leaves are long and shiny and not as stiff as those of the more common Y. aloifolia.

Zebrina
Spiderwort family
Commelinaceae

Zee-bry'na. There are only 2 species in the
genus *Zebrina*. One of them is perfectly
suited for hanging baskets in the house.

How to Grow
Zebrinas thrive in average temperatures but
to keep their color need bright light,
preferably with some direct sun. Let the soil
dry out slightly between waterings and
fertilize every 2 weeks when the plants are
actively growing. Pinch back the ends
frequently to keep the vine full. Repot when
the roots fill the pot, using an all-purpose
soil mix. After 2 years, take tip cuttings
from your plant, discard it, and pot up the
cuttings after they rot.

pendula pp. 83, 84
Wandering Jew; Inch Plant. This trailing
plant has beautiful silver and green striped
leaves. Cultivars include 'Purposii', with dark
red or red-green leaves, and 'Quadricolor',
with silvery leaves striped with green, red,
and white.

Appendices

Orchids

Orchids are so exotically beautiful that you may think only an expert could raise them. Actually, many species can be grown as houseplants with just a little more care than you'd give your begonias. This book features 32 different orchids, most of which are well within the horticultural grasp of any indoor gardener.

The orchid family, Orchidaceae, includes over 25,000 species, several hundred of which are large-flowered types, commonly grown commercially. Some home growers also enjoy collecting rare, small-flowered orchids. The commonly cultivated orchids come from the tropics of Africa, Asia, India, and Latin America. Their native surroundings range from torrid lowlands to temperate mountain slopes to elevations above 9,000 feet, where cool misty days are followed by chilly nights.

Orchid Names

Knowing an orchid's correct genus, species, and hybrid name is important in determining exactly how to care for it. Orchid names are written in a slightly different format from those of other houseplants. Genus and species names are written in italics, with only the genus name in initial caps—*Oncidium viperinum,* for example—as for other plants. The difference comes in hybrid names. Hybrids are given official names that do not carry single quotes as they would for other plants. *Oncidium* William Thurston is a hybrid of *O. triquetrum* × *O. desetorum.* A specific clone—a type derived from a single "parent"—can be given a further, "fancy" name, which does carry single quotes. *Oncidium* William Thurston 'Orchidglade' is a specific individual derived from the hybrid cross William Thurston. It is very common to see such lengthy names in orchid catalogues. They serve the practical purpose of allowing you to order a plant exactly like the one you've seen labeled.

You will also see long generic names, such as *Sophrolaeliocattleya,* which describe complex hybrids involving several genera—in this case, *Sophronitis, Laelia,* and *Cattleya.* These are usually given universally recognized abbreviations such as *Slc.*

The Indoor Environment

The guidelines given here are general tips on growing orchids indoors. Check the individual entries in the Encyclopedia of Houseplants for more detailed directions. The orchids included there were chosen because most are appropriate for home collections. They are easily available from commercial growers and adaptable to average home—or, in some cases, sun room or greenhouse—conditions. They have abundant, attractive flowers of appealing form, color, and often fragrance.

Temperature

As is true of most houseplants, orchids prefer daytime temperatures five to ten degrees higher than those at night for best growth and blooming. They can be grouped into three broad categories according to their nighttime temperature preferences. Some prefer cool nights, from 45 to 55° F; others do best in average temperatures of 55 to 65° F; and the third group thrives in warm, or 65 to 70° F, nights. When your orchids are actively growing, keep the temperatures toward the warmer end of the preference ranges. Orchids at rest, usually after flowering, will accept cooler environments. Hybrids are more adaptable than pure species to variations in temperature, so it is wise to start your collection with those.

It is important not only that the air be the right temperature, but also that it circulate freely around your orchids. Many are epiphytes, adapted to life on tree branches or mossy rocks. If your room is not large and relatively well-ventilated, consider using a fan to improve the circulation around your plants.

Light

Provide bright diffuse light for almost all orchid species. This means strong artificial light, indirect sunlight, or a combination of both. Thin-leaved orchids and those without water-storing pseudobulbs—the swollen stems that bear leaves or flower stalks—usually need less intense light than those species with thick leaves and pseudobulbs. Direct sun early and late in the day is usually safe for all orchids, but only a few types, such as some vandas, do well in full sun all day.

Many compact orchids and all orchid seedlings thrive under broad-spectrum fluorescent lamps. Some popular brands are Wide-Spectrum Gro-Lux, Vita-Lite, and Agro-Lite. Standard fixtures, available at hardware stores or by mail, are easy to install in your home—as supplements or even as the only source of light. Two 40-watt tubes are enough to add extra light; use four or more where there is no other light source.

Humidity

Orchids are more temperamental than most houseplants in demanding moist conditions. Most prefer 50 to 60 percent humidity, which is not often naturally available, especially in heated or air-conditioned homes. The more intense the light, the more careful you should be that the humidity level is maintained. Dry air causes the leaves of orchids to lose water faster than their roots can replace it. On sunny mornings many growers mist their orchids with lukewarm water to counteract this process.

Furnish extra humidity by placing your orchids above trays of water or moist pebbles or by growing them in an enclosed sunporch, where dampness can be trapped. Misting leaves is useful but should not be the only source of humidity. Do not mist at night; the foliage will stay wet too long, encouraging fungus rots.

You may need to purchase a humidifier if the air in your home

Orchids

This drawing shows
the most common
anatomical parts of a
cattleya-type orchid.

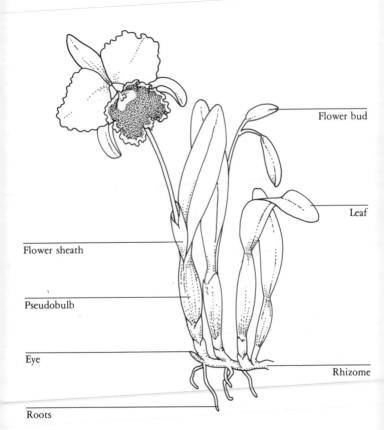

Flower bud

Leaf

Flower sheath

Pseudobulb

Eye

Rhizome

Roots

tends to be dry. Another attractive way to solve the problem—especially for some small species that need very high humidity—is to grow them in glass containers or terrariums. The plants will love their environment, and you will have a show-cased beauty on display.

Potting

Orchids can be terrestrial, such as paphiopedilums; semiterrestrial, like many cymbidiums and reed-stem epidendrums; or epiphytic, such as the cattleyas. There are potting mixtures tailored to each different growth habit.

Mixtures for epiphytic orchids are generally made with ground barks like cork and fir, tree fern, coarse perlite, and hardwood charcoal. Some epiphytes—phalaenopsis, for example—have no pseudobulbs to store water, so they need a mix that retains moisture well. Epiphytic genera that do have pseudobulbs, such as laelias or dendrobiums, do better in a lighter potting medium. The same materials may be used in mixtures for semiterrestrial plants, but add unmilled sphagnum moss and finer sizes of bark to retain more moisture. Terrestrial orchids thrive in mixes of rough compost and bark, often with sphagnum moss, fine-ground tree fern, or bark added.

In all cases, orchids in pots must have good drainage. Let the roots of most species dry out slightly between waterings. Some small species even grow well on slabs of cork or tree fern with no potting mix at all. They must have high humidity, however. Commercial growers will provide specific recommendations for potting the orchids they sell. Check the How to Grow descriptions for tips on potting those in this book.

Expanding Your Knowledge

When you are successful with your first orchids, you may become hooked and want to expand your collection. There are many mail order sources of plants; write the American Orchid Society (6000 South Olive Avenue, West Palm Beach, Florida 33405) for lists and other helpful information. There are also specialized magazines and books—including *All About Orchids,* by Charles Marden Fitch—geared toward enthusiasts and experts alike. Whether you grow one orchid or a whole roomful, these showy plants will be a special source of pride and pleasure.

Decorating with

Plants are as much a part of room decor these days as are furniture, curtains, and pictures on the wall. When you see a photograph of a room—any room—in an architecture or home magazine, you'll find plants located in all sorts of unlikely places. Most houseplant books, while paying lip service to a plant's needs, are often no better. In one, a laundry basket potted up with six giant blooming amaryllis bulbs sits on the counter a few inches away from the stove. The cook who can't use the stove presumably doesn't need the counter space anyway. In the same house it would be hard to take a bath because the tub is totally surrounded with pots of foliage and flowering plants.

While pictures like these are a source of ideas for placing plants in ways that enhance the appearance and ambience of a room, take them for what they are worth and then add the two elements that are always missing—the growing needs of the plants and the comfort of the people who live in the house with the plants.

If you have a greenhouse or any other room where you can bring plants into flower or keep them growing under ideal conditions, you can indeed bring out a perfect plant and put it on temporary display almost anywhere, returning it to its proper place after the guests leave. But if, as is more often the case, your plants must grow and look decorative in one place, you should make sure that you have chosen your plants well.

Using Plants as Sculpture

Most rooms have a corner that cries out for a large, dramatic specimen—a piece of living sculpture. These trees or large foliage plants are an investment, but well worth it if you can accommodate them. Consider adding a spotlight if the corner is dark, but never light a plant from the bottom, no matter how dramatic the effect may seem. Plants grow toward the light. A corner treatment that doesn't require a tree-sized plant is a tall plant stand or pedestal, on which you can place a handsome foliage plant or a fern that needs room for its fronds to droop gracefully. This may be a better solution if the light in the corner is poor, because there is probably a wider selection of low-light foliage plants than trees. And if the plant doesn't thrive, it will cost less to replace. When you are using plants for decoration, it is even more important than usual that they be well shaped and in luxuriant good health.

Placement, From Floor to Ceiling

Unless your ceiling has a skylight, it is not really possible to place plants above the top of a window. However, hanging plants in front of a window works very well and is a deservedly popular way of growing indoor plants. A swivel hook makes it easier to turn the plant regularly so all the growth isn't to one side.

Although large trees and plants in tubs sit naturally on the floor, they aren't the only plants that work well there. Many medium-sized

Plants

foliage plants, flowering bushes, or even large pots of orchids, look wonderful when placed below eye level. In the garden, of course, one looks down on most flowering plants. An upright plant that shows a good bit of leggy stems should never be placed above eye level, as on a mantelpiece. A hanging or trailing plant would look fine on that mantel.

When you place a plant in a room, stand back and look at it in the context of the entire space and its furnishings. Then sit down and see how the plant relates to the people in the room. If every aspect pleases, the only thing left to do is make sure that the plant can live comfortably where you have located it.

Grouping Plants

Large specimens or beautiful flowers of any size usually look best displayed alone. But a half-dozen small foliage plants of mixed parentage don't amount to much stationed separately around the house on any handy surface. Put them in matching white cachepots and line them up on a shelf, a windowsill, or a room divider, and you have a very attractive indoor garden. The pots, of course, don't have to be white, and the same group theme works equally well with flowering plants. It's the repetition and the restraint that makes a handsome decorative pattern.

A basket with a handle, large enough to hold two or three pots of flowering plants, makes a charming centerpiece for a dining table or coffee table. Try it with two or three cyclamens or streptocarpus, both of which hold their flowers gracefully above the foliage. To complete the natural effect, buy a bag of Spanish moss from a florist or garden shop to cover the tops of the plastic pots. When it is not on show, you can easily move a basketful of plants into better light, if necessary. And don't forget that baskets aren't waterproof; be sure to line the bottom with aluminum foil to prevent leakage.

These ideas are just the opposite of the windowsill-as-garden-junkyard that one sees so often—plants of every kind jammed together, in a miscellany of pots and saucers or even cottage cheese containers. A windowsill makes a perfect stage for an indoor garden. Choose the plants that you want to grow there with an eye for what they can do for the window as well as what the light can do for them, and then use restraint. One perfect plant is better than a dozen miscellaneous ones. If you want to take advantage of the sill as a nursery for developing plants, you can still make it an attractive one by using matching containers.

You might also consider turning a window into an indoor garden by putting up plant shelves across its entire expanse. These are easily purchased or can be built. Generally, glass shelves strong enough to hold pots are most desirable because they don't interfere with the light, airy look of the window. One caveat: If your window faces west or gets direct sun in summer, be sure to allow room for a translucent curtain to cut the hot, direct rays of the midday sun.

Dish Gardens

The first person who crammed a Snake Plant, a piece of ivy, a seedling dracaena, a peperomia, and a china bunny rabbit into a piece of glazed pottery and called this horticultural horror a dish garden has a lot to account for. Yet a real dish garden—a miniature landscape of compatible plants in a simple low container—can be a living work of art.

The plants most suited for a dish garden are small cacti and succulents. Singly or in a row of little pots, these plants are not much to look at. Mixed with other foliage plants, they may receive too much water and not enough light to suit their needs. But grouped sparsely in a sandy or gravelly bed, as they would be in nature, they can be very striking. Moreover, they will thrive in their garden because they are shallow-rooted and need very little water. Display the garden on a low table where it can be appreciated.

Decorative Containers

Plants deserve better than they usually get in pots. Except for unglazed clay, which has a natural integrity, most plants will be enhanced if you place the pots in which they're growing inside another, decorative container. The container should be large enough and deep enough to hide the pot completely, but its size should be in proportion to that of the plant. Natural materials are always appropriate—brass, pottery, wood, basketry—but remember that wood and baskets will not protect the floor or furniture, and that baskets will eventually rot. Use a lining or place a saucer inside the basket.

Simple materials are always appropriate, but a decorated pot or piece of fine china can make a beautiful display container for a single plant. Try miniature African violets or sinningias in demitasse cups. Use a few of them on the dinner table where you used to keep the cigarettes. Make sure that the colors enhance the foliage or flowers and that the whole effect of plant and pot is harmonious.

Buying Plants

Purchasing a plant is not the same as buying an inanimate object. In the latter case, what you see is usually what you get, and it is possible to judge whether a bargain is actually a bargain. The plant you see in the store, however, is going to grow and change—for better or worse—in your home, and the factors that will cause it to succeed or fail may not always be detectable. Gardeners are too apt to blame themselves for a plant's demise; sometimes the only thing they did wrong was to buy the plant in the first place.

It's always a good idea to patronize an established plant nursery or garden shop; it is most important to do so when you are buying any expensive plant, particularly a large foliage plant. Here is where you'll find the biggest discrepancy in prices and the most natural temptation to buy the "bargain." But let the buyer beware. The tropical or semitropical trees and large leafy plants that are sold out of the back of a truck or in a special promotion are just a few days away from the Florida or Texas fields where they were growing under 10,000 to 15,000 footcandles of natural light. To make these plants suitable for growing indoors, where they may receive as little as 150 footcandles of illumination, takes time. In business, time is money. To move a plant from a bright, sun-baked field directly into your home is a sure recipe for drastic leaf drop, if not worse.

The expensive plant probably spent two months in shade after it was dug up and then was further acclimated in a greenhouse to lower indoor light levels. When you buy the plant, you should continue the process by putting it in the brightest light you have, even if it is a plant that you will eventually grow in medium or low light. After a couple of weeks, move it to its permanent home.

When you buy flowering plants—especially the seasonal plants that you intend to discard after blooming—avoid those that are in full flower. Instead look for a plant that has lots of buds.

Any plant that you buy should look in vigorous good health; if it isn't flourishing in the ideal environment of a plant nursery, it will never do well in yours. Give the pot a shake to see whether the plant is actually growing in the pot or has just been potted up. You want one that is growing. At the same time, you don't want one that has so outgrown its pot that the bottom leaves are drooping and yellow. Since plants are often priced by pot size, you can sometimes get a bargain by buying a plant in a two-inch pot, for instance, and then promptly repotting it when you get home. You are taking a chance, but if the original investment isn't significant, it may be worth it.

Look at the leaves to make sure the edges have not been trimmed off. Brush against them; if a cloud of whiteflies rises from the plant, put it back and be careful about buying any plant in that greenhouse. Check the undersides of leaves for signs of insects or disease (see page 440 to learn how to identify these). As a final precaution isolate the new purchase for a week or so to be sure it isn't a carrier of insects or disease.

Pests & Problems

If you are careful to purchase healthy plants and give them the proper conditions and care, you should not have much trouble making them thrive. More houseplants die from neglect and improper care than from insect or disease damage. When problems do develop, it pays to be able to recognize the pests, diseases, or conditions that most often plague houseplants and to know how to control them.

Environmental Stresses
Many types of houseplant illness result from environment-related stress, such as insufficient or excess light, overwatering, or low humidity. Other problems are caused by excess fertilizer salts or inadequate feeding. Most of these injuries are avoidable if you choose the right plant for your environment and learn about its needs.

Diseases
Both fungi and bacteria are responsible for a variety of diseases, ranging from leafspots and wilts to root rot, but bacterial diseases usually make the affected plant tissues appear wetter than fungi do. Diseases caused by viruses, often transmitted by aphids, display such symptoms as mottled yellow or deformed leaves and stunted growth.

Insect Pests
Numerous insects attack plants. Sap-sucking insects—including aphids, whiteflies, mealybugs, and scale insects—suck plant juices. The affected plant becomes yellow, stunted, and misshapen. These insects produce honeydew, a sticky substance that attracts ants and sooty mold fungus growth. Other pests with rasping-sucking mouthparts, such as thrips and spider mites, scrape plant tissue and then suck the juices that well up in the injured areas.

Controlling Plant Problems
When buying plants, check leaves and stems for dead areas or off-color and stunted tissue. Make sure there are no signs of insect pests, and ask whether the plant you like is particularly susceptible to any health problems.

Routine Preventives
Making sure your plants have the proper soil, water, humidity, nutrients, light, and containers is the first and biggest step toward keeping them healthy. It is especially important to avoid overwatering, which is the number one cause of houseplant death. Use clay pots when possible, since they allow evaporation from the sides as well as the top of the pot, and be sure that any pot you use has adequate drainage. Spray plants with water and wipe off the leaves from time to time to dislodge insect pests and remove suffocating dust. Pick off larger insects by hand. To discourage

fungal and bacterial leafspots, mist plants lightly but do not let
water sit on the leaves. For the same reason, provide adequate air
circulation around leaves and stems.

If you put plants outdoors in the summer, be sure to check them
carefully for insects and diseases before bringing them back inside.
Spray them with plain or soapy water, dry them, and then keep
them separated from your other houseplants for several weeks to be
sure no unwanted houseguests appear.

If you watch over your plants from day to day, you will notice signs
of trouble in time to prevent serious problems. Pesticides may not
be very effective once the culprit has become established on a plant.

Insecticides and Fungicides
To protect plant tissue from injury due to insects and diseases, a
number of insecticides and fungicides are available especially for use
on houseplants. However, few products control diseases due to
bacteria and viruses. Always check the pesticide label to be sure that
it is registered for use on the pest and plant you are dealing with.
Follow the label recommendations for safety precautions, dosage, and
frequency of application. Some pesticides are for use only on outdoor
plants and should never be used indoors. In recent years products
called insecticidal soaps have been introduced, and they are useful in
controlling many insect pests.

Any pesticide you use may be toxic to certain plants, so test it on a
few leaves before spraying the entire plant. You can make a pesticide
spray at home by dissolving a few drops of mild dishwashing soap in
one quart of water. Be sure to rinse the plant off after applying this
homemade solution.

One application of pesticide spray is usually not enough. You will
have to spray any control—chemical or soap solution—once to kill
the adult pests and again one to two weeks later to destroy any eggs
or hatching young. Further applications may be required depending
on the severity of the attack.

Recognizing Distress Signals
Learning to recognize the insects, diseases, and environmental
stresses that plague houseplants is not difficult, but some of the same
general symptoms—discolored, dropping, or wilted leaves; stunted or
weak growth—can be signs of different problems. Read through the
whole chart on the following pages before deciding what your
problem is. There you will find descriptions of the most common
pests, diseases, and disorders, the damage they cause, and how to
control them.

Pest or Problem

Aphids

Bacterial Leafspots

Cyclamen Mites

Fungal Leafspots

Low Humidity

Description	Damage	Control
Tiny green, brown, or reddish, pear-shaped, soft-bodied insects in clusters on buds, shoots, and undersides of leaves.	Suck plant juices, causing stunted or deformed blooms and leaves. Some transmit plant viruses.	Spray with pyrethrum, rotenone, or insecticidal soap.
Dark, water-soaked areas on leaves due to bacteria.	Leaves covered with watery spots. Lesions may spread to stem.	Destroy severely affected plants. Avoid misting plants.
Tiny, eight-legged mites that attack cyclamens, gesneriads, and many other plants.	Suck juices from new buds and leaves, causing stunted plants. New leaves and flowers are misshapen. Buds turn black.	Immerse plant and pot in 110° F water for 30 minutes or use Kelthane.
Spots on leaves caused by fungi encouraged by high humidity.	Tan, brown, or black spots on leaves. If serious, leaves may drop from plant.	Increase air circulation around plants. Remove badly diseased leaves. Spray with zineb or benomyl if serious. Do not mist plants.
Drying or death of leaves due to insufficient moisture in air.	Leaf edges and tips turn brown. Leaves may fall suddenly.	Increase humidity around plants by use of pebble trays. Lower room temperature.

Pest or Problem

Mealybugs

Nutritional Deficiencies

Oedema

Powdery Mildew

Root- or Pot-bound

Description	Damage	Control
White, waxy, oval, soft-bodied insects on leaves, leaf axils, and shoots. Produce sticky honeydew.	Suck plant juices, causing off-color and stunted plants.	Clean foliage frequently. Pick off bugs with alcohol swab. Spray with insecticidal soap or pyrethrum.
Plant is not growing properly due to lack of nutrients.	Plants off-color and stunted. Leaf veins may be colored.	Apply an all-purpose fertilizer lightly once a month.
Irregular leaf growth caused by overwatering.	Swellings on leaves. Spots have a corklike texture.	Remove damaged leaves. Cut down on watering and be sure pot drains well.
White, powdery fungal disease on aerial plant parts.	Reddish spots and powdery fungal growth. Leaves may be distorted and drop. Stems, buds, and flowers also affected.	Remove badly infected leaves. Increase air circulation. Spray with benomyl.
Roots emerge at top and/or from drainage holes of pot. Water runs through pot very quickly.	Plant too large for pot, so roots are constricted and plant growth is slowed.	Transplant to pot of next largest size.

Pest or Problem

Root Rot

Salt Buildup

Scale

Shock

Sooty Mold

Description	Damage	Control
Fungal or bacterial disease, usually soilborne, often encouraged by overwatering.	Wilting, off-color plants. Roots dark and dry or mushy rather than firm and white.	Avoid overwatering. Be sure pots have good drainage.
White, dusty deposit on soil and/or pot.	Leaf edges turn brown. Plant may be spindly.	Leach salts from pot by gently running water through and draining, or repot into fresh soil. Fertilize less often and use deionized water.
Small, waxy, soft- or hard-bodied stationary insects on shoots and leaves. May be red, white, brown, black, or gray.	Suck plant juices, causing stunted, off-color plants.	Pick off scale. Spray with malathion, which is best used outdoors.
Loss of leaves due to temperature extremes, repotting, or change in location.	Leaves drop suddenly from plant.	Avoid extremes of temperature, light conditions, humidity. Keep drafts from plants. Introduce plants gradually to new locations.
Black, sooty fungus growth on leaves.	Unsightly black mold growth indicates infestation by sucking insects.	Control sucking insects with methods recommended for aphids.

448

Pests & Problems

Pest or Problem

Spider Mites

 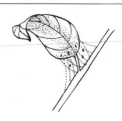

Thrips

Too Little or Too Much Light

Viruses

Whiteflies

Description	Damage	Control
Tiny golden, red, or brown arachnids on undersides of leaves. Profuse fine webs seen with heavy infestations.	Scrape leaves and suck plant juices. Leaves become pale and dry. Plant may be stunted.	Spray leaves with water or insecticidal soap.
Very small, slender, brown, yellow, or black insects with narrow, fringed wings. Rasping-sucking mouthparts.	Scrape and suck plant tissue. Cause browning, white flecking, and gumminess. Sometimes deform flowers, buds, and leaves.	Remove infested flowers and buds. Spray with pyrethrum.
Light too low or too high to allow proper growth.	In low light, plant stems very long, leaves unusually light green, or flowers not blooming. In bright light, leaves yellow, brown-spotted, dry, or curled.	Move plant into correct light. Pinch off damaged parts.
Various diseases, including mosaics, that cause off-color, stunted plants. May be transmitted by aphids.	Crinkled, mottled, deformed leaves, stunted plants, poor growth.	Remove and destroy infected plants. Control aphids if present. Buy only healthy plants.
Tiny flies with white, powdery wings. Fly up in large numbers when disturbed. Secrete honeydew.	Suck plant juices. Plants look yellow, sickly, and stunted.	Spray with pyrethrum or insecticidal soap.

Glossary

Air Layering
A method of propagation in which a stem is cut into, causing roots to form. The stem is severed below the new roots and grown separately from the parent plant.

Annual
A plant whose life span is encompassed in a single growing season.

Areole
A raised or sunken spot on the stem of a cactus, usually bearing spines.

Axil
The angle formed by a leafstalk and the stem from which it grows.

Bract
A modified and often scale-like leaf, usually located at the base of a flower. Many houseplants, including the bromeliads, Moses-in-the-Cradle, and bougainvillea, are grown for their decorative bracts rather than for their insignificant flowers.

Bromeliad
A member of the family Bromeliaceae, characterized by rosettes of leaves and colorful bracts surrounding small flowers. Many are epiphytes.

Bud
A young and undeveloped leaf, flower, or shoot, usually covered tightly with scales.

Bulb
A short underground stem, the swollen portion consisting mostly of fleshy, food-storing scale leaves.

Cactus
A member of the family Cactaceae, characterized by succulent stems and branches with scales or spines rather than typical leaves. Most are native to dry or desert regions.

Clone
A population of plants all originating by vegetative propagation from a single plant, and therefore genetically identical to it and to one another.

Creeping
Prostrate or trailing over the ground or over other plants.

Cultivar
A manmade plant variety, produced by selective breeding.

Cutting
A piece of plant without roots that, set in a rooting medium, develops roots and can then be potted as a new plant.

Division
Propagation of a plant by separating it into two or more pieces, each of which has at least one bud and some roots.

Double-flowered
Having more than the usual number of petals, most often arranged in extra rows.

Dwarf
A plant low in stature or with small parts.

Epiphyte
A plant whose roots do not need soil surrounding them for nutrition; often called air plant or tree-percher.

Fern
A perennial, flowerless plant that reproduces by means of spores.

Frond
The leaf of a fern or palm.

Genus
A group of closely related species; plural, genera.

Germinate
To sprout.

Gesneriad
A member of the large tropical family Gesneriaceae, mostly showy-flowered greenhouse plants, including the gloxinias, lipstick plants, and African violets.

Glaucous
Covered with a waxy bloom or fine pale powder that rubs off easily.

Humus
Partly or wholly decomposed vegetable matter.

Hybrid
A plant resulting from a cross between two parent plants belonging to different species, subspecies, or genera.

Leaf
A structure borne laterally on a stem, and having a bud on its axil.

Leaflet
One of the subdivisions of a compound leaf, resembling a leaf but not having a bud in its axil.

Leaf margin
The edge of a leaf.

Midrib
The primary rib or mid-vein of a leaf or leaflet.

Node
The place on the stem where a leaf or branch is attached.

Offset
A short, lateral shoot arising near the base of the plant, readily producing new roots, and useful in propagation.

Peat moss
Partially decomposed plants, useful in cultivating houseplants because of its high capacity to hold water. It is the main component of soilless mixes.

Perennial
A plant whose life span extends over several growing seasons.

Pistil
The female reproductive organ of a flower.

Plantlet
An offset produced on a plant's stems or leaves.

Potting mix
The medium in which plants are grown, which may or may not contain soil.

Propagate
To produce new plants, either by vegetative means involving rooting pieces of a plant, or by sowing seeds.

Pseudobulb
The thickened stem of an orchid plant, which stores energy and moisture.

Rhizome
A horizontal stem running underground or in the soil, distinguished from a root by the presence of nodes, and often enlarged for food storage.

Root ball
The dense mass of matted roots and the potting mixture trapped in them.

Rosette
A circular, crowded cluster of leaves.

Runner
A horizontal, above-ground stem that produces buds at its nodes, from which new shoots and roots sprout.

Seed
A fertilized, ripened ovule.

Seedling
A young plant soon after seed germination, while still with a single, unbranched stem.

Shoot
A young growing branch.

Spadix
A dense spike of tiny flowers, usually enclosed in a spathe.

Spathe
A bract or pair of bracts, often large and enclosing the flowers, as in members of the Arum family.

Species
A population of plants or animals whose members are at least potentially able to breed with each other, but which is reproductively isolated from other populations.

Spore
The reproductive cell of a fern or moss. Ferns usually carry spores in raised brown patches called sori on the undersides of the fronds.

Stamen
The male reproductive organ of a flower.

Stolon
An unthickened rhizome, which produces a plantlet where it touches the surface of the soil.

Succulent
A plant with fleshy leaves or stems that contain abundant water storage tissue. Cacti and aloes are examples.

Sucker
A young shoot emerging from roots of a plant that forms its own leaves and roots.

Tropical plant
A plant whose native habitat is somewhere between the Tropic of Cancer and the Tropic of Capricorn. Most houseplants are tropical.

Tuber
A swollen, mostly underground stem that bears buds and serves as a storage site for food.

Variegated
Marked, striped, or blotched with some color other than green.

Variety
A naturally occurring population of plants that differ consistently from the typical form of the species; more loosely applied in popular usage to forms produced in cultivation. See Cultivar.

Vegetative propagation
Propagation by means other than seed.

Index

Numbers in boldface
refer to pages on which
color plates appear.

A
Abutilon, 290
hybridum, **180,** 290
Acalypha, 290
hispida, **183,** 291
wilkesiana, **116,** 291
Acorus, 291
gramineus pusillus,
292
gramineus
'Variegatus', **226,**
292
Adiantum, 292
capillus-veneris, **251,**
292
raddianum, **251,** 292
Aechmea, 293
chantinii, **158,** 293
fasciata, **159,** 293
lueddemanniana, **273,**
293
Aeonium, 294
arboreum, **212,** 294
arboreum 'Black
Rose', **286,** 294
tabuliforme, **285,** 294
Aeschynanthus, 294
pulcher, 294
radicans, **86,** 294
**African Violet, 166,
167, 168, 174,** *411,*
412
Agave, 295
filifera, 295
leopoldii, **281,** 295
schidigera, 295
victoriae-reginae, **281,**
295
Aglaonema, 295
commutatum, **98,** 296
commutatum
'Treubii', **98,** 296
costatum, **91,** 296
Airplane Plant, 335
Allamanda, 296
cathartica, **193,** 296
Aloe
Barbados, **280,** 297

Kaniedood, **278,** 297
Medicinal, 297
Partridge-breast, 297
Pheasant's-wing, 297
Aloe, 296
barbadensis, **280,** 297
variegata, **278,** 297
vera, 297
**Aluminum Plant,
99,** *401*
Ananas, 297
comosus 'Variegatus',
237, 297
Angelwings, 108,
401
Angraecum, 298
sesquipedale, **136,
137,** 298
Ansellia, 298
africana, **132, 133,**
299
gigantea, 298
**Anthurium,
Crystal, 104,** *300*
Anthurium, 299
crystallinum, **104,** *300*
scherzeranum, **155,** *300*
Aphelandra, *300*
squarrosa 'Louisae',
109, *300*
Aporocactus, 301
flagelliformis, **266,**
301
Aralia
Balfour, **202, 203,**
406
False, **222,** *346*
Ming, **220,** *406*
Araucaria, 301
bidwillii, **221,** *301*
excelsa, 302
heterophylla, **221,** 302
Ardisia, 302
crenata, **216,** 302
**Arrowhead Vine,
103,** *422*
**Artillery Plant,
253,** *401*

Ascocenda, 303, *426*
Meda Arnold, 303
Yip Sum Wah, 303
Ascocentrum, 303
curvifolium, **122,
123,** 303
Asparagus, 303
densiflorus 'Myers',
245, 304
densiflorus
'Sprengeri', **245,** 304
plumosus, 304
setaceus, **247,** 304
Aspasia, 305
epidendroides, **140,
141,** 305
principissa, 305
Aspidistra, 306
elatior, **228,** 306
elatior variegata, **225,**
306
Asplenium, 306
bulbiferum, **250,** 307
daucifolium, 307
nidus, **242,** 307
nidus 'Antiquum',
243, 307
**Aspoglossum
Copper Butte,** 305
Aucuba, 307
japonica 'Variegata',
214, 307

B
Basket Grass, 252,
389
Bead Vine, 336
Beaucarnea, 308
recurvata, **236,** 308
Beef Plant, 117, *371*
Beefsteak Plant, 291
Begonia
Angel-wing, **179,**
309
Bedding, 310
Beefsteak, **106, 169,**
309
Elatior Hybrids, 309

Eyelash, **102**, *309*
Iron-cross, **100**, *310*
Kidney, *309*
Polka Dot, **204**, *310*
Rex, **110, 111, 112, 115**, *310*
Rieger, **162**, *309*
Strawberry, *414*
Superba hybrids, *309*
Trailing
Watermelon, **82**, *396*
Troutleaf, **208**, *310*
Wax, **80, 169, 186**, *310*
Winter-flowering, *309*
Begonia, *308*
boweri, **102**, *309*
coccinea, **179**, *309*
'Di-Erna', **178**, *309*
× *erythrophylla*, **106, 169**, *309*
× *hiemalis*, **162**, *309*
'Lana', **179**, *309*
maculata 'Wightii', **204**, *310*
masoniana, **100**, *310*
'Medora', **208**, *310*
× *rex-cultorum*, **110, 111, 112, 115**, *310*
× *semperflorens-cultorum*, **169, 186**, *310*
× *semperflorens-cultorum* 'Charm', **80**, *310*
Begonia Vine, Trailing, 81, *328*
Belgian Evergreen, 224, *347*
Beloperone guttata, *372*
Billbergia, *310*
'Theodore L. Mead', **178**, *311*
Black-eyed Susan Vine, 194, *423*

Blechnum, *311*
gibbum, **244**, *311*
moorei, *311*
Bleeding-heart Vine, 330
Botanical-wonder, 357
Bougainvillea, *311*
'Barbara Karst', **197**, *312*
glabra 'Sanderana Variegata', **198**, *312*
Brake
Cretan, **241**, *407*
Ribbon, *407*
Victoria, **249**, *408*
Brassaia, *312*
actinophylla, **213**, *312*
Brassavola, *313*
nodosa, **134, 135**, *313*
Brassia, *313*
gireoudiana, **134, 135**, *314*
Bromeliad, Blushing, 161, *384*
Broughtonia, *314*
negrilensis × *sanguinea*, **146, 147**, *315*
Browallia, *315*
speciosa, **174**, *316*
Bulbophyllum, *316*
blumei, **126, 127**, *316*
Burro's Tail, 267, *415*
Busy Lizzy, 170, 171, *370*
Buttons-on-a-string, 284, *336*

C
Cactus
Barrel, **256, 257**, *349, 350*
Bird's-nest, **258**, *379*
Christmas, **270**, *415*

Cob, **258, 262**, *377*
Easter, **270**, *409*
Easter-lily, *350*
Golden Ball, *349*
Hedgehog, *350*
Mistletoe, **272**, *410*
Mule-crippler, *349*
Old-lady, *379*
Old-man, **261**, *324*
Old-woman, **260**, *379*
Peanut, **266**, *325*
Powder-puff, *379*
Rainbow, **262**, *350*
Rattail, **266**, *301*
Red Orchid, **271**, *352*
Scarlet Crown, **259**, *408*
Snowball, **260, 261**, *379*
Strawberry, **259**, *379*
Thanksgiving, *415*
Wickerware, **271**, *410*
Caladium, Fancy-leaved, 109, 112, 113, *317*
Caladium, *316*
× *hortulanum*, *317*
× *hortulanum* 'Candidum', **109**, *317*
× *hortulanum* 'Crimson Glow', **112**, *317*
× *hortulanum* 'Rosalie', **113**, *317*
Calathea, *317*
makoyana, **99**, *318*
picturata, **97**, *318*
roseopicta, **104**, *318*
vittata, **103**, *318*
zebrina, **100**, *318*
Calceolaria, *319*
herbeohybrida, **162**, *319*
Camellia, *319*
japonica, **192**, *319*

Capsicum, 320
annuum, **194,** *320*
Carissa, 320
grandiflora, **191,** *320*
Caryota, 321
mitis, **229,** *321*
urens, 321
Cast-iron Plant,
225, 228, *306*
Cattail, Red-hot,
291
Cattleya, 322
aclandiae, 322
mossiae, 323
violacea, **148, 149,**
323
walkeriana, **148,**
149, *323*
Cattleytonia, 315
Cephalocereus, 323
senilis, **261,** *324*
Ceropegia, 324
woodii, **87,** *324*
Chamaecereus, 325
sylvestri, **266,** *325*
Chamaedorea, 325
elegans, **231,** *325*
elegans 'Bella', **230,**
325
Chamaerops, 326
humilis, **233,** *326*
Chenille Plant, 183,
291
Chlorophytum, 326
comosum, **85,** *327*
Christmas Cactus,
270, *415*
Christmas Pepper,
194, *320*
Chrysalidocarpus,
327
lutescens, **232,** *327*
Cigar Flower, 182,
337
Cissus, 328
antarctica, **76,** *328*
discolor, **81,** *328*
rhombifolia, 328

rhombifolia 'Ellen
Danica', **207,** *328*
Citrus, 329
× *citrofortunella*
mitis, **218,** *329*
limon 'Meyer', **218,**
329
Cleistocactus, 329
strausii, **263,** *330*
Clerodendrum, 330
thomsoniae, **193,** *330*
Clivia, 330
miniata, **155,** *331*
Codiaeum, 331
variegatum pictum,
204, *331*
variegatum pictum
'Fascination', **224,**
331
variegatum pictum
'Punctatum
Aureum', **223,** *332*
Coffea, 332
arabica, **217,** *332*
Coleus, 332
blumei, 333
× *hybridus,* **114,** *333*
× *hybridus* 'Lacey
Leaf', **96,** *333*
× *hybridus*
'Reasoner's Fancy
Leaf', **95,** *333*
× *hybridus* 'Red
Lace Leaf', **113,** *333*
× *hybridus* 'Wizard
Mixture', **114,** *333*
Columnea, 333
'California Gold',
185, *334*
hirta, **269,** *334*
Copperleaf, *291*
Coralberry, 216,
302
Cordyline, 334
terminalis, **116,** *334*
Corn Plant, 226,
347

Crassula, 335
argentea, **287,** *335*
falcata, **283,** *335*
lycopodioides, **265,** *335*
rupestris, **284,** *336*
Creeping Charlie,
86, *401*
Crossandra, 336
infundibuliformis,
188, *336*
Croton, 204, 223,
224, *331*
Crown of Thorns,
170, 197, *355*
Cryptanthus, 336
acaulis, **276,** *337*
bivittatus, **274,** *337*
bivittatus 'Pink
Starlight', **274,** *337*
bivittatus 'Starlite',
275, *337*
zonatus, **275,** *337*
Cuphea, 337
ignea, **182,** *337*
Cyanotis, 338
kewensis, **110,** *338*
somaliensis, 338
Cycas, 338
revoluta, **230,** *339*
Cyclamen, 339
persicum 'Shell Pink',
168, *340*
purpurascens, 339
Cymbidium, 340
Gainesville × Dan
Carpenter, **130, 131,**
341
Cyperus, 341
alternifolius, **233,** *341*
alternifolius gracilis,
342
papyrus, 341
Cypress, Toy, *335*
Cyrtomium, 342
falcatum, **240,** *342*

D
Dagger Plant, *428*

Davallia, 342
fejeensis, **250,** *343*
trichomanoides, **247,**
343
Dendrobium,
Antelope, *343*
Dendrobium, *343*
gouldii, *343*
nobile, *343*
phalaenopsis, *343*
primulinum, **146,**
147, *344*
Tangerine ×
Mushroom Pink,
130, 131, *344*
Desert Fan, 234,
427
Dieffenbachia, *344*
amoena, **97,** *345*
'Camille', **96,** *345*
maculata, **203,** *345*
Dizygotheca, *345*
elegantissima, **222,**
346
veitchii, *346*
Donkey's Tail, *415*
Dracaena, Striped,
227, *347*
Dracaena, *346*
deremensis
'Warneckii', **227,**
347
fragrans
'Massangeana', **226,**
347
godseffiana, *348*
marginata, **236,** *347*
sanderana, **224,** *347*
surculosa, **91,** *347*
Dracuvallia, *380*
Dragon Tree, 236,
347
Drunkard's Dream,
246, *365*
Dumb Cane, *344*
Spotted, **203,** *345*
Dutch Wings, 278,
362

Dyckia, *348*
fosterana, **282,** *348*

E
Eagle Claws, 257,
349
Easter Cactus, 270,
409
Echeveria, *348*
'Black Prince', **286,**
348
elegans, **268,** *349*
runyonii, **285,** *349*
Echinocactus, *349*
grusonii, **257,** *349*
horizonthalonius, **257,**
349
Echinocereus, *350*
pectinatus, **262,** *350*
Echinopsis, *350*
multiplex, **256,** *350*
Elephant Bush,
287, *407*
Elephant-foot Tree,
308
Elf, Hawaiian, *367*
Emerald Feather,
245, *304*
Encyclia, *351*
Epicattleya hybrids,
351
Epidendrum, *350*
atropurpureum, **351**
cochleatum
'Cockleshell', *351*
conopseum, *350*
cordigera, **150, 151,**
351
ibaguense, *352*
radicans, **124, 125,**
351
Epiphyllum, *352*
ackermannii, **271,** *352*
Epipremnum, *353*
aureum, **92,** *353*
aureum 'Marble
Queen', **93,** *353*

Episcia, *353*
cupreata, **108,** *354*
Euanthe sanderana,
426
Euonymous, *354*
japonica
'Mediopicta', **215,**
354
Euphorbia, *354*
milii, **170, 197,** *355*
pulcherrima, **199,** *355*
tirucalli, **272,** *356*
Evergreen, Belgian,
224, *347*
Exacum, *356*
affine, **175,** *356*

F
Fatshedera, *357*
lizei, **207,** *357*
Fatsia, Japanese,
210, *358*
Fatsia, *357*
japonica, **210,** *358*
Fern
Asparagus, **247,** *304*
Bird's-nest, **242,**
243, *307*
Boston, **248,** *385*
Button, **252,** *395*
Deer's-foot, *342*
Dish, *407*
Erect Sword, *385*
Foxtail Asparagus,
245, *304*
Hare's-foot, *406*
Hart's-tongue, **242,**
400
Hen-and-chickens,
250, *307*
Holly, **240,** *342*
Leather, **248,** *411*
Mother, *307*
Parsley, *307*
Peacock, **249,** *416*
Rabbit's-foot, **241,**
250, *343, 406*

Squirrel's-foot, **247,** *343*
Staghorn, **240,** *403*
Sword, **244,** *385*
Table, *407*
Ficus, 358
benjamina, **216,** *359*
benjamina 'Variegata', **90,** *359*
carica, 358
deltoidea, **219,** *359*
diversifolia, 359
elastica, **205,** *359*
'Elegante', **219,** *359*
lyrata, **205,** *359*
pumila, **208,** *360*
Fiddle-leaf Plant, *398*
Fig
Climbing, *360*
Creeping, **208,** *360*
Fiddle-leaf, **205,** *359*
Java, *359*
Mistletoe, **219,** *359*
Weeping, **90, 216,** *359*
Firecracker Flower, **188,** *336*
Firecracker Plant, *337*
Fire-dragon, *291*
Fittonia, 360
verschaffeltii
argyroneura, **107,** *360*
Flame-of-the-woods, **187,** *371*
Flamingo Flower, **155,** *300*
Flaming Sword, **158,** *427*
Freckle-face, *369*
Friendship Plant, *401*
Fuchsia, 360
× *hybrida,* **176, 177,** *361*

G
Gardenia, 189, *362*
Gardenia, 361
jasminoides, **189,** *362*
Gasteria, 362
liliputana, **278,** *362*
Geranium
Bedding, *394*
Hanging, *394*
Ivy, **172, 173,** *394*
Jungle, *371*
Martha Washington, *394*
Oak-leaved, *394*
Peppermint, **180,** *394*
Strawberry, *414*
Zonal, **94, 199,** *394*
Gesneria, 362
cuneifolia, **182,** *363*
Glory-bower, Bleeding, 193, *330*
Gloxinia
Florist, **163,** *418*
Tree, **181,** *373*
Gold-dust Plant, 91, *347*
Gold-dust Tree, 214, *307*
Golden Trumpet, 193, *296*
Goldfish Plant, 185, 269, *334*
Granadilla, Red, *393*
Grass, Basket, 252, *389*
Green Curls, *369*
Grevillea, 363
robusta, **222,** *363*
Guzmania, 363
'Cherry', **156,** *364*
lingulata, **156,** *364*
Gymnocalcium, 364
mihanovichii, **256,** *364*
Gynura, 364
aurantiaca, **117,** *365*
sarmentosa, 365

H
Hairy Toad Plant, **264,** *420*
Hatiora, 365
salicornioides, **246,** *365*
Hawkinsara, 315
Haworthia, Zebra, **279,** *366*
Haworthia, 365
fasciata, **279,** *366*
margaritifera, **279,** *366*
Hearts-on-a-string, **87,** *324*
Hedera, 366
helix, **79, 178,** *366*
helix 'Harald', **78,** *366*
helix 'Ripples', **77,** *366*
helix 'Sagittaefolia', *366*
Heptapleurum, 367
arboricola, **211,** *367,* *414*
Hibiscus, Chinese, **188,** *367*
Hibiscus, 367
rosa-sinensis, **188,** *367*
Hindu-rope, 267, *369*
Holly
Dwarf, *379*
False, **215,** *390*
Miniature, **253,** *379*
Singapore, *379*
Howea, 368
belmoreana, **232,** *368*
forsterana, 368
Hoya, 368
bella, 369
carnosa, **80,** *369*
carnosa 'Krinkle Kurl', **267,** *369*
sanguinolenta, 369
Hurricane Plant, *383*

Hypoestes, 369
phyllostachya, **214,** 369

I
Impatiens, 369
New Guinea Hybrid,
198, 370
wallerana, **171,** 370
wallerana 'Super
Elfin Blush', **170,**
370
wallerana 'Twinkles',
171, 370
Inch Plant, 429
Iresine, 370
herbstii, **117,** 371
Ivy
Aralia, **207,** 357
Devil's, 353
English, 77, 78, 79,
366
Grape, **207,** 328
Swedish, **176,** 403
Tree, 357
Ixora, 371
coccinea, **187,** 371

J
Jacob's-coat, 116,
291
Jade, Baby, 407
Jade Plant, **287,** 335
Jasmine
Angel-wing, **190,**
372
Arabian, **190,** 372
Cape, 362
Star, **191,** 372, 425
Winter, **192,** 372
Jasminum, 371
ilicifolium, 372
nitidum, **190,** 372
polyanthum, **192,** 372
sambac 'Maid of
Orleans', **190,** 372
Justicia, 372
brandegeana, **184,**
372

K
Kalanchoe, 373
blossfeldiana, **187,**
373
pumila, **283,** 373
tomentosa, **282,** 373
Kale, Indian, **105,**
428
Kangaroo Vine, **76,**
328
King's Mantle, **195,**
423
Kohleria, 373
'Dark Velvet', **181,**
373

L
Lacefern, 304
Lady of the Night,
134, 135, 313
Lady's Ear-drop,
176, 177, 361
Laelia, 374
anceps, **150, 151,** 374
purpurata, 374
rupestris, 374
Laeliocattleya, 322
Park Ridge, **142,**
143, 322
Lantana, 375
camara, **185, 189,**
375
Lantern, Chinese,
180, 290
Laurel, Australian,
402
Leadwort, Cape,
195, 405
Lemon, Meyer, **218,**
329
Lily
Boat, 411
Kaffir, **155,** 331
Lipstick Plant, **86,**
294
Lithops, 375
lesliei, **284,** 376

Living Stones, **284,**
376
Living Vase Plant,
159, 293
Livistona, 376
chinensis, **234,** 376
Lobivia, 377
arachnacantha, **262,**
377
leucomalla, **258,** 377
Lycaste, 377
cruenta, **128, 129,**
378
skinneri, 377

M
Maidenhair, Delta,
251, 292
Malpighia, 378
coccigera, **253,** 379
Mammillaria, 379
bocasana, **260, 261,**
379
camptotricha, **258,**
379
guelzowiana, **259,** 379
hahniana, **260,** 379
Maranta, 380
leuconeura, **101,** 380
leuconeura kerchoviana,
101, 380
Masdevallia, 380
Marguerite 'Selby',
126, 127, 381
Match-me-if-you-can,
291
Measles Plant, 369
Medusa, Philippine,
291
Mexican Gem, **268,**
349
Milkbush, **272,** 356
Miltonia, 381
flavescens, **136, 137,**
382
Miltoniopsis, 381
Monkey Puzzle
Tree, **221,** 301

Monstera, 382
deliciosa, 211, *383*
obliqua, 92, *383*
Moonstones, 268,
391
Mosaic Plant, 107,
360
Moses-in-a-boat, *411*
Moses-in-the-
bulrushes, *411*
Moses-in-the-cradle,
227, *411*
**Mother-in-law's
Tongue, 277,** *413*
Mother-of-thousands,
106, *414*

N
Neanthe bella
'Bella', *325*
Nematanthus, 383
'Castanet', **184,** *383*
'Tropicana', **183,**
384
Neoregelia, 384
carolinae 'Meyendorfii
Flandria', **161,** *384*
carolinae 'Tricolor',
161, *384*
Nephrolepis, 384
cordifolia, 244, *385*
exaltata
'Bostoniensis', **248,**
385
Nephthytis, 422
Nerium, 385
indicum, 386
odorum, 386
oleander, 196, *386*
Nerve Plant, *360*
Nettle, Painted, 95,
96, 113, 114, *333*
Nidularium, 386
billbergioides, **157,**
386
'Ra Ru' × 'Sao
Paulo', **157,** *386*

O
Oak, Silk, 222, *363*
Odontioda, 387
Memoria Len Page,
142, 143, *387*
Odontoglossum, 387
bictoniense, 387
bilobum, **140, 141,**
387
Oleander, Common,
196, *386*
Olive
Fragrant, *390*
Holly, *390*
Sweet, 90, *390*
Oncidium, 388
Equitant Hybrids,
120, 121, *388*
Golden Sunset ×
Orglade's Rose
Claret, **120, 121,**
388
maculatum, **132,**
133, *389*
sphacetatum, 388
viperinium, **128, 129,**
389
William Thurston
'Orchidglade', **120,**
121, *388*
Oplismenus, 389
hirtellus 'Variegatus',
252, *389*
Opuntia, 389
microdasys, **263,** *390*
subulata, **265,** *390*
Osmanthus, 390
fragrans, 90, *390*
heterophyllus
'Variegatus', **215,**
390
Orange
Calamondin, **218,**
329
Mock, *402*
Orchid
Darwin, **136, 137,**
298

Lady Slipper, **138,**
392
Moth, **138,** *398*
Spice, **150,** *351*
Spider, **134,** *313*
Oyster Plant, *411*

P
Pachyphytum, 391
oviferum, **268,** *391*
Palm
Areca, **232,** *327*
Bamboo, **229,** *409*
Bottle, *308*
Burmese Fishtail,
229, *321*
Butterfly, *327*
Chinese Fan, **234,**
376
Chinese Fountain,
376
Curly, *368*
European Fan, **233,**
326
Kentia, *368*
Miniature Date, **231,**
400
Parlor, **230, 231,**
325
Petticoat, *427*
Pygmy Date, *400*
Sago, **230,** *339*
Sentry, **232,** *368*
Slender Lady, *409*
Yellow, *327*
Panamiga, 102, *401*
Pandanus, 391
veitchii, **237,** *391*
Panda Plant, 206,
373, 398
Paper Flower, 197,
198, *312*
Paphiopedilum, 392
Maudiae, **138, 139,**
392
niveum, 392
Passiflora, 393
caerulea, **209,** *393*

coccinea, **209,** *393*
Passionflower
Blue, **209,** *393*
Red, **209,** *393*
Patient Lucy, *370*
Peacock Plant, 99, *318*
Pearl Elegans, *349*
Pearl Plant, 279, *366*
Pelargonium, 393
Cascade hybrids, **172, 173,** *394*
domesticum hybrids, *394*
hortorum hybrids, **94, 199,** *394*
× *hortorum* 'Mrs. Parker', **94,** *394*
peltatum hybrids, **172, 173,** *394*
quercifolium, 394
'Sofie-Cascade', **172,** *394*
tomentosum, **180,** *394*
Pellaea, 395
rotundifolia, **252,** *395*
Pellionia, 395
daveauana, **82,** *396*
Pencil Tree, *356*
Peperomia
Emerald Ripple, **107,** *396*
Philodendron, **95,** *396*
Watermelon, **105,** *396*
Peperomia, 396
argyreia, **105,** *396*
caperata, **107,** *396*
obtusifolia, **93,** *396*
scandens 'Variegata', **95,** *396*
Pepper, Christmas, 194, *320*
Pepper Face, *396*
Phalaenopsis, 397
amabilis, 397

Carnival Queen ×
Zauberot, **144, 145,** *398*
stuartiana, **138, 139,** *398*
violacea, 397
Philodendron
Blushing, *399*
Fernleaf, **246,** *399*
Heart-leaf, **76,** *399*
Red-leaf, **206,** *399*
Split-leaf, *383*
Philodendron, 398
bipennifolium, **206,** *398*
cordatum, 399
erubescens, **206,** *399*
oxycardium, 399
pinnatilobum
'Fernleaf', **246,** *399*
'Pluto', **243,** *399*
scandens, **76,** *399*
selloum, **210,** *399*
Phoenix, 399
roebelenii, **231,** *400*
Phyllitis, 400
scolopendrium
'Crispum', **242,** *400*
Piggyback Plant, 77, *424*
Pilea, Watermelon, *401*
Pilea, 401
cadierei, **99,** *401*
involucrata, **102,** *401*
microphylla, **253,** *401*
nummularifolia, **86,** *401*
spruceana 'Norfolk', **108,** *401*
Pine
Buddhist, *405*
Norfolk Island, **221,** *302*
Screw, **237,** *391*
Pineapple, Variegated, 237, *297*

Pittosporum, Japanese, 212, *402*
Pittosporum, 402
tobira, **212,** *402*
Platycerium, 402
bifurcatum, **240,** *403*
Plectranthus, 403
australis, **176,** *403*
australis 'Purple Majesty', **81,** *403*
coleoides 'Marginatus', **94,** *404*
Pleomele, 404
recurva, 404
reflexa, **228,** *404*
reflexa 'Variegata', **225,** *404*
Plum, Natal, 191, *320*
Plumbago, 404
auriculata, **195,** *405*
capensis, 404
Pocketbook Plant, *319*
Podocarpus, 405
macrophyllus, **223,** *405*
Poinsettia, 199, *355*
Polka-dot Plant, 214, *369*
Polypodium, 405
aureum, **241,** *406*
Polyscias, 406
balfouriana, **202,** *406*
balfouriana 'Marginata', **202,** *406*
balfouriana 'Pennockii', **203,** *406*
fruiticosa, **220,** *406*
paniculata 'Variegata', **217,** *406*
Polystichum, 411
Pomegranate, 220, *408*
Ponytail, 236, *308*
Portulacaria, 407
afra, **287,** *407*
Pothos, 92, 93, *353*

Prayer Plant, 101, *380*

Primrose, Cape, 164, 165, 175, *421*

Propeller Plant, 283, *335*

Pteris, 407

cretica 'Alexandrae', 241, *407*

ensiformis 'Victoriae', 249, *408*

Punica, 408

granatum 'Nana', 220, *408*

Purple-heart, 83, *417*

Purple Velvet Plant, 117, *365*

Pussy Ears, 282, *338, 373*

R

Rattail, 265, *335*

Rebutia, 408

kupperana, 259, *408*

Rechsteineria, 417

Rhapis, 409

excelsa, 229, *409*

humilis, 409

Rhipsalidopsis, 409

gaertneri, 270, *409*

Rhipsalis, 409

baccifera, 272, *410*

cassutha, 410

crispata, 271, *410*

rhombea, 269, *410*

Rhoeo, 410

spathecea, 227, *411*

Rhyncholaelia, 313

Rice Tree, Formosa, *358*

Rosary Vine, 324, *336*

Rose-of-China, *367*

Rosebay, *386*

Rubber Plant, 205, *359*

American, *396*

Baby, **93**, *396*

Rumohra, 411

adiantiformis, 248, 411

S

Saffron Spike, *300*

Sage, Yellow, 185, 189, *375*

Saintpaulia, 411

'Alabama', 166, *412*

'Hawaii', 167, *412*

'Jelly Bean', 168, *412*

'New Mexico', 168, *412*

Optimara hybrids, 166, 167, *412*

'Pendula', 174, *412*

'Wisconsin', 167, *412*

Sansevieria, Bird's-nest, 276, 277, *413*

Sansevieria, 412

trifasciata 'Golden Hahnii', 277, *413*

trifasciata 'Hahnii', 276, *413*

trifasciata 'Laurentii', 277, *413*

Saxifraga, 413

sarmentosa, 414

stolonifera, 106, *414*

Schefflera, 213, *312*

Dwarf, 211, *367*

Schefflera, 414

actinophylla, 312

arboricola, 213, *414*

digitata, 414

Schlumbergera, 414

bridgesii, 270, *415*

truncata, 415

Sedum, 415

morganianum, 267, *415*

Selaginella, 416

willdenovii, 249, *416*

Senecio, 416

macroglossus 'Variegatum', 79, *416*

rowleyanus, 87, *416*

Setcreasea, 417

pallida 'Purple Heart', 83, *417*

purpurea, 417

Shrimp Plant, 184, *372*

Sickle Plant, *335*

Silver Torch, 263, *330*

Sinningia, 417

aggregata, 418

cardinalis, 418

concinna, 163, *418*

leucotricha, 418

Miniature hybrids, 181, *418*

pusilla, 418

speciosa 'Kiss of Fire', 163, *418*

Slipper Plant, 162, *319*

Snake Plant, 277, *413*

Snowball, Mexican, *349*

Sophrolaeliocattleya, 323

Jewel Box, 122, 123, *323*

Sophronitis, 418

cernua, 124, 125, *419*

coccinea, 419

Spanish-Bayonet, 235, *428*

Spanish Moss, *423*

Spathiphyllum, 419

'Mauna Loa', 154, *420*

wallisii, 154, *420*

Spiceberry, *302*

Spider Plant, 85, *327*

Spindle Tree, 215, 354
Spoon Flower, 428
Stapelia, 420
hirsuta, 264, 420
leendertziae, 280, 420
variegata, 264, 421
Starfish Plant, 276, 337, 421
Streptocarpus, 421
'Constant Nymph', 165, 421
'Good Hope', 175, 421
'John Innes' hybrids, 164, 165, 422
'Wiesmoor' hybrids, 164, 422
String-of-beads, 87, 416
String-of-hearts, 324
Sweet Flag, Japanese, 226, 292
Swiss-cheese Plant, 211, 383
Syngonium, 422
podophyllum, 103, 422

T
Teddy-bear Plant, 110, 338
Thunbergia, 422
alata, 194, 423
erecta, 195, 423
Ti Plant, 116, 334
Tillandsia, 423
caput-medusae, 273, 423
cyanea, 160, 423
didisticha, 160, 423
usneoides, 423
Toad Plant, 264, 421
Tolmiea, 424
menziesii, 77, 424
Trachelospermum, 424
jasminoides, 191, 425

Tradescantia, 425
fluminensis, 425
fluminensis 'Quicksilver', 82, 425
fluminensis 'Variegata', 85, 425
Trailing Begonia Vine, 81, 328

U
Umbrella Plant, 233, 341
Umbrella Tree, 312
Australian, 213, 312, 414
Urn Plant, 293

V
Vanda, 425
Rothschildiana, 426
sanderiana, 144, 145, 426
Velvet Slipper Plant, 418
Venus-hair, 251, 292
Vine
Arrowhead, 103, 422
Bead, 336
Black-eyed Susan, 194, 423
Bleeding-heart, 330
Kangaroo, 76, 328
Rosary, 324, 336
Trailing Begonia, 81, 328
Violet
African, 166, 167, 168, 174, 411, 412
Amethyst, 316
Arabian, 356
Bush, 174, 316
German, 356
Persian, 175, 356
Vriesea, 427
ensiformis, 159, 427
splendens, 158, 427

W
Wandering Jew, 82, 83, 84, 85, 425, 429
Washingtonia, 427
filifera, 234, 427
Wax Plant, 80, 369
Miniature, 369
Waxvine, Variegated, 79, 416

X
Xanthosoma, 428
lindenii, 105, 428

Y
Yew
Japanese, 405
Southern, 223, 405
Yucca, Spineless, 235, 428
Yucca, 428
aloifolia, 235, 428
elephantipes, 235, 428

Z
Zebra Haworthia, 279, 366
Zebra Plant, 100, 109, 275, 300, 318, 337
Zebrina, 429
pendula, 84, 429
pendula 'Purposii', 83, 429
pendula 'Quadricolor', 84, 429